Project Management Institute

W9-BJE-183

THE STANDARD FOR PROGRAM MANAGEMENT

Second Edition

An American National Standard
ANSI/PMI 08-002-2008

The Standard for Program Management — Second Edition

ISBN: 978-1-933890-52-4

Published by:
Project Management Institute, Inc.
14 Campus Boulevard
Newtown Square, Pennsylvania 19073-3299 USA.
Phone: +1-610-356-4600
Fax: +1-610-356-4647
E-mail: customercare@pmi.org
Internet: www.PMI.org

PMI Publications welcomes corrections and comments on its books. Please feel free to send comments on typographical, formatting, or other errors. Simply make a copy of the relevant page of the book, mark the error, and send it to: Book Editor, PMI Publications, 14 Campus Boulevard, Newtown Square, PA 19073-3299 USA.

To inquire about discounts for resale or educational purposes, please contact the PMI Book Service Center.

PMI Book Service Center
P.O. Box 932683, Atlanta, GA 31193-2683 USA
Phone: 1-866-276-4764 (within the U.S. or Canada) or +1-770-280-4129 (globally)
Fax: +1-770-280-4113
E-mail: book.orders@pmi.org

The paper used in this book complies with the Permanent Paper Standard issued by the National Information Standards Organization (Z39.48—1984).

10 9 8 7 6 5 4 3

NOTICE

TABLE OF CONTENTS

PREFACE TO THE SECOND EDITION XXI

SECTION I - THE PROGRAM MANAGEMENT FRAMEWORK 1

CHAPTER 1 - INTRODUCTION 3

    1.1   Purpose of *The Standard for Program Management* 4
    1.2   What is a Program? 5
    1.3   What is Program Management? 6
    1.4   Relationships among Project, Program, and Portfolio 6
        1.4.1   The Relationship between Program Management and Project Management 8
        1.4.2   The Relationship between Program Management and Portfolio Management 9
        1.4.3   The Interactions among Portfolio, Program, and Project Management .. 10
    1.5   Program Management Office 11
    1.6   Role of the Program Manager 12
        1.6.1   Program Manager Knowledge and Skills 12
    1.7   Program-External Factors 14
        1.7.1   Organizational Process Assets 14
        1.7.2   Enterprise Environmental Factors 14
        1.7.3   Enterprise External Factors 15

CHAPTER 2 - PROGRAM LIFE CYCLE AND BENEFITS MANAGEMENT 17

    2.1   The Program Life Cycle – Overview 17
        2.1.1   Characteristics of the Program Life Cycle 18
        2.1.2   Relationship to a Product's Life Cycle 19
        2.1.3   Program Life Cycle and Benefits Management 20
        2.1.4   Program Governance across the Life Cycle 21
    2.2   Program Life Cycle Phases 22
        2.2.1   Pre-Program Preparations 22
        2.2.2   Program Initiation 24
        2.2.3   Program Setup 26
        2.2.4   Delivery of Program Benefits 28
        2.2.5   Program Closure 29

2.3   **Program Benefits Management** 30

    2.3.1   **Delivering and Managing Benefits** 30

    2.3.2   **Organizational Differences** 31

    2.3.3   **Benefits Sustainment** 31

SECTION II - THE STANDARD FOR PROGRAM MANAGEMENT 33

CHAPTER 3 - PROGRAM MANAGEMENT PROCESSES 35

3.1   **Common Program Management Process Interactions** 36

    3.1.1   **Common Inputs and Outputs** 38

3.2   **Program Management Process Groups** 40

3.3   **Initiating Process Group** 42

    3.3.1   **Initiate Program** 43

    3.3.2   **Establish Program Financial Framework** 43

3.4   **Planning Process Group** 44

    3.4.1   **Plan Program Scope** 46

    3.4.2   **Define Program Goals and Objectives** 47

    3.4.3   **Plan and Establish Program Governance Structure** 47

    3.4.4   **Identify Program Stakeholders** 47

    3.4.5   **Develop Program Management Plan** 48

    3.4.6   **Develop Program Infrastructure** 48

    3.4.7   **Develop Program Requirements** 48

    3.4.8   **Develop Program Architecture** 49

    3.4.9   **Develop Program WBS** 49

    3.4.10 **Develop Program Schedule** 49

    3.4.11 **Develop Program Financial Plan** 50

    3.4.12 **Estimate Program Costs** 50

    3.4.13 **Budget Program Costs** 51

    3.4.14 **Plan Program Procurements** 51

    3.4.15 **Plan Program Stakeholder Management** 51

    3.4.16 **Plan Communications** 52

    3.4.17 **Plan for Audits** 52

    3.4.18 **Plan Program Quality** 53

    3.4.19 **Plan Program Risk Management** 53

    3.4.20 **Identify Program Risks** 54

    3.4.21 **Analyze Program Risks** 54

    3.4.22 **Plan Program Risk Responses** 55

3.5   Executing Process Group 55

    3.5.1   Direct and Manage Program Execution 56

    3.5.2   Manage Program Resources 57

    3.5.3   Manage Program Architecture 57

    3.5.4   Manage Component Interfaces 57

    3.5.5   Engage Program Stakeholders 58

    3.5.6   Distribute Information 58

    3.5.7   Conduct Program Procurements 59

    3.5.8   Approve Component Initiation 59

3.6   Monitoring and Controlling Process Group 59

    3.6.1   Monitor and Control Program Performance 60

    3.6.2   Monitor and Control Program Scope 61

    3.6.3   Monitor and Control Program Schedule 61

    3.6.4   Monitor and Control Program Financials 62

    3.6.5   Manage Program Stakeholder Expectations 62

    3.6.6   Monitor and Control Program Risks 63

    3.6.7   Administer Program Procurements 63

    3.6.8   Manage Program Issues 64

    3.6.9   Monitor and Control Program Changes 64

    3.6.10 Report Program Performance 65

    3.6.11 Provide Governance Oversight 65

    3.6.12 Manage Program Benefits 66

3.7   Closing Process Group 66

    3.7.1   Close Program 67

    3.7.2   Approve Component Transition 68

    3.7.3   Close Program Procurements 68

SECTION III - THE PROGRAM MANAGEMENT KNOWLEDGE AREAS 69

CHAPTER 4 - PROGRAM INTEGRATION MANAGEMENT 71

4.1   Initiate Program 74

    4.1.1   Initiate Program: Inputs 76

    4.1.2   Initiate Program: Tools and Techniques 77

    4.1.3   Initiate Program: Outputs 78

4.2 Develop Program Management Plan 79

    4.2.1 Develop Program Management Plan: Inputs 81

    4.2.2 Develop Program Management Plan: Tools and Techniques 82

    4.2.3 Develop Program Management Plan: Outputs 83

4.3 Develop Program Infrastructure 84

    4.3.1 Develop Program Infrastructure: Inputs 84

    4.3.2 Develop Program Infrastructure: Tools and Techniques 85

    4.3.3 Develop Program Infrastructure: Outputs 86

4.4 Direct and Manage Program Execution 86

    4.4.1 Direct and Manage Program Execution: Inputs 88

    4.4.2 Direct and Manage Program Execution: Tools and Techniques 89

    4.4.3 Direct and Manage Program Execution: Outputs 90

4.5 Manage Program Resources 91

    4.5.1 Manage Program Resources: Inputs 92

    4.5.2 Manage Program Resources: Tools and Techniques 92

    4.5.3 Manage Program Resources: Outputs 93

4.6 Monitor and Control Program Performance 93

    4.6.1 Monitor and Control Program Performance: Inputs 94

    4.6.2 Monitor and Control Program Performance: Tools and Techniques 94

    4.6.3 Monitor and Control Program Performance: Outputs 95

4.7 Manage Program Issues 95

    4.7.1 Manage Program Issues: Inputs 97

    4.7.2 Manage Program Issues: Tools and Techniques 97

    4.7.3 Manage Program Issues: Outputs 97

4.8 Close Program 98

    4.8.1 Close Program: Inputs 99

    4.8.2 Close Program: Tools and Techniques 100

    4.8.3 Close Program: Outputs 100

CHAPTER 5 - PROGRAM SCOPE MANAGEMENT 103

5.1 Plan Program Scope 104

    5.1.1 Plan Program Scope: Inputs 105

    5.1.2 Plan Program Scope: Tools and Techniques 106

    5.1.3 Plan Program Scope: Outputs 106

5.2   **Define Program Goals and Objectives** 107
     5.2.1   **Define Program Goals and Objectives: Inputs** 108
     5.2.2   **Define Program Goals and Objectives: Tools and Techniques** 108
     5.2.3   **Define Program Goals and Objectives: Outputs** 109
5.3   **Develop Program Requirements** 110
     5.3.1   **Develop Program Requirements: Inputs** 110
     5.3.2   **Develop Program Requirements: Tools and Techniques** 111
     5.3.3   **Develop Program Requirements: Outputs** 112
5.4   **Develop Program Architecture** 112
     5.4.1   **Develop Program Architecture: Inputs** 113
     5.4.2   **Develop Program Architecture: Tools and Techniques** 113
     5.4.3   **Develop Program Architecture: Outputs** 114
5.5   **Develop Program WBS** 114
     5.5.1   **Develop Program WBS: Inputs** 115
     5.5.2   **Develop Program WBS: Tools and Techniques** 116
     5.5.3   **Develop Program WBS: Outputs** 117
5.6   **Manage Program Architecture** 117
     5.6.1   **Manage Program Architecture: Inputs** 118
     5.6.2   **Manage Program Architecture: Tools and Techniques** 118
     5.6.3   **Manage Program Architecture: Outputs** 119
5.7   **Manage Component Interfaces** 119
     5.7.1   **Manage Component Interfaces: Inputs** 120
     5.7.2   **Manage Component Interfaces: Tools and Techniques** 120
     5.7.3   **Manage Component Interfaces: Outputs** 121
5.8   **Monitor and Control Program Scope** 121
     5.8.1   **Monitor and Control Program Scope: Inputs** 122
     5.8.2   **Monitor and Control Program Scope: Tools and Techniques** 123
     5.8.3   **Monitor and Control Program Scope: Outputs** 123

CHAPTER 6 - PROGRAM TIME MANAGEMENT 125
6.1   **Develop Program Schedule** 127
     6.1.1   **Develop Program Schedule—Inputs** 128
     6.1.2   **Develop Program Schedule: Tools and Techniques** 129
     6.1.3   **Develop Program Schedule: Outputs** 130

6.2   Monitor and Control Program Schedule 131

     6.2.1   Monitor and Control Program Schedule: Inputs 132

     6.2.2   Monitor and Control Program Schedule: Tools and Techniques 133

     6.2.3   Monitor and Control Program Schedule: Outputs 134

CHAPTER 7 - PROGRAM COST MANAGEMENT 135

CHAPTER 8 - PROGRAM QUALITY MANAGEMENT 137

CHAPTER 9 - PROGRAM HUMAN RESOURCE MANAGEMENT 139

CHAPTER 10 - PROGRAM COMMUNICATION MANAGEMENT 141

   10.1   Plan Communications 142

     10.1.1   Plan Communications: Inputs 144

     10.1.2   Plan Communications: Tools and Techniques 145

     10.1.3   Plan Communications: Outputs 146

   10.2   Distribute Information 147

     10.2.1   Distribute Information: Inputs 149

     10.2.2   Distribute Information: Tools and Techniques 150

     10.2.3   Distribute Information: Outputs 151

   10.3   Report Program Performance 152

     10.3.1   Report Program Performance: Inputs 153

     10.3.2   Report Program Performance: Tools and Techniques 155

     10.3.3   Report Program Performance: Outputs 156

CHAPTER 11 - PROGRAM RISK MANAGEMENT 157

   11.1   Plan Program Risk Management 160

     11.1.1   Plan Program Risk Management: Inputs 161

     11.1.2   Plan Program Risk Management: Tools and Techniques 163

     11.1.3   Plan Program Risk Management: Outputs 163

   11.2   Identify Program Risks 164

     11.2.1   Identify Program Risks: Inputs 166

     11.2.2   Identify Program Risks: Tools and Techniques 166

     11.2.3   Identify Program Risks: Outputs 168

   11.3   Analyze Program Risks 169

     11.3.1   Analyze Program Risks: Inputs 171

     11.3.2   Analyze Program Risks: Tools and Techniques 172

     11.3.3   Analyze Program Risks: Outputs 176

11.4 Plan Program Risk Responses 176

    11.4.1 Plan Program Risk Responses: Inputs 177

    11.4.2 Plan Program Risk Responses: Tools and Techniques 178

    11.4.3 Plan Program Risk Responses: Outputs 179

11.5 Monitor and Control Program Risks 180

    11.5.1 Monitor and Control Program Risks: Inputs 181

    11.5.2 Monitor and Control Program Risks: Tools and Techniques 182

    11.5.3 Monitor and Control Program Risks: Outputs 183

CHAPTER 12 - PROGRAM PROCUREMENT MANAGEMENT 185

12.1 Plan Program Procurements 187

    12.1.1 Plan Program Procurements: Inputs 189

    12.1.2 Plan Program Procurements: Tools and Techniques 189

    12.1.3 Plan Program Procurements: Outputs 190

12.2 Conduct Program Procurements 192

    12.2.1 Conduct Program Procurements: Inputs 193

    12.2.2 Conduct Program Procurements: Tools and Techniques 194

    12.2.3 Conduct Program Procurements: Outputs 197

12.3 Administer Program Procurements 198

    12.3.1 Administer Program Procurements: Inputs 200

    12.3.2 Administer Program Procurements: Tools and Techniques 200

    12.3.3 Administer Program Procurements: Outputs 203

12.4 Close Program Procurements 203

    12.4.1 Close Program Procurements: Inputs 204

    12.4.2 Close Program Procurements: Tools and Techniques 205

    12.4.3 Close Program Procurements: Outputs 206

CHAPTER 13 - PROGRAM FINANCIAL MANAGEMENT 207

13.1 Establish Program Financial Framework 210

    13.1.1 Establish Program Financial Framework: Inputs 211

    13.1.2 Establish Program Financial Framework: Tools and Techniques 212

    13.1.3 Establish Program Financial Framework: Outputs 213

13.2 Develop Program Financial Plan 213

    13.2.1 Develop Program Financial Plan: Inputs 215

    13.2.2 Develop Program Financial Plan: Tools and Techniques 216

    13.2.3 Develop Program Financial Plan: Outputs 216

13.3 Estimate Program Costs... 217

    13.3.1 Estimate Program Costs: Inputs 219

    13.3.2 Estimate Program Costs: Tools and Techniques.................................... 219

    13.3.3 Estimate Program Costs: Outputs 220

13.4 Budget Program Costs 221

    13.4.1 Budget Program Costs: Inputs 222

    13.4.2 Budget Program Costs: Tools and Techniques 222

    13.4.3 Budget Program Costs: Outputs.. 222

13.5 Monitor and Control Program Financials.. 223

    13.5.1 Monitor and Control Program Financials: Inputs 224

    13.5.2 Monitor and Control Program Financials: Tools and Techniques 225

    13.5.3 Monitor and Control Program Financials: Outputs................................. 226

CHAPTER 14 - PROGRAM STAKEHOLDER MANAGEMENT 227

14.1 Plan Program Stakeholder Management.. 228

    14.1.1 Plan Program Stakeholder Management: Inputs 229

    14.1.2 Plan Program Stakeholder Management: Tools and Techniques 230

    14.1.3 Plan Program Stakeholder Management: Outputs.................................. 231

14.2 Identify Program Stakeholders 231

    14.2.1 Identify Program Stakeholders: Inputs... 232

    14.2.2 Identify Program Stakeholders: Tools and Techniques......................... 233

    14.2.3 Identify Program Stakeholders: Outputs 234

14.3 Engage Program Stakeholders 236

    14.3.1 Engage Program Stakeholders: Inputs... 237

    14.3.2 Engage Program Stakeholders: Tools and Techniques......................... 238

    14.3.3 Engage Program Stakeholders: Outputs.. 238

14.4 Manage Program Stakeholder Expectations 239

    14.4.1 Manage Program Stakeholder Expectations: Inputs.............................. 240

    14.4.2 Manage Program Stakeholder Expectations: Tools and Techniques..... 241

    14.4.3 Manage Program Stakeholder Expectations: Outputs 241

CHAPTER 15 - PROGRAM GOVERNANCE 243

15.1 Plan and Establish Program Governance Structure... 245

    15.1.1 Plan and Establish Program Governance Structure: Inputs.................. 247

    15.1.2 Plan and Establish Program Governance Structure: Tools and
           Techniques 248

    15.1.3 Plan and Establish Program Governance Structure: Outputs 249

15.2 **Plan for Audits** **251**

    15.2.1 **Plan for Audits: Inputs** **253**

    15.2.2 **Plan for Audits: Tools and Techniques** **253**

    15.2.3 **Plan for Audits: Outputs** **254**

15.3 **Plan Program Quality** **254**

    15.3.1 **Plan Program Quality: Inputs** **255**

    15.3.2 **Plan Program Quality: Tools and Techniques** **256**

    15.3.3 **Plan Program Quality: Outputs** **256**

15.4 **Approve Component Initiation** **257**

    15.4.1 **Approve Component Initiation: Inputs** **258**

    15.4.2 **Approve Component Initiation: Tools and Techniques** **259**

    15.4.3 **Approve Component Initiation: Outputs** **259**

15.5 **Provide Governance Oversight** **259**

    15.5.1 **Provide Governance Oversight: Inputs** **261**

    15.5.2 **Provide Governance Oversight: Tools and Techniques** **262**

    15.5.3 **Provide Governance Oversight: Outputs** **262**

15.6 **Manage Program Benefits** **263**

    15.6.1 **Manage Program Benefits: Inputs** **264**

    15.6.2 **Manage Program Benefits: Tools and Techniques** **264**

    15.6.3 **Manage Program Benefits: Outputs** **266**

15.7 **Monitor and Control Program Changes** **267**

    15.7.1 **Monitor and Control Program Changes: Inputs** **268**

    15.7.2 **Monitor and Control Program Changes: Tools and Techniques** **268**

    15.7.3 **Monitor and Control Program Changes: Outputs** **268**

15.8 **Approve Component Transition** **269**

    15.8.1 **Approve Component Transition: Inputs** **270**

    15.8.2 **Approve Component Transition: Tools and Techniques** **270**

    15.8.3 **Approve Component Transition: Outputs** **270**

SECTION IV - APPENDICES **273**

APPENDIX A - SECOND EDITION CHANGES **275**

A.1   **Structural Changes** **275**

A.2   **Addition of Knowledge Areas** **276**

A.3   **Elimination of Themes** **276**

A.4   **Writing Styles** **276**

A.5   **Chapter 1 – Introduction Changes** **276**

A.6   Chapter 2 – Program Life Cycle and Benefits Management 277

A.7   Chapter 3 – Program Management Processes Changes 278

A.8   Chapters 4 through 15 Changes 281

A.9   Chapters 4 – 15 Knowledge Area Summaries 284

A.10 Glossary 284

APPENDIX B - EVOLUTION OF PMI'S *THE STANDARD FOR PROGRAM MANAGEMENT* 285

B.1   Introduction 285

B.2   Preliminary Work 285

B.3   Drafting *The Standard for Program Management* 286

B.4   Delivering the Initial *The Standard for Program Management* 286

    B.4.1   *The Standard for Program Management* Project Core Team 287

    B.4.2   Significant Contributors 287

    B.4.3   *The Standard for Program Management* Project Team Members 288

    B.4.4   Final Exposure Draft Reviewers and Contributors 293

    B.4.5   PMI Project Management Standards Program Member
    Advisory Group 293

    B.4.6   Production Staff 294

B.5   *The Standard for Program Management*—Second Edition 294

**APPENDIX C - CONTRIBUTORS AND REVIEWERS OF *THE STANDARD FOR PROGRAM
MANAGEMENT* – SECOND EDITION 295**

C.1   *The Standard for Program Management* – Second Edition
Project Core Team 295

C.2   *The Standard for Program Management* – Second Edition
Project Sub-Teams 296

C.3   Significant Contributors 296

C.4   Operation Team Members 296

C.5   *The Standard for Program Management* – Second Edition
Project Content Reviewers 297

C.6   *The Standard for Program Management* – Second Edition
Project Team Members 297

C.7   Final Exposure Draft Reviewers and Contributors 299

C.8   PMI Standards Member Advisory Group (MAG) 300

C.9   Staff Contributors 300

APPENDIX D - SUMMARY OF PROGRAM MANAGEMENT KNOWLEDGE AREAS...................301

D.1   **Chapter 4 – Program Integration Management**.....................................301

D.2   **Chapter 5 – Program Scope Management**...302

D.3   **Chapter 6 – Program Time Management**..302

D.4   **Chapter 7 – Program Cost Management** 303

D.5   **Chapter 8 – Program Quality Management** 303

D.6   **Chapter 9 – Program Human Resource Management**................................303

D.7   **Chapter 10 – Program Communication Management**...............................303

D.8   **Chapter 11 – Program Risk Management** 303

D.9   **Chapter 12 – Program Procurement Management** 304

D.10 **Chapter 13 – Program Financial Management**....................................304

D.11 **Chapter 14 – Program Stakeholder Management**.................................305

D.12 **Chapter 15 – Program Governance Management**................................305

SECTION V - GLOSSARY AND INDEX...307

GLOSSARY 309

1.   **Inclusions and Exclusions**..309

2.   **Common Acronyms** 309

3.   **Definitions**..309

INDEX 315

LIST OF TABLES AND FIGURES

Figure 1-1.   Portfolio, Program, and Project Management Interactions.................................7

Figure 1-2.   Interaction between Program Management and Project Management 9

Figure 1-3.   Portfolios, Programs and Projects—High-Level View.................................10

Table 1-1.   Comparative Overview of Project, Program, and Portfolio Management......................11

Figure 1-4.   Required Blend of Skills and Competence in a Program Manager.........................13

Figure 2-1.   Program Component Overlap 18

Figure 2-2.   Program Life Cycle and Program Benefits Management 20

Figure 2-3.   A Representative Program Life Cycle 21

Figure 2-4.   Pre-Program Preparations 22

Figure 2-5.   Program Initiation...24

Figure 2-6.   Program Setup...26

Figure 2-7.   Delivery of Program Benefits 28

Figure 2-8.   Program Closure 29

Figure 3-1.   Program Management Process Interactions 37

Table 3-1.   Program Management Process Groups and Knowledge Areas Mapping......................41

Figure 3-2.   Initiating Process Group..43

Figure 3-3.   Initiate Program: Inputs and Outputs 43

Figure 3-4.   Establish Program Financial Framework: Inputs and Outputs 44

Figure 3-5.   Planning Process Group 45

Figure 3-6.   Plan Program Scope: Inputs and Outputs...46

Figure 3-7.   Define Program Goals and Objectives: Inputs and Outputs............................47

Figure 3-8.   Plan and Establish Program Governance Structure: Inputs and Outputs 47

Figure 3-9.   Identify Program Stakeholders: Inputs and Outputs..................................47

Figure 3-10.   Develop Program Management Plan: Inputs and Outputs................................48

Figure 3-11.   Develop Program Infrastructure: Inputs and Outputs.................................48

Figure 3-12.   Develop Program Requirements: Inputs and Outputs...48

Figure 3-13.   Develop Program Architecture: Inputs and Outputs 49

Figure 3-14.   Develop Program WBS: Inputs and Outputs 49

Figure 3-15.   Develop Program Schedule: Inputs and Outputs..49

Figure 3-16.   Develop Program Financial Plan: Inputs and Outputs..50

Figure 3-17.   Estimate Program Costs: Inputs and Outputs 50

Figure 3-18.   Budget Program Costs: Inputs and Outputs 51

Figure 3-19.   Plan Program Procurements: Inputs and Outputs..51

Figure 3-20.   Plan Program Stakeholder Management: Inputs and Outputs 51

Figure 3-21.   Plan Communications: Inputs and Outputs 52

Figure 3-22.   Plan for Audits: Inputs and Outputs..52

Figure 3-23.   Plan Program Quality: Inputs and Outputs 53

Figure 3-24.   Plan Program Risk Management: Inputs and Outputs..53

Figure 3-25.   Identify Program Risks: Inputs and Outputs 54

Figure 3-26.   Analyze Program Risk: Inputs and Outputs..54

Figure 3-27.   Plan Program Risk Responses: Inputs and Outputs...55

Figure 3-28.   Executing Process Group 56

Figure 3-29.   Direct and Manage Program Execution: Inputs and Outputs......................................56

Figure 3-30.   Manage Program Resources: Inputs and Outputs..57

Figure 3-31.   Manage Program Architecture: Inputs and Outputs 57

Figure 3-32.   Manage Component Interfaces: Inputs and Outputs..57

Figure 3-33.   Engage Program Stakeholders: Inputs and Outputs 58

Figure 3-34.   Distribute Information: Inputs and Outputs..58

Figure 3-35.   Conduct Program Procurements: Inputs and Outputs 59

Figure 3-36.   Approve Component Initiation: Inputs and Outputs..59

Figure 3-37.   Monitoring and Controlling Process Group 60

Figure 3-38.   Monitor and Control Program Performance: Inputs and Outputs.................................60

Figure 3-39. Monitor and Control Program Scope: Inputs and Outputs 61

Figure 3-40. Monitor and Control Program Schedule: Inputs and Outputs 61

Figure 3-41. Monitor and Control Program Financials: Inputs and Outputs 62

Figure 3-42. Manage Program Stakeholder Expectations: Inputs and Outputs 62

Figure 3-43. Monitor and Control Program Risks: Inputs and Outputs 63

Figure 3-44. Administer Program Procurements: Inputs and Outputs 63

Figure 3-45. Manage Program Issues: Inputs and Outputs 64

Figure 3-46. Monitor and Control Program Changes: Inputs and Outputs 64

Figure 3-47. Report Program Performance: Inputs and Outputs 65

Figure 3-48. Provide Governance Oversight: Inputs and Outputs 65

Figure 3-49. Manage Program Benefits: Inputs and Output 66

Figure 3-50. Closing Process Group 67

Figure 3-51. Close Program: Inputs and Outputs 67

Figure 3-52. Approve Component Transition: Inputs and Outputs 68

Figure 3-53. Close Program Procurements: Inputs and Outputs 68

Figure 4-1. Program Integration Management Overview 73

Figure 4-2. Change Control Process Links Between Components, Program Management, and Program Governance 74

Figure 4-3. Initiate Program: Inputs, Tools & Techniques, and Outputs 75

Figure 4-4. Initiate Program: Data Flow Diagram 76

Figure 4-5. Develop Program Management Plan: Inputs, Tools & Techniques, and Outputs 80

Figure 4-6. Develop Program Management Plan: Data Flow Diagram 80

Figure 4-7. Develop Program Infrastructure: Inputs, Tools & Techniques, and Outputs 84

Figure 4-8. Develop Program Infrastructure: Data Flow Diagram 84

Figure 4-9. Direct and Manage Program Execution: Inputs, Tools & Techniques, and Outputs 88

Figure 4-10. Direct and Manage Program Execution: Data Flow Diagram 88

Figure 4-11. Manage Program Resources: Inputs, Tools & Techniques, and Outputs 91

Figure 4-12. Manage Program Resources: Data Flow Diagram 92

Figure 4-13.   Monitor and Control Program Performance: Inputs, Tools & Techniques, and Outputs..93

Figure 4-14.   Monitor and Control Program Performance: Data Flow Diagram 94

Figure 4-15.   Manage Program Issues: Inputs, Tools & Techniques, and Outputs 96

Figure 4-16.   Manage Program Issues: Data Flow Diagram 96

Figure 4-17.   Close Program: Inputs, Tools & Techniques, and Outputs..99

Figure 4-18.   Close Program: Data Flow Diagram 99

Figure 5-1.   Program Scope Management Overview 104

Figure 5-2.   Plan Program Scope: Inputs, Tools & Techniques, and Outputs 105

Figure 5-3.   Plan Program Scope Process Data Flow 105

Figure 5-4.   Define Program Goals and Objectives: Inputs, Tools & Techniques, and Outputs.........107

Figure 5-5.   Define Program Goals and Objectives Process Data Flow 107

Figure 5-6.   Develop Program Requirements: Inputs, Tools& Techniques, and Outputs 110

Figure 5-7.   Develop Program Requirements Data Flow Diagram..110

Figure 5-8.   Develop Program Architecture: Inputs, Tools & Techniques, and Outputs 113

Figure 5-9.   Develop Program Architecture Process Data Flow 113

Figure 5-10.   Develop Program WBS: Inputs, Tools & Techniques, and Outputs................................115

Figure 5-11.   Develop Program WBS Data Flow Diagram 115

Figure 5-12.   Manage Program Architecture: Inputs, Tools & Techniques, and Outputs 117

Figure 5-13.   Manage Program Architecture Data Flow Diagram 118

Figure 5-14.   Manage Component Interfaces: Inputs, Tools & Techniques, and Outputs 119

Figure 5-15.   Manage Component Interfaces Data Flow Diagram...120

Figure 5-16.   Monitor and Control Program Scope: Inputs, Tools & Techniques, and Outputs...........122

Figure 5-17.   Monitor and Control Program Scope Process Data Flow Diagram.................................122

Figure 6-1.   Program Time Management Overview...126

Figure 6-2.   Program Time Management Data Flow Diagram 126

Figure 6-3.   Develop Program Schedule: Inputs, Tools & Techniques, and Outputs 127

Figure 6-4.   Develop Program Schedule: Data Flow Diagram..128

Figure 6-5.   Monitor and Control Program Schedule: Inputs, Tools & Techniques, and Outputs......131

Figure 6-6.   Monitor and Control Program Schedule: Data Flow Diagram.......................132

Figure 10-1.   Program Communication Management Overview.......................142

Figure 10-2.   Plan Communications: Inputs, Tools & Techniques, and Outputs.....................143

Figure 10-3.   Plan Communications Data Flow Diagram 143

Figure 10-4.   Distribute Information: Inputs, Tools & Techniques and Outputs 148

Figure 10-5.   Distribute Information Data Flow Diagram.......................148

Figure 10-6.   Report Program Performance: Inputs, Tools & Techniques, and Outputs.....................152

Figure 10-7.   Report Program Performance Data Flow Diagram 153

Figure 11-1.   Program Risk Management Overview 159

Figure 11-2.   Plan Program Risk Management: Inputs, Tools & Techniques, and Outputs.................161

Figure 11-3.   Plan Program Risk Management Data Flow Diagram.......................161

Figure 11-4.   Identify Program Risks: Inputs, Tools & Techniques, and Outputs 165

Figure 11-5.   Identify Program Risks Data Flow Diagram 165

Figure 11-6.   Analyze Program Risks: Inputs, Tools & Techniques, and Outputs.......................170

Figure 11-7.   Analyze Program Risks Data Flow Diagram 170

Figure 11-8.   Threats and Opportunities.......................171

Figure 11-9.   WBS—RBS Correlation Matrix Diagram 174

Figure 11-10.   Program—Project Interdependencies 175

Figure 11-11.   Plan Program Risk Responses: Inputs, Tools & Techniques, and Outputs 176

Figure 11-12.   Plan Program Risk Response Data Flow Diagram 177

Figure 11-13.   Monitor and Control Program Risks: Inputs, Tools & Techniques, and Outputs............180

Figure 11-14.   Monitor and Control Program Risks Data Flow Diagram.......................181

Figure 12-1.   Program Procurement Management Overview 186

Figure 12-2.   Program Procurement Management Data Flow Diagram 187

Figure 12-3.   Plan Program Procurements: Inputs, Tools & Techniques, and Outputs 188

Figure 12-4.   Plan Program Procurements Data Flow Diagram.......................188

Figure 12-5.   Conduct Program Procurements: Inputs, Tools & Techniques, and Outputs.................192

Figure 12-6.   Conduct Program Procurements Process Data Flow Diagram.......................193

Figure 12-7.   Administer Program Procurements: Inputs, Tools & Techniques, and Outputs............199

Figure 12-8.   Administer Program Procurements Data Flows.........................199

Figure 12-9.   Close Program Procurements: Inputs, Tools & Techniques, and Outputs....................204

Figure 12-10. Close Program Procurements Data Flow Diagram.......................204

Figure 13-1.   Program Financial Management Overview..............................208

Figure 13-2.   Program Financial Management Data Flow Diagram.....................209

Figure 13-3.   Establish Program Financial Framework Inputs, Tools & Techniques, and Outputs.....210

Figure 13-4.   Establish Program Financial Framework Data Flow Diagram.................211

Figure 13-5.   Develop Program Financial Plan: Inputs, Tools & Techniques, and Outputs.................213

Figure 13-6.   Contractor Payment Time Lag..............................214

Figure 13-7.   Develop Program Financial Plan Data Flow Diagram.....................215

Figure 13-8.   Estimate Program Costs Inputs, Tools & Techniques, and Outputs.................218

Figure 13-9.   Estimate Program Costs Data Flow Diagram..........................218

Figure 13-10. Budget Program Costs Inputs, Tools & Techniques, and Outputs....................221

Figure 13-11. Budget Program Costs Data Flow Diagrams....................221

Figure 13-12. Monitor and Control Program Financials Inputs, Tools & Techniques, and Outputs.....224

Figure 13-13. Monitor and Control Program Financials Data Flow Diagram.................224

Figure 14-1.   Program Stakeholder Management Overview..........................228

Figure 14-2.   Plan Program Stakeholder Management: Inputs, Tools & Techniques, and Outputs....229

Figure 14-3.   Plan Stakeholder Management Data Flow Diagram.....................229

Figure 14-4.   Identify Program Stakeholders: Inputs, Tools & Techniques, and Outputs.................232

Figure 14-5.   Identify Program Stakeholders Data Flow Diagram.....................232

Figure 14-6.   Engage Program Stakeholders: Inputs, Tools & Techniques, and Outputs....................236

Figure 14-7.   Engage Program Stakeholders Data Flow Diagram.....................237

Figure 14-8.   Manage Program Stakeholder Expectations: Inputs, Tools & Techniques, and Outputs..........................239

Figure 14-9.   Manage Program Stakeholder Expectations Data Flow Diagram..................................240

Figure 15-1.   Program Governance Overview..244

Figure 15-2.   Plan and Establish Program Governance Structure: Inputs, Tools & Techniques,
                and Outputs..246

Figure 15-3.   Plan and Establish Program Governance Structure: Data Flow Diagram 246

Figure 15-4.   Plan for Audits: Inputs, Tools & Techniques, and Outputs 252

Figure 15-5.   Plan for Audits: Data Flow Diagram..252

Figure 15-6.   Plan Program Quality: Inputs, Tools & Techniques, and Outputs..................................255

Figure 15-7.   Plan Program Quality: Inputs, Tools & Techniques, and Outputs..................................255

Figure 15-8.   Approve Component Initiation: Inputs, Tools & Techniques, and Outputs.....................257

Figure 15-9.   Approve Component Initiation: Data Flow Diagram 258

Figure 15-10.   Provide Governance Oversight: Inputs, Tools & Techniques, and Outputs 260

Figure 15-11.   Provide Governance Oversight: Data Flow Diagram 260

Figure 15-12.   Manage Program Benefits: Inputs, Tools & Techniques, and Outputs...........................263

Figure 15-13.   Manage Program Benefits: Data Flow Diagram 263

Figure 15-14.   Monitor and Control Program Changes: Inputs, Tools & Techniques, and Outputs 267

Figure 15-15.   Monitor and Control Program Changes: Data Flow Diagram..267

Figure 15-16.   Approve Component Transition: Inputs, Tools & Techniques, and Outputs...................269

Figure 15-17.   Approve Component Transition: Inputs, Tools & Techniques, and Outputs...................270

Table A1.   Structural Changes..275

Table A2.   Chapter 1 Summary of Changes 277

Table A3.   Chapter 2 Summary of Changes 278

Table A4.   Chapter 3 Summary of Changes 279

Table A5.   Chapter 4 Program Integration Management Changes..282

Table A6.   Chapter 5 Program Scope Management Changes...282

Table A7.   Chapter 6 Program Time Management Changes...282

Table A8.   Chapter 10 Program Communication Management Changes..282

Table A9.   Chapter 11 Program Risk Management Changes 283

Table A10. **Chapter 12 Program Procurement Management Changes** 283

Table A11. **Chapter 13 Program Financial Management Changes**...283

Table A12. **Chapter 14 Program Stakeholder Management Changes**...283

Table A13. **Chapter 15 Program Governance Changes**...284

PREFACE TO THE SECOND EDITION

This document supersedes the first publication of *The Standard for Program Management*. Since its initial publication in May 2006, the Project Management Institute (PMI) has received many valuable recommendations for improvements to this standard. These recommendations, as well as those received during the Exposure Draft process, were taken into consideration during the development of the second edition.

The team responsible for developing, reviewing, and editing the second edition included more than 150 volunteers from around the world and from many different industry segments, for example, construction, aerospace, IT, pharmaceuticals, petroleum/chemicals, and others.

In order to achieve the goal of providing a standard that was useful for program managers from diverse areas, the team followed the consensus processes required by the American National Standards Institute (ANSI):

In addition to these ANSI requirements, the management team had specific goals from PMI to:

1. Revise the standard so that it would not conflict with other PMI standards such as *A Guide to the Project Management Body of Knowledge (PMBOK® Guide)* – Fourth Edition, *The Standard for Portfolio Management* – Second Edition, and the revision to the *Organizational Project Management Maturity Model (OPM3®)*. All of these standards were being developed in parallel with each other.

2. Ensure that the information contained in the standard was cohesive in concept and clear in writing style, and that terminology was well-defined and congruous with the other standards' terminology.

3. Ensure that all processes in the standard were consistent and congruent with those of the *Organizational Project Management Maturity Model (OPM3®)* – Second Edition.

The most significant difference between the first and second edition is in the development of program-specific Knowledge Areas. These included Knowledge Areas that are critical to successful program management as well as Knowledge Areas that are significantly different at a program level than at a project level.

A second significant difference between the two editions was in the removal of "themes" that were introduced in the first edition. The theme of Program Stakeholder Management was expanded into a Knowledge Area. The theme of Program Governance was significantly expanded and also became a Knowledge Area. The theme of Benefits Management was incorporated into the body of the document.

One last area of note is that there are three areas: Cost Management, Quality Management, and Human Resource Management, that were determined to be better discussed at the project level rather than at the higher program level as stand-alone Knowledge Areas. These areas reference the *PMBOK® Guide*—Fourth Edition for the reader. At a program level, Chapter 13 discusses how to manage program finances while leaving the discussion of project costing and budgeting to the project level. Similarly, program-level quality is discussed under the umbrella of program governance, with detailed discussions of quality deferred to the project level.

Section I: The Project Management Framework provides a basis for understanding program management. There are two chapters in this section.

Chapter 1: Introduction presents a basis and purpose for the standard. It defines what a program is, how it differs from a project, and discusses program management and the relationship among project, program, and portfolio management. It introduces the Program Management Office and describes the external influences on programs. The chapter includes:

- Purpose of *The Standard for Program Management*
- What is a Program?
- What is Program Management?
- Relationships Among Project, Program, and Portfolio
- Program Management Office
- Role of the Program Manager
- Program-External Factors

Chapter 2: Program Life Cycle and Benefits Management describes the basic phases of a program and important considerations that can help a program manager to be able to adapt the life cycle model to satisfy requirements assigned to the program. Programs are a means of achieving organizational goals and objectives that are so large scale that they cannot be achieved by single projects. This chapter describes basic phases of a program and important considerations that can help a program manager to be able to adapt the life cycle model to satisfy requirements assigned to the program. The chapter includes:

- The Program Life Cycle—Overview
- Program Life Cycle Phases
- Program Benefits Management

Section II: *The Standard for Program Management* defines the program management processes and defines the inputs and outputs for each process within the context of the Process Groups.

Chapter 3: Program Management Processes defines the five Process Groups: Initiation, Planning, Executing, Monitoring and Controlling, and Closing. It shows the major relationships among the Process Groups as well as inputs and outputs that are common to multiple processes. This chapter also shows the specific processes within each Process Group. The chapter includes:

- Common Program Management Process Interactions
- Program Management Process Groups

- Initiating Process Group
- Planning Process Group
- Executing Process Group
- Monitoring and Controlling Process Group
- Closing Process Group

Section III: The Program Management Knowledge Areas describes the new Program Management Knowledge Areas, lists the program management processes and defines the inputs, tools and techniques, and outputs for each area. Each of the chapters focus on a specific Knowledge Area.

Chapter 4: Program Integration Management includes the processes and activities needed to identify, define, combine, unify, and coordinate multiple components within the program as well as coordinate the various processes and program management activities within the Program Management Process Groups. This chapter includes:

- Initiate Program
- Develop Program Management Plan
- Develop Program Infrastructure
- Direct and Manage Program Execution
- Manage Program Resources
- Monitor and Control Program Performance
- Manage Program Issues
- Close Program

Chapter 5: Program Scope Management identifies the deliverables, estimates the major risks, and establishes the relationship between product scope and program scope while setting standards for clear achievable objectives. This chapter includes:

- Plan Program Scope
- Define Program Goals and Objectives
- Develop Program Requirements
- Develop Program Architecture
- Develop Program WBS
- Manage Program Architecture
- Manage Component Interfaces
- Monitor and Control Program Scope

Chapter 6: Program Time Management involves processes for scheduling the defined program components and entities necessary to produce the final program deliverables. It includes determining the order in which the individual components are executed, the critical path for the program, and the milestones to be measured to keep the overall program on track and within the defined constraints. This chapter includes:

- Develop Program Schedule
- Monitor and Control Program Schedule

Chapter 7: Program Cost Management—Refer to the *PMBOK® Guide* – Fourth Edition

Chapter 8: Program Quality Management—Refer to the *PMBOK® Guide* – Fourth Edition.

Chapter 9: Program Human Resource Management—Refer to the *PMBOK® Guide* – Fourth Edition.

Chapter 10: Program Communications Management includes the processes for ensuring timely and appropriate generation, collection, distribution, storage, retrieval, and ultimate disposition of program information. The Program Communication Management processes provide the critical links between people and information that are necessary for successful communications. This chapter includes:

- Plan Communications
- Distribute Information
- Report Program Performance

Chapter 11: Program Risk Management describes the processes involved with identifying, analyzing, and controlling risks for the program. This chapter includes:

- Plan Program Risk Management
- Identify Program Risks
- Analyze Program Risks
- Plan Program Risk Responses
- Monitor and Control Program Risks

Chapter 12: Program Procurement Management describes the processes, inputs, tools and techniques, and outputs associated with performing procurement for a program. This chapter includes:

- Plan Program Procurements
- Conduct Program Procurements

- Administer Program Procurements

- Close Program Procurements

Chapter 13: Program Financial Management includes all of the processes involved in identifying the program's financial sources and resources, integrating the budgets of the individual program components, developing the overall budget for the program, and controlling costs throughout the life cycle of both the component and program. This chapter includes:

- Establish Program Financial Framework

- Develop Program Financial Plan

- Estimate Program Costs

- Budget Program Costs

- Monitor and Control Program Financials

Chapter 14: Program Stakeholder Management defines program stakeholders as individuals and organizations whose interests may be affected by the program outcomes, either positively or negatively. This chapter includes:

- Plan Program Stakeholder Management

- Identify Program Stakeholders

- Engage Program Stakeholders

- Manage Program Stakeholder Expectations

Chapter 15: Program Governance ensures decision-making and delivery management activities are focused on achieving program goals in a consistent manner, addressing appropriate risks and fulfilling stakeholder requirements. This chapter includes:

- Plan and Establish Program Governance Structure

- Plan for Audits

- Plan Program Quality

- Approve Component Initiation

- Provide Governance Oversight

- Manage Program Benefits

- Monitor and Control Program Changes

- Approve Component Transition

Section IV:

   Appendices

Section V:

   Glossary

   Index

The Standard for Program Management – Second Edition was presented in an exposure draft early in 2008. Most of the recommendations sent in by reviewers were incorporated into this final release either entirely or slightly modified for internal consistency.

SECTION I

THE PROGRAM MANAGEMENT FRAMEWORK

Chapter 1

- Introduction

Chapter 2

- Program Life Cycle and Benefits Management

CHAPTER 1

INTRODUCTION

The Standard for Program Management provides guidelines for managing programs within an organization. It defines program management and related concepts, describes the main generic phases of the program management life cycle, and outlines related processes. This standard is an expansion of information in and a companion to *A Guide to the Project Management Body of Knowledge* (*PMBOK® Guide*) – Fourth Edition. The *PMBOK® Guide* is the accepted standard describing the processes of project management and the management of individual projects throughout their life cycle. The *PMBOK® Guide* briefly addresses the management of multiple projects and other activities beyond the scope of managing individual projects.

This chapter defines and explains several key terms and provides an overview of the rest of the document. It includes the following major sections:

1.1 Purpose of *The Standard for Program Management*

1.2 What is a Program?

1.3 What is Program Management?

1.4 Relationships among Project, Program, and Portfolio

1.5 Program Management Office

1.6 Role of the Program Manager

1.7 Program-External Factors

The terms *program* and *program management* are used in different ways by different organizations. Some organizations and industries refer to ongoing or cyclical streams of operational or functional work as programs. An example of this is a social program funded by a government. The recognized disciplines of operational or functional management address this type of work; therefore, this form of program is out of the scope of this standard.

Other organizations refer to large projects as programs. These "programs" include large individual projects or a large project that is broken into more easily managed subprojects. These efforts remain within the discipline of project management, and as such, are already covered in the *PMBOK® Guide.* When the management of these efforts results in collective benefits and control is not achievable through managing individual projects, the effort becomes a program. *The Standard for Program Management* is applicable to managing these efforts.

Some groups define programs by the manner in which the projects are related. This standard defines a program as a group of related projects managed in a coordinated way to obtain benefits and control not available when managing them individually. All projects within a program are related through a common goal. If the projects have separate goals and are only related by common funding, technology, stakeholders, or resources, then these efforts are better managed as a portfolio rather than as a program. *The Standard for Portfolio Management* – Second Edition addresses the management of project portfolios.

1.1 Purpose of *The Standard for Program Management*

The Standard for Program Management presents materials that are specific and relevant to program management. This standard is an important and essential link in understanding how to drive the strategy of the organization by enhancing the delivery capabilities of interrelated components. It also provides information on program management that is clear, complete, relevant, and generally recognized as good practices on most programs, most of the time. "Generally recognized" means the knowledge and practices described are applicable to most projects most of the time, and there is consensus about their value and usefulness. "Good practice" means that there is general agreement that the application of these skills, tools, and techniques can enhance the chances of success over a wide range of projects. Good practice does not mean the knowledge described should always be applied uniformly to all projects; the organization and/or project management team is responsible for determining what is appropriate for any given project.

This standard is aligned with:

- *PMBOK® Guide* – Fourth Edition,
- *The Standard for Portfolio Management* – Second Edition, and
- *The Organizational Project Management Maturity Model (OPM3®)* – Second Edition.

The primary purpose of *The Standard for Program Management* is to describe generally recognized good practices and place program management in the context of portfolio and project management. The processes documented within this standard are generally accepted as the necessary steps to successfully manage a program. In addition, this standard promotes efficient and effective communication and coordination by providing a common lexicon leading to a detailed understanding of program management among the following groups:

- Project managers, so they can understand the role of program managers and the relationship and interface between project and program managers;
- Program managers, to enable them to understand how to effectively manage programs;
- Portfolio managers, in order for them to understand the role of program managers and the relationship and interface between program and portfolio managers (when the program is part of an actively managed portfolio); and
- Stakeholders, to help them understand the role of program managers and how they engage the various stakeholder groups (e.g., users, executive management, client).

This introductory chapter provides an overview of *The Standard for Program Management* by assisting the reader in understanding where program management fits in the management spectrum. Furthermore, the introduction lists the benefits that can be gained by utilizing it.

In addition to the standards that establish guidelines for project management processes, tools, and techniques, the *Project Management Institute Code of Ethics and Professional Conduct,* guides practitioners of the profession of project management and describes the expectations practitioners have of themselves and others. The *Project Management Institute Code of Ethics and Professional Conduct* is specific about the basic obligation of responsibility, respect, fairness and honesty. It requires that practitioners demonstrate a commitment to ethical and professional conduct. It carries the obligation to comply with laws, regulations and organizational and professional policies. Since practitioners come from diverse backgrounds and cultures, the *Code of Ethics and Professional Conduct* applies globally. When dealing with any stakeholder, practitioners should be committed to honest and fair practices and respectful dealings. The *Project Management Institute Code of Ethics and Professional Conduct* is posted on the PMI website (http://www.pmi.org). Acceptance of the code is a requirement for the PMP® certification by PMI.

1.2 What is a Program?

A program is a group of related projects managed in a coordinated way to obtain benefits and control not available from managing them individually. Programs may include elements of related work outside of the scope of the discrete projects in the program. Programs are comprised of various components. Most of these components are the separate projects within the program, but another component is the management effort and infrastructure needed to manage the program. Thus, programs may include elements of related work (e.g. managing the program itself) outside the scope of the discrete projects in a program.

Programs and projects deliver benefits to organizations by enhancing current capabilities or developing new capabilities for the organization to use. A benefit is an outcome of actions and behaviors that provides utility to the organization.

Programs, like projects, are a means of achieving organizational goals and objectives, often in the context of a strategic plan. Some projects within a program can deliver useful incremental benefits to the organization before the program itself has completed. An example of this is an organization-wide process improvement program with multiple projects within the program.

For many programs, all of the benefits come at the very end of the program and are delivered at once. These programs are best exemplified by the construction industry, aerospace and military development programs, public works construction projects, shipbuilding, and other areas.

1.3 What is Program Management?

Program management is the centralized coordinated management of a program to achieve the program's strategic objectives and benefits. It involves aligning multiple projects to achieve the program goals and allows for optimized or integrated cost, schedule, and effort.

Projects within a program are related through a common outcome or a collective capability that is delivered. If the relationship among the projects is only that of a shared client, seller, technology, or resources, the effort should be managed as a portfolio of projects rather than as a program. In programs, it is important to integrate, monitor, and control the interdependencies among the components. Program management focuses on these project interdependencies and helps to determine the optimal approach for managing them. Actions related to these interdependencies may include:

- Coordinating the supply of components, work, or phases as experienced in the construction of bridges, skyscrapers, or aircraft;
- For internal programs, resolving resource constraints and/or conflicts that affect multiple projects within the program;
- Mitigating risk activities that run across components, such as contingency planning;
- Aligning organizational/strategic direction that affects project and program goals and objectives; and
- Resolving issues and scope/cost/schedule/quality changes within a shared governance structure.
- Tailoring program management processes and interfaces across a global program to handle culture, language, time, and distance differences.

Through structured governance, program management enables appropriate planning, scheduling, executing, monitoring, and controlling across the projects within the program to achieve program benefits. Program management provides a framework for managing related projects considering key factors such as strategic benefits, coordinated planning, complex interdependencies, deliverable integration, and optimized pacing.

See Section 1.4 for definitions and relationships among projects, programs, and portfolios.

1.4 Relationships among Project, Program, and Portfolio

In understanding program management, it is important to distinguish among project management, portfolio management, and program management. These relationships are shown graphically in Figure 1-1. A project is defined as a temporary endeavor undertaken to create a unique product, service or result. Project management is the application of knowledge, skills, tools, and techniques to project activities to meet the project requirements.

A program is comprised of multiple related projects that are initiated during the program's life cycle and are managed in a coordinated fashion. The program manager coordinates efforts between projects but does not directly manage the individual projects.

A portfolio is a collection of components (i.e., projects, programs, portfolios, and other work such as maintenance and related ongoing operations) that are grouped together to facilitate the effective management of that work in order to meet strategic business objectives. The projects or programs of the portfolio may not necessarily be interdependent or directly related.

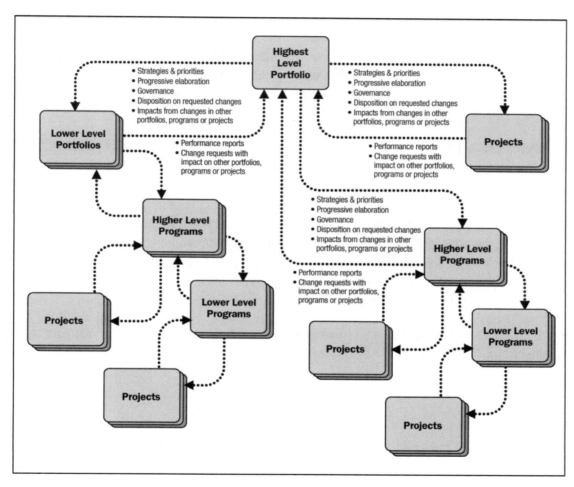

Figure 1-1. Portfolio, Program, and Project Management Interactions

1.4.1   The Relationship between Program Management and Project Management

During a program's life cycle, projects are initiated and the program manager oversees and provides direction and guidance to the project managers. Program managers coordinate efforts between projects but do not manage them. Essential program management responsibilities include the identification, monitoring and control of the interdependencies between projects; dealing with the escalated issues among the projects that comprise the program; and tracking the contribution of each project and the non-project work to the consolidated program benefits.

The integrative nature of program management processes involves coordinating the processes for each of the projects or program. This applies through all the Process Groups of Initiating, Planning, Executing, Monitoring and Controlling, and Closing, and involves managing the processes at a level higher than those pertaining to a project. An example of this type of integration is the management of issues and risks needing resolution at the program level, because they involve multiple projects or otherwise cross project boundaries and therefore cannot be addressed at the individual project level.

The interactions between a program and its components tend to be iterative and cyclical. During the early phases of initiating and planning, information flows from the program to the components, and then flows from the components to the program in the later phases of planning and in the executing, monitoring and controlling, and closing. Early in the life cycle, the program guides and directs the project domain on desired goals and benefits. The program domain also influences the approach for managing the individual projects within it. Later in the life cycle, the project domain reports to the program domain on project status, risks, changes, costs, issues and other information affecting the program. An example of such an interaction can be found during schedule development, where a detailed review of the overall schedule at the component level is needed to validate information at the program level.

Figure 1-2 shows the interaction of information flow between program management and project management.

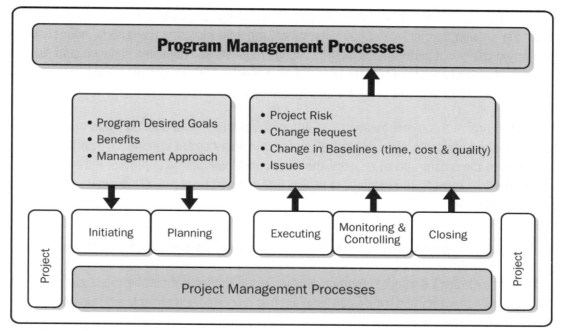

Figure 1-2. Interaction between Program Management and Project Management

1.4.2   The Relationship between Program Management and Portfolio Management

A portfolio is a collection of components (i.e., projects, programs, portfolios, and other work such as maintenance and ongoing operations) that are grouped together to facilitate the effective management of that work in order to meet strategic business objectives. The projects or programs within a portfolio may not necessarily be interdependent or directly related and in fact are normally unrelated, although they may share a common resource pool or compete for funding.

A project portfolio always exists within an organization that has projects in progress. It is comprised of the set of current initiatives, which may or may not be related, interdependent, or even managed as a portfolio. Projects may have been created by management efforts to benefit one part of the organization without regard to overall strategic objectives or risks. With portfolio management, the organization is able to align the portfolio to strategic objectives, approve only components that directly support business objectives, and take into account the risk of the component mix in a portfolio at any given time. Components may be deferred by the organization when the risk of adding them to the current portfolio would unreasonably upset the balance and exceed the organizational risk tolerance. The portfolio is a snapshot of the organization's projects in work, reflecting the organizational goals at the time the projects were selected.

Like the interactions between program and project domains, portfolio management and program management domains interact in their Process Groups. If the organization is actively managing its portfolio, the program's Initiating and Planning Process Groups receive inputs from the portfolio domain. These inputs include strategic goals and benefits, funding allocations, requirements, timelines, and constraints that the program team translates into the program scope, deliverables, budget, and schedule. The direction of control usually flows from the portfolio to the program.

Similarly, the program's Executing, Monitoring and Controlling, and Closing Process Groups provide inputs to the portfolio domain that include status information, program performance reports, budget and schedule updates, earned value cost performance reports, change requests and approved changes, and escalated risks and issues. The type and frequency of these interactions is specified by the portfolio management or governance team, and influenced by the program review and update cycles.

A portfolio is one of the truest measures of an organization's intent, direction, and progress. It is where investment decisions are made, resources are allocated, and priorities are identified. If a portfolio's components are not aligned to the organizational strategy, the components will not be approved. If the strategic direction changes, the portfolio must be re-examined to ensure that its constituent projects are still viable and expending resources is worthwhile.

1.4.3   The Interactions among Portfolio, Program, and Project Management

The distinctions among portfolio, program, and project management can be made clearer through their interaction. Portfolio management focuses on assuring that programs and projects are selected, prioritized, and staffed with respect to their alignment with organizational strategies. Programs focus on achieving the benefits aligned with the portfolio and, subsequently, organizational objectives. Programs are comprised of projects that focus on achieving their individual requirements. Figure 1-3 depicts the often-complex relationship between portfolios, programs, projects, and related work.

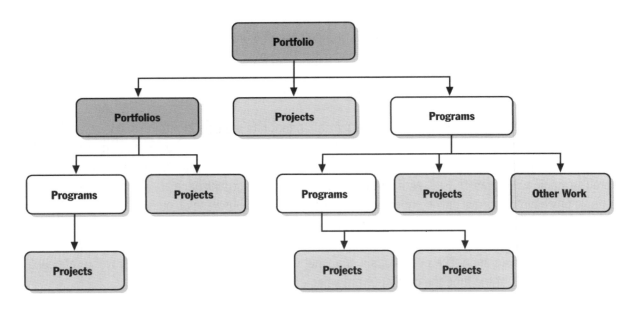

Figure 1-3. Portfolios, Programs and Projects—High-Level View

Table 1-1 summarizes some of the differences among portfolios, programs, and projects.

Table 1-1. Comparative Overview of Project, Program, and Portfolio Management

	PROJECTS	PROGRAMS	PORTFOLIOS
Scope	Projects have defined objectives. Scope is progressively elaborated throughout the project life cycle.	Programs have a larger scope and provide more significant benefits.	Portfolios have a business scope that changes with the strategic goals of the organization.
Change	Project managers expect change and implement processes to keep change managed and controlled.	The program manager must expect change from both inside and outside the program and be prepared to manage it.	Portfolio managers continually monitor changes in the broad environment.
Planning	Project managers progressively elaborate high-level information into detailed plans throughout the project life cycle.	Program managers develop the overall program plan and create high-level plans to guide detailed planning at the component level.	Portfolio managers create and maintain necessary processes and communication relative to the aggregate portfolio.
Management	Project managers manage the project team to meet the project objectives.	Program managers manage the program staff and the project managers; they provide vision and overall leadership.	Portfolio managers may manage or coordinate portfolio management staff.
Success	Success is measured by product and project quality, timeliness, budget compliance, and degree of customer satisfaction.	Success is measured by the degree to which the program satisfies the needs and benefits for which it was undertaken.	Success is measured in terms of aggregate performance of portfolio components.
Monitoring	Project managers monitor and control the work of producing the products, services or results that the project was undertaken to produce.	Program managers monitor the progress of program components to ensure the overall goals, schedules, budget, and benefits of the program will be met.	Portfolio managers monitor aggregate performance and value indicators.

1.5 Program Management Office

The program management office (PMO) is a crucial portion of the program's infrastructure. The PMO supports the program manager with the management of multiple, unrelated projects. While there are many varieties of PMOs within organizations, for the purposes of this standard the PMO provides support to the program manager by:

- Defining the program management processes that will be followed,
- Managing schedule and budget at the program level,
- Defining the quality standards for the program and for the program's components,
- Providing document configuration management, and
- Providing centralized support for managing changes and tracking risks and issues.

In addition, for long, risky, or complex programs, the program management office may provide additional support in the areas of managing personnel resources, managing contracts and procurements (especially international procurements), legal support, and other support as required. Some programs continue for years and assume many aspects of normal operations that overlap with the larger organization's operational management.

1.6 Role of the Program Manager

The role of the program manager is separate and distinct from that of the project manager. The program manager interacts with each project manager to provide support and guidance on the individual projects as well as to convey the important relationship of each project to the bigger picture, including the larger program and the organizational performance objectives. The program manager is responsible for ensuring that the overall program structure and program management processes enable the component teams to successfully complete their work and that the components' deliverables can be integrated into the program's end product, service, results and/or benefits. Program managers also ensure projects are organized and executed in a consistent manner and/or fulfilled within established standards. The PMO supports the program manager by providing the information needed to make decisions that guide the program and by providing administrative support in managing schedules, budgets, risks, and the other areas required for effective program management.

Program managers should have a broad view both of program objectives and organizational culture and processes. Leverage of resources among program's projects, evaluation of total ownership costs, and requirements and configuration management across projects are main issues for program managers.

1.6.1 Program Manager Knowledge and Skills

Program management requires a special blend of technical program management skills, time management abilities, and a solid foundation of people skills, including political skills. The most important competence, however, is communication. A program manager must have strong communication skills to deal with various stakeholders—team members, sponsors, managing directors, customers, vendors, senior management, and other program stakeholders.

The program manager must identify stakeholders, understand their needs and expectations, and develop a stakeholder management plan to engage affected stakeholders, manage their expectations, and improve their acceptance of program objectives. The program manager must also recognize committed stakeholders from those that are only interested. Some stakeholders are professionally committed, some are both professionally and emotionally committed to the program's success or failure, and others are only interested. The program manager must recognize the dynamic human aspects of each program and manage accordingly. This can be extremely difficult in programs that have an impact on the public, such as highway, bridge, or dam construction. Many stakeholders will be against the program because it may have a negative impact on their particular interests. Yet the program manager cannot ignore these special interests and will often find that dealing with them requires a great deal of time and effort to communicate program goals, manage their expectations, and establish buy-in to ensure the success of the program.

The program communications management plan should address stakeholder needs and expectations, providing key messages in a timely fashion and in the correct format to all interested parties. It is important to initiate, engage and maintain stakeholder relationships to effectively manage the program and achieve desired benefits. Active management of stakeholder relationships can help to build support for the program.

Leadership skills are needed for managing multiple program teams throughout the program life cycle. Program managers lead the program management team in establishing program direction, identifying interdependencies, communicating program requirements, tracking progress, making decisions, and resolving conflicts and issues. Program managers work with component managers and often with functional managers to gain support, resolve conflicts, and lead individual program team members by providing specific work directions. Leadership is embedded in the program manager's job and happens throughout the program life cycle. Figure 1-4 highlights the skills and competence required to be an effective program manager.

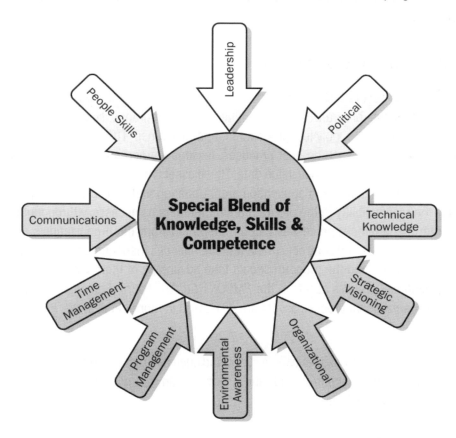

Figure 1-4. Required Blend of Skills and Competence in a Program Manager

Programs often require strategic visioning and planning skills to align program goals and benefits with the long-term goals of the organization. Once the program goals and benefits have been defined, structured plans are developed to execute the individual components. While project managers lead the work on their components, it is the program manager's responsibility to ensure alignment of the individual plans with the program goals and benefits.

Consideration should be given to the political relationships that need to be observed and fostered within a program. The program manager may not be able to affect or influence it during the life cycle of a project or even a program. Understanding the political climate and temperature of a program is important in achieving a positive relationship, and setting the ground work for when the benefits from the program will be transitioned to the supporting organization.

1.7 Program-External Factors

There are often influences outside the program that can have a significant impact on the program's management and ultimate success. Some of these enterprise environmental factors come from outside the program but are internal to the larger organization, and some of these influences come from completely external sources. The program manager is responsible for identifying these influences as much as possible, and taking them into account when managing the program.

1.7.1   Organizational Process Assets

Organizational process assets include any or all processes related to the assets, from any or all of the organizations involved in the program that can influence the program's success. These process assets include formal and informal plans, policies, procedures, and guidelines. The process assets also include the organizations' knowledge bases such as best practices, lessons learned and historical information, such as completed schedules, risk data, and earned value data. These assets may take many different forms depending on the type of industry, organization, and application area. Updating and adding to the organizational process assets is generally the responsibility of the program team members as necessary throughout the program life cycle. Many program management processes can be supported from the organization's operations groups. Processes such as procurement and contracts management, financial management, quality control, and others often exist in the organization and the program should take advantage of them whenever possible. These are referred to as organizational process assets in the *PMBOK® Guide* – Fourth Edition, and apply to programs as well as to projects. Organizational process assets are discussed in more detail in the *PMBOK® Guide* – Fourth Edition.

Many program management processes can be supported such as procurement and contracts management, financial management and quality control, and others that exist in the organization so that the program can take advantage of them wherever possible.

1.7.2   Enterprise Environmental Factors

Outside of the program there are organizational factors that influence the selection, design, funding, and management of the program. The program has been selected and prioritized according to how well it supports the strategic goals of the organization. However, strategic goals can change. A change in direction of the organization can cause the program to no longer support the new strategic goals. In this case the program may be changed or cancelled completely regardless of how well it was doing with regard to the old strategic direction.

There are many parts of the larger organization that can influence program success or failure. The organization should have well-defined and documented processes, tools, and templates for managing programs and projects. These documented processes form internal standards that programs should follow. Deviations from these standards will require approval by the governance organization. Tools and templates should be available for the program manager so that he or she does not have to create documents from new when similar documents have been produced in the past.

1.7.3 Enterprise External Factors

Both the program and its performing organization can be impacted by environmental influences that are external to both. Examples include:

- Changes in governmental regulations can have an immediate impact on the organization and any efforts it has in work;

- Changes in market conditions may cause a program to be cancelled, slowed down, or sped up;

- Changes in the funding organization can cause a redesign of the product to save money;

- Changes in military threat levels may cause weapons programs in progress to be cancelled and new programs begun;

- Changes in interest rates can cause funds to be made less available;

- Changes in the political climate can cause stakeholder resistance to new highway construction; and

- New stakeholders may appear from external sources and change the direction of a current program.

CHAPTER 2

PROGRAM LIFE CYCLE AND BENEFITS MANAGEMENT

As stated in Chapter 1, programs deliver benefits to organizations developing new capabilities or by enhancing current capabilities. The program manager must understand this wider context to be able to adapt the life cycle model and program benefits to satisfy the needs for which the program was created.

This chapter describes the basic phases of a program and important considerations that can help a program manager to be able to adapt the life cycle model to satisfy requirements assigned to the program. Programs are means of achieving organizational goals and objectives that are so large scale that they cannot be achieved by single projects. This chapter describes basic phases of a program and important considerations that can help a program manager to be able to adapt the life cycle model to satisfy requirements assigned to the program.

This chapter describes some of the key life cycle considerations in the program management context. The topics include:

2.1 The Program Life Cycle -- Overview

2.2 Program Life Cycle Phases

2.3 Program Benefits Management

2.1 The Program Life Cycle – Overview

Programs have both a life cycle and a set of Process Groups. In addition, programs generally require an infrastructure that supports the program manager and provides information on schedule and budget performance, risks, inter-component status and issues, stakeholder communications, and all other information needed to effectively manage the program. Because of the often complex nature and duration of programs, program managers spend a proportionally larger amount of effort in stakeholder communications and management than project managers do.

Programs, just as projects, have an initiation effort, a development effort, and an end. The details within those three spans are dependent on the type of program. The program begins either when funding is approved or when the program manager is assigned. The program is ended by the steering committee when all components within the program have successfully produced their deliverable, or are at the stage whereby they can deliver these benefits in the future, and they have been incorporated into the final product; and that final product is either delivered to the customer or transitioned into an operations phase. Quite often a significant amount of program work occurs during the integration effort when the multiple deliverables from the components are tied together into a final integration product. Integration testing can require a significant amount of time and cost to ensure the different pieces work together as a unified system.

The components within the program can begin at any time after the program begins and generally end before the program itself ends. The product of these components is integrated into the final product being developed by the program. This is shown in Figure 2-1.

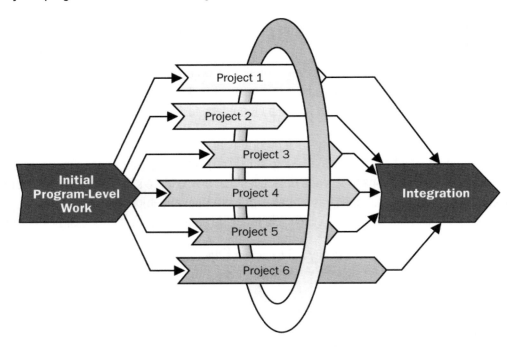

Figure 2-1. Program Component Overlap

These phases facilitate program governance, enhanced control, and coordination of program and component schedule and budget and overall risk management.

To ensure that the program delivers the expected benefits, there is management oversight of a program through governance, often by means of regular status updates, audits, phase-gate reviews, and change control. In the context of a program, some projects may produce benefits that can be realized immediately whereas other projects may deliver capabilities that must be integrated with the capabilities delivered by other projects before the associated benefits can be realized.

2.1.1   Characteristics of the Program Life Cycle

Organizations and their project managers recognize that current best practice in project control involves breaking the project into discrete stages or phases. The management of programs has the same requirement. To assure effective program control, the program moves through discrete, though often overlapping phases. These phases facilitate program governance, enhanced control and coordination of program and project resources, and overall risk management.

The type of program being managed may influence a program life cycle—construction programs have different life cycles than business process improvement programs do. However, the major life cycle phases and their deliverables remain similar. Five main phases are identified in a program life cycle:

1. Pre-Program Preparations

2. Program Initiation

3. Program Setup

4. Delivery of Program Benefits

5. Program Closure

This high-level view provides a common frame of reference for all programs regardless of their nature and industry.

As stated previously, a significant part of the definition of a program is that it is comprised of multiple components. Each component begins at the appropriate time in the program schedule and delivers its product to the program. That product is incorporated into the overall product being developed by the program. Component initiation and component closure are significant milestones on the program schedule.

2.1.2   Relationship to a Product's Life Cycle

While there are various approaches to the product life cycle, the most typical phase categories include: conception, design, manufacturing, service, and divestment.

The specific product being developed can influence the phase and progress through the phases of the program life cycle. For example, a large program with a single product, such as the development and construction of a large building complex, a simple model of the product life cycle in its four phases (build, commission, operate, maintain) represents the progression of the product as it moves through its life. As the product progresses from phase to phase, the program management of the product will also be following its life cycle. The movement from phase to phase in the product life cycle, from a schedule, cost, benefits, and stakeholder management perspective can be impacted by changes. If, for example, during commissioning of the building complex, a major unplanned change requires some reconstruction, then this impact will be felt in the program life cycle as well as in the product life cycle. Similarly, if during the build phase progress is moving more swiftly than expected, this also influences the program life cycle, while being subject to its own product life cycle.

In programs where multiple versions of a product are expected, the products would follow their product life cycle while at the same time fulfilling differing objectives. For example, Boeing's 777 program includes several products: the 777-200, 777-200ER, 777-200 LR, 777-300, 777-300LR, and the 777-F. Although each of these products have different missions and are designed with different features, they share the same product life cycle, in this case: design, build, commission, operate, maintain, decommission, and dispose. Each of these products in their various phases on the product life cycle can have major or minor influence on the phases of the overall program life cycle, and should be monitored accordingly.

2.1.3 Program Life Cycle and Benefits Management

The program life cycle complies with the needs of corporate governance and also ensures that the expected benefits are realized in a predictable and coordinated manner. As will be discussed later, benefits management requires the establishment of processes and measures for tracking and assessing benefits throughout the program life cycle. For programs that deliver incremental benefits, the management of these benefits has a life cycle of its own which runs parallel to that of the program, a relationship that is illustrated in Figure 2-2.

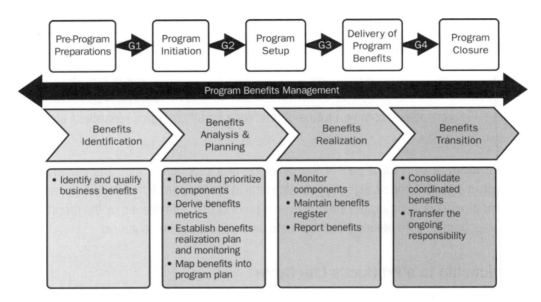

Figure 2-2. Program Life Cycle and Program Benefits Management

Program life cycle and program benefits management begins during pre-program preparations with benefits identification, and continues throughout the Program Setup life cycle phases. There should be a clear definition and agreement among stakeholders on the factors contributing to these identified benefits, as well as a supporting structure and processes to help plan, manage, measure, track, and realize the benefits. The benefits expected from each project should be defined in the project business case before the project is initiated, and combined together with the benefit tracking and assessment processes at the program level.

During Program Setup, phase capabilities for recording, tracking, and evaluating benefits should be established in accordance with the benefits definition and assessment processes defined in the preceding phase.

During program phase-gate reviews and at the Program Closure phase, benefits management includes reporting planned versus actual benefits at the current point in time, as well as forecasting their ongoing value, reasons for any deviations, and recommendations on how gaps can be bridged.

2.1.4   Program Governance across the Life Cycle

While it is not a specific phase in the program management life cycle, governance spans all of the program life cycle phases. Program governance oversees the progress of the program and the delivery of the coordinated benefits from its components.

Programs are often too complex to be managed by a single individual, which is why appropriate implementation of program governance is critical for a program to succeed. Program governance assists in managing risks, stakeholders, benefits, resources, and quality across program life cycle.

Program governance provides an appropriate organizational structure and the policies and procedures necessary to support program delivery through formal program reviews. This is facilitated by the regular and phase-gate-based oversight of deliverables, performance, risks, and issues by the program board.

This section highlights governance activities, and how it should be applied throughout the program management life cycle. The mechanisms for doing so are described in Chapter 15.

Program governance monitors and reviews the progress of the program and the delivery of the coordinated benefits from its component projects.

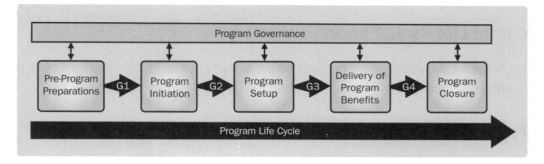

Figure 2-3. A Representative Program Life Cycle

A common oversight approach is to monitor progress by means of predefined milestones such as phase-gate reviews. The phase-gate review approach, common in new product development, is focused on strategic alignment, investment appraisal, monitoring and control of opportunities and threats, benefit assessment, and monitoring program outcomes. In cases where the program was initiated as part of a portfolio, these reviews will be carried out within the context of the corresponding portfolio.

Phase-gate reviews (Figure 2-3) are recommended to assist program control and management as well as to facilitate program governance. Phase-gate reviews are carried out at key decision points in the program life cycle. The purpose of phase-gate reviews is to provide an objective check against the exit criteria of a completed phase to determine readiness to proceed to the next phase in the program life cycle. Phase-gate reviews also provide an opportunity to assess the program with respect to a number of strategic and quality-related criteria including:

- Program and its constituent projects are aligned with the organization's strategy,

- Expected benefits are in line with the business case,

- Level of risk remains acceptable to the organization,

- Generally accepted good practices are being followed (e.g., efficient resource utilization, effective decision making, appropriate accountability and oversight, stakeholder engagement, etc.), and

- The program/projects within it are still relevant to the organization.

Phase-gate reviews are often based upon the core investment decisions within the life cycle. The focus of each phase-gate review is specific to the phase just completed by the program. Each phase-gate review functions as a "go" or "no-go" decision point on the program as a whole. In the case of phase-gate G4, shown in Figure 2-3, it is a convention to indicate confirmation of program closure.

2.2 Program Life Cycle Phases

This section defines the phases of the program life cycle. These phases apply to most programs most of the time. The durations of these phases will vary depending on unique program requirements.

2.2.1   Pre-Program Preparations

The objective of work done before the program is approved identifies the needs supported by a valid business case that lead to a program being created. This enables the program to be justified and prioritized which prepares the groundwork for initiating the program (Figure 2-4).

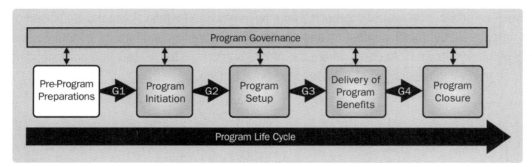

Figure 2-4. Pre-Program Preparations

In program management, there is typically a selection process that determines whether an organization will approve a program. This selection process varies from a very informal to formal using a standardized approach. The more mature an organization is in terms of program management, the more likely it is to have a formalized selection process. A strategic decision-making body in the form of portfolio review board or executive steering group may issue a program mandate which defines the strategic objectives and benefits that the program is expected to deliver. This program mandate confirms the commitment of organizational resources to determine if a program is the most appropriate approach to achieve these objectives, and also triggers the program initiation phase.

The pre-program work focuses on the analysis of the available information about organizational and business strategies, internal and external influences, program drivers, and the benefits that involved parties expect to realize. The program is defined in terms of expected results, resources needed, and the complexity for delivering the changes needed to implement new capabilities across the organization. The range of activities in this phase includes:

- Understanding the strategic benefits of the program,
- Developing a plan to initiate the program,
- Defining the program objectives and their alignment with the organization's goals, and
- Developing a high-level business case demonstrating an understanding of the needs, business benefits, feasibility and justification of the program.
- Agreeing to"check points" throughout the program, to ensure it is on track.

Internal programs such as enterprise-wide process improvement programs are undertaken by organizations as a catalyst for change. In this case, program plans should provide a clear understanding of and integration with generally accepted methods of organizational change management. Once the strategic area to be addressed is understood, and the stakeholders with whom communication must be established are identified, then a high-level approach or plan is developed. This plan must show that the program manager clearly understands the stimuli that triggered the program, the program objectives, and how the objectives align with the organization.

2.2.2 Program Initiation

The primary objective of the Program Initiation phase is to develop in greater detail how a program can be structured and managed to deliver the desired outcomes that were identified in the program mandate (Figure 2-5).

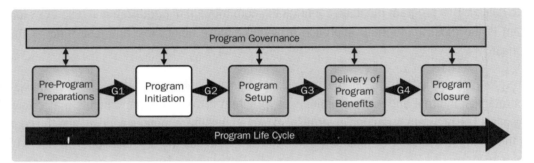

Figure 2-5. Program Initiation

All of the considerations listed in the pre-program work are analyzed and used to produce a program charter. The program charter is the formal document that consolidates all the available information about the program. The content of the program charter usually consists of the following sections:

- **Justification**—Why is the program important and what does it needs to achieve?
- **Vision**—What will the end state look like and how will it benefit the organization?
- **Strategic fit**—What are the key strategic drivers, and the program's relationship with organizational strategic objectives and with other on going strategic initiatives?
- **Outcomes**—What are the key program outcomes required to achieve the vision?
- **Scope**—What is included within the program and what is outside the scope?
- **Benefit strategy**—What are the key benefits sought and how are their realization envisioned?
- **Assumptions and constraints**—What are the assumptions, constraints, dependencies, and external factors considered to shape the program?
- **Components**—How are the projects and other program components configured to deliver the program? This may also include a high-level program plan for all components.
- **Risks and issues**—What are the initial risks and issues identified during the preparation of the program brief?
- **Time scale**—What is the total length of the program, including all key milestone dates?
- **Resources needed**—What are the estimated program cost and resources (staff, training, accommodation, etc.) needed?
- **Stakeholder considerations**—Who are the identified stakeholders, who are the most important stakeholders, and what is their attitude towards the program and what is the initial strategy to manage them? This should be complemented with a draft of the program communications management plan.

- **Program governance**—What is the recommended governance structure to manage, control, and support the program? What are the recommended governance structures to manage and control projects and other program components, including reporting requirements?

- **Initial high-level roadmap**—What is the high-level roadmap for the program moving forward?

The program charter is the primary document analyzed by the strategic governing board to decide if the delivery of the program is approved. Once approved, the program charter provides the basis to progress to program setup, the development of the program's full business case, detailed program plans, and component charters. Typically, the following factors are considered when selecting and approving programs:

- Desired outcomes;

- Benefits analysis, which identifies and plans for their realization;

- Strategic fit within the organization's long-term goals;

- Total available resources (i.e., funding, equipment or people);

- Estimated time scale, costs and effort required to set-up, manage and deliver the program; and

- Risks inherent in this program.

The results from this phase of the life cycle are:

- Approval from the strategic governing board to proceed to the next program phase (program setup);

- Program charter or program mandate that documents, for example:

  - Vision, key objectives, and success criteria,

  - Expected outcomes and benefits,

  - Program assumptions and constraints,

  - High-level program plan, and

  - Known risks and issues.

- Identification of suitable business change managers with the ability to influence business change;

- Identification of potential members of the sponsoring group or program board;

- Identification of the key decision makers/stakeholders in the program and their expectations and interests;

- Identification of candidate projects and other potential program components;

- Appointment of the executive sponsor and the program manager;

- Creation of the infrastructure to manage the program; and

- Identification and commitment of key resources needed for setting up the program.

2.2.3 Program Setup

At this stage, the program has passed the second phase-gate review (G2) and has received "approval in principle" from a selection committee to proceed to program setup. A program manager has been identified and the key input into this phase—a program brief or charter defining high-level scope, objectives, visions, and constraints—has been generated (Figure 2-6).

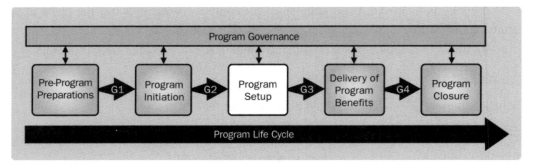

Figure 2-6. Program Setup

The purpose of the program setup phase is to progressively elaborate the program charter and develop the foundation for the program by establishing an infrastructure and building a detailed "roadmap" that provides direction on how the program will be managed and defines its key deliverables (Figure 2-6).

The desired outcome of this phase is approval authorizing execution of the program management plan. To achieve that outcome, the program management plan contains answers to the following questions:

- What is the end result and expectations?
- When will it be ready and accomplish the program benefits?
- What will be the program budget?
- What are the risks and issues?
- What dependencies, assumptions, and constraints?
- How will the program and program components be managed?
- What are the other services required?
- How will the program be managed/executed?

This phase determines the components that need to be included in the program, if not already defined. It also identifies any feasibility studies that may need to be conducted to address program issues. Activities in this phase may include:

- Aligning the mission, vision, and values for the program with the organization's objectives;
- Developing an initial detailed cost and schedule plan for setting up the program and outline plans for the remainder of the program;

- Conducting feasibility studies, where applicable, to assess the proposed program for technical and economic feasibility, as well as ethical feasibility or acceptability;

- Establishing rules for make/buy decisions as well as those for selecting subcontractors to support the program;

- Developing a program architecture that maps out how the projects within the program will deliver the capabilities that result in the required benefits;

- Developing a business case for each project in the program which addresses the technical, investment and regulatory/legislative factors which may pertain to each project; and

- Communicating with stakeholders and getting support.

During this phase, the program manager and the program team establish the infrastructure in which work will occur. More so than projects, programs usually have a supporting infrastructure in place, including the following:

- Program-specific governance areas such as processes and procedures;

- Program-specific tools such as program management tools, time/expense reporting tools and processes, earned value management processes and tools;

- Program management office;

- Program facilities; and

- Other tools, processes, and techniques as necessary to manage the program.

Key results from this stage of the life cycle revolve around the program-level planning processes:

- Scope definition and planning;

- Requirements definition, decomposition, validation, and management;

- Benefits definition, decomposition, management, cost and realization;

- Activity definition and sequencing;

- Duration estimates;

- Schedule;

- Procurement of external resources;

- Contracting and procurement;

- Human resources and staffing;

- Cost estimates/budgeting;

- Risk management consolidation;

- Constituent component identification and definition;

- Program management office to support the program;

- Approval of the program management plan, based upon the individual business cases and supporting feasibility studies;

- Program governance mechanism with approval and reporting procedures;

- Program control framework for monitoring and controlling both the projects and the measurement of benefits within the program;

- Facilities and other required infrastructure to support the program; and

- IT systems and communication technologies with the necessary support arrangements to sustain the program throughout its life cycle.

2.2.4   Delivery of Program Benefits

The purpose of this phase is to initiate the component projects of the program and manage the development of the program benefits which were identified during initial phases. Some programs deliver benefits incrementally, other programs deliver all of the benefits at the end (Figure 2-7).

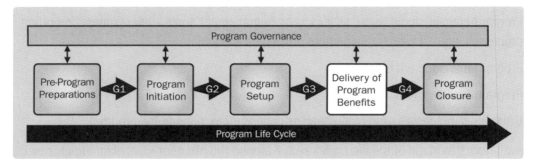

Figure 2-7. Delivery of Program Benefits

At this point in the program's life cycle, the program has passed another phase-gate review (G3) and the core work of the program—through its components—begins. The phase ends only when the planned benefits of the program have been achieved, delivered and accepted or a decision is made to terminate the program.

The program management team is responsible for managing this group of related components in a consistent and coordinated way in order to achieve results that could not be obtained by managing the components as stand-alone efforts. The following activities are performed during this phase:

- Establishing a project governance structure to monitor and control the projects;

- Initiating projects in order to meet program objectives;

- Ensuring component deliverables meet the requirements;

- Analyzing progress to plan;

- Identifying environmental changes which may impact the program management or its anticipated benefits;

- Ensuring that shared resources, common activities and other dependencies across the components are coordinated;

- Identifying risks and ensuring appropriate actions have been taken to manage positive and negative risks;

- Identifying issues and ensuring corrective actions are taken;

- Measuring benefits reutilization;

- Reviewing change requests and authorizing additional work as appropriate;

- Maintaining thresholds and initiating corrective action when results are not delivered per expectations; and

- Communicating with stakeholders and with the program governance board.

Program managers ensure and check alignment; project managers keep the detail of each project under control.

In the context of a program, some components may produce immediately, whereas other components may deliver capabilities that must be integrated with the capabilities delivered by other components before the associated benefits can be realized.

2.2.5 Program Closure

The purpose of this phase is to execute a controlled closedown of the program.

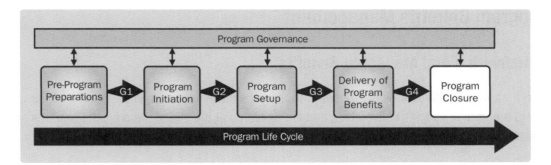

Figure 2-8. Program Closure

The last phase of a program begins after a phase-gate review (G4). All program work is completed and benefits are accruing. The activities in this phase lead to the shutdown of the program organization and infrastructure. For many programs, the product is delivered and/or accepted to the customer and the program is shut down. For other programs, the product transitions into an operation phase and is managed by normal operations (Figure 2-8).

Program closure can also be due to circumstances within the organization, in the instance of premature closure before benefits are realized, the same controlled project closure should be followed.

There are a number of key activities that must be executed when a program arrives at the end of its life cycle to ensure that the closure is smooth and safe.

- Review status of benefits with the stakeholders;

- Disband the program organization;

- Disband the program team and ensure arrangements are in place for appropriate redeployment of all human resources;

- Dismantle the infrastructure and ensure arrangements are in place for appropriate redeployment of all physical resources (e.g., facilities, equipment, etc.);

- Provide customer support assuring that guidance and maintenance will be provided in the event that an issue arises or a defect is detected after the program deliverables are delivered and accepted by the customer. This assurance is generally defined by contract;

- Document lessons learned in the organizational database so they can be referenced in the future by similar programs. Lessons learned are generally expressed as weaknesses or areas to improve and as strengths and best practices of the performing organization to be utilized in the future;

- Provide feedback and recommendations on changes identified during the program's life but beyond the scope of the program that may benefit the organization to pursue;

- Store and index all program-related documents to facilitate reuse in the future or possible future audits; and

- Manage any required transition to operations.

2.3 Program Benefits Management

2.3.1 Delivering and Managing Benefits

Both programs and projects deliver benefits to the organization. For projects, those benefits are usually produced in the form of specific deliverables that are delivered at the end of the project. Programs are created by organizations to create benefits that are much larger than single projects can deliver.

Unlike projects, which usually deliver all of their benefits at the end of the project, programs can deliver benefits either all at once at the end of the program or incrementally during the program itself. Examples of programs which deliver all of their benefits at the end include major construction efforts; public works programs such as roads, dams, or bridges; aerospace programs; aircraft and ship developments; and others. Examples of programs which deliver incremental benefits include business process improvement initiatives and major IT projects such as enterprise resource planning implementations or large-scale IT infrastructure programs.

Good benefits management assesses the value of the program's benefits, identifies the interdependencies of benefits being delivered among various projects within the program and assigns responsibilities and accountability for the actual realization of benefits from the program.

Benefits realization planning is a part of program initiation that includes: intended interdependencies between benefits; alignment with the strategic goals of the organization; benefit delivery scheduling; metrics and measurement; responsibility for delivery of the final and intermediate benefits within the program; and benefit realization. The interdependencies, benefit delivery scheduling and responsibility for delivery, lie within the program management domain.

Expected benefits should be derived from the business case on which the program is based. The benefits realization plan for the program is based on this information and is the main output from the program initiation process. This plan is part of the program management plan and helps to determine how benefits will subsequently be realized as well as providing a baseline for tracking progress and reporting any variances.

At the end of the program, the benefits delivered should always be compared against those promised in the business case to ensure that the program actually delivered the full benefits for which it was created.

2.3.2　Organizational Differences

In some organizations, benefits delivery is considered to be the responsibility of operations management rather than program management. Once the program's output is delivered, the program ends and the effort to obtain benefits from the delivered product is an operational responsibility. An example of this is a business process improvements program that makes multiple business processes within the enterprise more efficient. Once the new process is delivered by the program, utilizing and optimizing it to obtain the greatest benefit is an operational responsibility.

Other organizations keep the program name even after the final product has been delivered. The Space Shuttle Program, for instance, included both the development effort of the space shuttle and all related ground support facilities and also included the operations of the program itself.

For these types of organizations, the name may remain the same but true program management principles are no longer useful to operate the end product. The day to day operations now become a function of normal operations management and not program management.

2.3.3　Benefits Sustainment

The delivered benefits need to be sustained after the program is over. These sustainment elements may include:

- Assuring that, in the project and program environments, the creation of a new product or service is accompanied by the development and deployment of support for that output;

- Assuring that the demands for continuing delivery/deployment are understood so that resources can be appropriately applied to maintain the schedule and satisfy customer expectations;

- Assuring that ongoing product support adds value by managing the post-production product life cycle. Project management is often used to deliver upgrades to the product during its product life cycle;

- Assuring that upstream projects (the performing organization or the project that creates the product) define and otherwise provide life-cycle information to support benefits product support for management of the product life cycle;

- Assuring that there is ongoing benchmarking of support practices;

- Assuring that ongoing product support representation is present at beginning of the project that produces the product;

- Assuring that there is a customer support organization;

- Assuring that support is properly scheduled when changes are made to the deployed product so that customers will be able to support the updated products;

- Assuring the availability of training for support staff to understand product support requirements; and

- Assuring that repair/return facilities/processes requirements are developed and implemented.

SECTION II

THE STANDARD FOR PROGRAM MANAGEMENT

Chapter 3

- Program Management Processes

CHAPTER 3

PROGRAM MANAGEMENT PROCESSES

Program management is the centralized coordinated management of a program to achieve the program's strategic objectives and benefits. Good program management requires visionary, entrepreneurial, and motivational zeal, combined with sound management processes.

A process is a set of interrelated actions and activities performed to achieve a pre-specified outcome. Each program management process is characterized by its inputs, the tools and techniques that can be applied, and the resulting outputs. The process definitions and terminology at the program level are similar to the processes at the project level. However, program management processes address issues at a higher level and involve less detailed project-level analysis. The program level seeks to resolve issues between projects, and enable a synergistic approach, so as to deliver program benefits. Similar to project management processes, program management processes require coordination with other functional groups in the organization as well as stakeholder management in general—but in a broader context.

A guiding rule for applying program management processes is to ensure that the program manager effectively delegates authority, autonomy, and responsibility for day-to-day management of the projects to the designated project managers.

Program management processes are primarily integrative in that they coordinate the outputs of various projects to derive the desired program outcomes. For this reason, the program management processes can be mapped in terms of the various knowledge areas similar to the ones outlined in *A Guide to the Project Management Body of Knowledge (PMBOK® Guide)* – Fourth Edition.

This chapter includes the following major sections:

3.1 Common Program Management Process Interactions

3.2 Program Management Process Groups

3.3 Initiating Process Group

3.4 Planning Process Group

3.5 Executing Process Group

3.6 Monitoring and Controlling Process Group

3.7 Closing Process Group

3.1 Common Program Management Process Interactions

There are many interactions among program management processes. Processes receive inputs from processes that logically precede them and send outputs to successor processes. In some cases, an output from a process becomes an input to the same process; for example, when a planning process iteratively updates a plan over time.

There are cases where an output of a process may pass through several other processes in succession before returning as an input to its originating process, and more typically, cases where an output from a process travels along a "one-way street." An example of this is lessons learned, produced as output from many processes and flowing to a single closing process, close program, to be analyzed, incorporated into a program closure report and then archived.

The complexity of the program management process model is increased when inputs and outputs flow between the project domain, the program domain and the portfolio domain. This can be illustrated with a few examples:

- Project schedules flow to the program domain as inputs to the program schedule control process in order to update the program's integrated master schedule. Project risks flow to the program risk management planning and analysis process in a similar manner to create a comprehensive view of risks to the program. Corrective actions may be created by program management processes and flow back to the project domain.

- Funding availability outputs flow from the portfolio domain to the program cost estimating and budgeting process as inputs to the program budget, while cost performance reports from the program flow back to the portfolio domain.

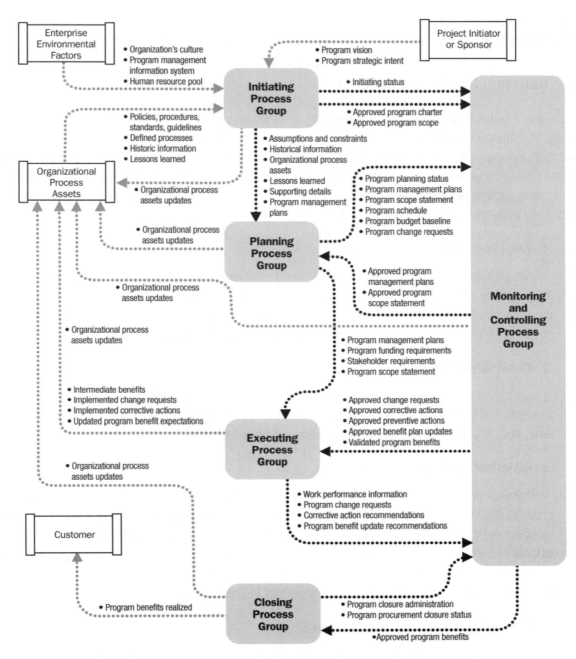

Figure 3-1. Program Management Process Interactions

Each of the program management processes may have components (inputs, tools and techniques, and outputs) that are unique to that process, but there are also components that are common to many processes throughout the Program Management Process Groups. Among these are inputs and outputs such as assumptions, constraints, historical information, lessons learned and supporting details, and controls such as policies, procedures, and reviews.

Instead of repeating these components in many process descriptions, they have been described and explained below in terms of how they apply to the program management process approach in general.

3.1.1 Common Inputs and Outputs

There are a number of inputs and outputs that are common to most program management processes. Generally, the common inputs fall into a category that can be considered common knowledge within the organization. For example, assumptions or constraints could be inputs to almost any process. Some of the inputs common to many program management processes are presented below. Included in here are an organization's best practices, such as updated lessons learned and historical information. In addition, others can be identified and observed while studying the program management processes.

.1 Assumptions (Input and Output)

Assumptions are factors that, for planning purposes, are considered true, real, or certain. Assumptions affect all aspects of program planning and are part of the progressive elaboration of the program. Program teams frequently identify, document, and validate assumptions as part of their planning process. Due to their uncertainty, assumptions generally involve a degree of risk.

.2 Constraints (Input)

Constraints are factors that limit the program team's options. They are factors external to the program that limit the flexibility of the program manager. Constraints generally fall in the categories of time, cost, resources, or specific deliverables or program benefits.

.3 Historical Information (Input)

Previous programs can be a source of lessons learned and best practices for a new program. This is particularly true for programs where a substantial amount of work is done by virtual means or when work involves multicultural interaction. Historical information includes all artifacts, metrics, risks, and estimations from previous programs and projects that are pertinent to the current program. Historical information describing the successes, failures, and lessons learned on past programs with respect to integrating multiple projects is especially important to program planning and management.

.4 Organizational Process Assets (Input)

Organizational process assets, sometimes called a process asset library (PAL), are composed of the set of formal and informal program management process-related plans, policies, procedures, and guidelines that are developed, documented, and institutionalized by the organization. These assets may include an organization's knowledge bases, such as lessons learned and historical information. Assets may exist as paper documents or in electronic form in an automated repository.

.5 Lessons Learned (Output)

Lessons learned include causes of variances from the program management plan, corrective actions taken and their outcomes, risk mitigations, and other information of value to management and stakeholders of future programs. Lessons learned should be identified and documented throughout the program management processes, and flow to the Program Closure process for analysis and archiving.

.6 Supporting Details (Output)

Supporting details vary by process and program size. Supporting details consist of documentation and information not included in formal program artifacts but deemed necessary to the successful management of the program.

.7 Information Requests (Output)

Requests for information on various aspects of a program are initiated continuously and frequently by the program's external and internal stakeholders and are outputs from many of its program management processes. Information requests flow to the Information Distribution process, which creates the appropriate responses as outputs.

.8 Program Management Plan Updates (Output)

Many processes update the program management plan as the program evolves and matures. The program manager should always be aware of these updates and the potential interdependencies.

.9 Program Status Reports and Performance Reports (Inputs and Outputs)

On a regular basis, status and performance reports are generated by the program and by the components of the program. Program status reports communicate the current state of specific areas such as schedule, budget, and so on. Program performance reports include status information but often communicate other information, such as accomplishments, component completions, and more general information. There is no strict line between the two and the words are often used interchangeably. In this standard, we will generally refer to program performance reports.

3.2 Program Management Process Groups

This section identifies and describes the five Program Management Process Groups. These Process Groups align with those defined in the *PMBOK® Guide* – Fourth Edition, and are independent of application areas or industry focus.

These Process Groups are not linear and they do overlap. Interaction occurs both within a Process Group and between Process Groups. It is important to note that these Process Groups do not bear any direct relationship to phases of a program life cycle. In fact, one or more processes from each Process Group will normally be executed at least once in every phase of a program life cycle. The five Program Management Process Groups are briefly discussed below:

- **Initiating Process Group.** Defines and authorizes the program or a project within the program, and produces the program benefits statement for the program.

- **Planning Process Group.** Plans the best alternative course of action to deliver the benefits and scope that the program was undertaken to address.

- **Executing Process Group.** Integrates projects, people and other resources to carry out the program plan and deliver the program's benefits.

- **Monitoring and Controlling Process Group.** Requires that the program and its component projects be monitored against the benefit delivery expectations and that their progress be regularly measured to identify variances from the program management plan. This Process Group also coordinates corrective actions to be taken when necessary to achieve program benefits.

- **Closing Process Group.** Formalizes acceptance of a product, service, or benefit/result and brings the program or program component (e.g. project) to an orderly end.

In Table 3-1, the program management processes are aligned with their respective Process Groups and correlated to the nine Knowledge Areas in which most of the activities associated with the program occur.

Table 3-1. Program Management Process Groups and Knowledge Areas Mapping

Knowledge Areas	Initiating Process Group	Planning Process Group	Executing Process Group	Monitoring and Controlling Process Group	Closing Process Group
4. Program Integration Management	4.1 Initiate Program	4.2 Develop Program Management Plan 4.3 Develop Program Infrastructure	4.4 Direct and Manage Program Execution 4.5 Manage Program Resources	4.6 Monitor and Control Program Performance 4.7 Manage Program Issues	4.8 Close Program
5. Program Scope Management		5.1 Plan Program Scope 5.2 Define Program Goals and Objectives 5.3 Develop Program Requirements 5.4 Develop Program Architecture 5.5 Develop Program WBS	5.6 Manage Program Architecture 5.7 Manage Component Interfaces	5.8 Monitor and Control Program Scope	
6. Program Time Management		6.1 Develop Program Schedule		6.2 Monitor and Control Program Schedule	
7. Program Cost Management*	*	*	*	*	*
8. Program Quality Management*	*	*	*	*	*
9. Program Human Resource Management*	*	*	*	*	*
10. Program Communication Management		10.1 Plan Communications	10.2 Distribute Information	10.3 Report Program Performance	
11. Program Risk Management		11.1 Plan Program Risk Management 11.2 Identify Program Risks 11.3 Analyze Program Risks 11.4 Plan Program Risk Responses		11.5 Monitor and Control Program Risks	
12. Program Procurement Management		12.1 Plan Program Procurements	12.2 Conduct Program Procurements	12.3 Administer Program Procurements	12.4 Close Program Procurements
13. Program Financial Management	13.1 Establish Program Financial Framework	13.2 Develop Program Financial Plan 13.3 Estimate Program Costs 13.4 Budget Program Costs		13.5 Monitor and Control Program Financials	
14. Program Stakeholder Management		14.1 Plan Program Stakeholder Management 14.2 Identify Program Stakeholders	14.3 Engage Program Stakeholders	14.4 Manage Program Stakeholder Expectations	
15. Program Governance		15.1 Plan and Establish Program Governance Structure 15.2 Plan for Audits 15.3 Plan Program Quality	15.4 Approve Component Initiation	15.5 Provide Governance Oversight 15.6 Manage Program Benefits 15.7 Monitor and Control Program Changes	15.8 Approve Component Transition

* These Knowledge Areas are not included as part of The Standard for Program Management

3.3 Initiating Process Group

Initiation of a program occurs as the result of a strategic plan to fulfill an initiative within a portfolio, or as the result of a decision to bid for a contract from an external customer. There may be a number of activities performed before program initiation, resulting in the development of concepts (for products or services), scope frameworks, initial requirements, timelines, deliverables, and guidelines as to acceptable costs.

Initiating a program can entail configuring or grouping proposed projects and existing projects into a program based on specific benefit delivery or other criteria. Program initiation also requires obtaining formal acceptance of the program concept from the stakeholders. Such acceptance acknowledges the necessity of the program as a way to achieve the desired portfolio or strategic benefits.

Program initiation generally calls for order-of-magnitude estimates of scope, effort, and cost. Such estimates are often called feasibility studies or concept development and can be done in the business case. A feasibility study may occur before a formal initiation of a program. This depends on the culture of the organization and the type of program under consideration. In either case, the results of the activities are used as inputs to one or more of the initiating and planning processes.

The Initiate Program process (Figure 3-2) takes into account the organization's strategic plan and its business needs, as documented in a business case and investment analysis, which are developed external to the program domain. The business case and investment analysis define the way in which those business needs will be achieved.

Programs are typically chartered and authorized by an organizational executive committee, steering committee, or a portfolio management body.

The key output from this process is the program charter. The program charter links the program to the ongoing work of the organization. The charter often contains the vision statement that defines the desired organizational end state to follow successful completion of the program, and is used as the vehicle to authorize the program and officially commence planning.

Program funding is required to support the program through the initiating and planning phases until cost and budget estimates are complete. Significant resources can be required for these early activities.

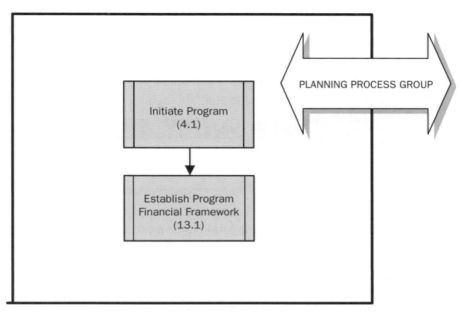

Figure 3-2. Initiating Process Group

3.3.1 Initiate Program

Often, the starting point for a program is an organizational concept for a future state to fit in with a future organizational environment. Initially, this concept may be inadequately defined and the purpose of the Initiate Program process (Figure 3-3) is to provide a process that helps define the benefit expectations of the program. Program initiation ensures that the authorization and initiation of the program are linked to the organization's ongoing work and strategic priorities.

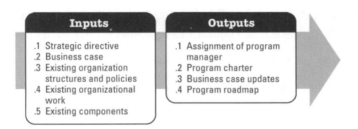

Figure 3-3. Initiate Program: Inputs and Outputs

3.3.2 Establish Program Financial Framework

This process identifies the overall financial environment for the program as well as the funds available according to identified program milestones (Figure 3-4). Establishing the program's financial framework must occur at the very beginning of the program and is done in conjunction with the financing organization. To a much greater extent than in projects, costs occur earlier in programs, often years earlier, than benefits. Because of the large amount of money involved in most programs, the funding organization has significant inputs to the program management and to the decisions made by both the technical leaders and by the program manager. The financial environment in which a program exists depends on the type of program and whether it is being funded entirely within a single organization, managed within a single organization but funded separately, or entirely funded and managed from outside the parent organization. The program financial framework varies both by the type of program, but also by the size of the program itself.

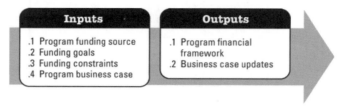

Figure 3-4. Establish Program Financial Framework: Inputs and Outputs

3.4 Planning Process Group

The program planning Process Group contains the processes needed to lay the groundwork for the program and to position it for successful execution. These processes involve formalizing the scope of the work to be accomplished by the program and identifying the deliverables that will satisfy the program's goals and deliver its benefits.

The key program-level deliverable is the program management plan, which defines the tactical means by which the program will be carried out. Included in the program management plan, either as components within the document or as subsidiary plans, are the plans that drive the basic elements of managing the program. These plans include and address:

- Organization of the program;

- Program work breakdown structure that formalizes the program scope in terms of deliverables and the work needed to produce those deliverables/benefits via the components;

- All aspects of scope, technology, risks, and costs;

- Program schedule that establishes the timeline for program milestones and deliverables;

- Program budget that defines the monetary plan for the program in terms of outlays of funds over the program life cycle and the purposes to which those funds will be applied;

- Means by which the required quality of the program deliverables will be assured;

- Plans for defining metrics and systems to track benefit realization and sustainability;

- Communications with stakeholders both internal and external to the program;

- Approach and methodology used to manage risks associated with the program;

- Procurement management plan created during the first iteration of the procurement planning process, and then updated as needed in subsequent iterations of the conduct procurement process;

- Plans for procurement of facilities, goods, services, and other external resources needed to accomplish the program, and to manage contractual vehicles for procurement; and

- Interrelationships between projects and non-project tasks within the program, between the program and its projects or with factors external to the program.

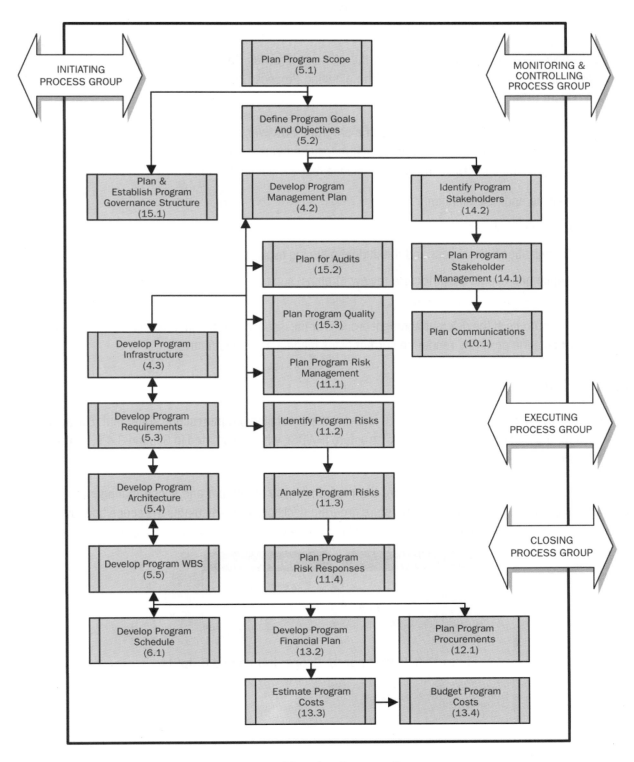

Figure 3-5. Planning Process Group

The program planning processes are iterative and are dependent upon information generated at the project level. During this iterative process, a combination of top-down and bottom-up approaches may be the most suitable. Re-planning is required at points in the program's performance when scope changes or other unplanned circumstances dictate the need.

Interactions among the processes within the planning Process Group can vary based on the nature and complexity of the program. The activities of the planning Process Group include interaction with the portfolio domain (Figure 3-5).

Planning is performed in the early phase of a program. However, due to the extended length and the multi-project nature of programs, there are additional milestones where plans should be revisited and updated to ensure ongoing usefulness. These milestones include, but are not limited to:

- New component initiation;

- Component closure;

- Organization's fiscal year and the budget planning cycle for the program;

- Unplanned events that trigger a review of plans, such as acquisitions and mergers and other major organizational changes; and

- The outputs of the risk management process or the issue management process, if an event sufficiently affects the program, rendering current plans inadequate or ineffective.

3.4.1   Plan Program Scope

The objective of this process (Figure 3-6) is to develop a detailed program scope statement. The appropriate approach for the program work breakdown structure (PWBS), which is created in Section 3.4.9, is also defined in this section.

The primary outputs of this process are the program scope statement and scope management plan. The program scope statement is the basis for future program decisions and articulates the scope boundaries of the program. The scope management plan identifies how scope will be managed throughout the program.

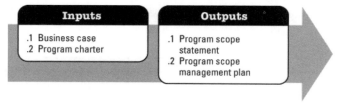

Figure 3-6. Plan Program Scope: Inputs and Outputs

3.4.2　Define Program Goals and Objectives

Define Program Goals and Objectives is the process for establishing the overall goals and objectives of the program and ultimately what is to be delivered (Figure 3-7).

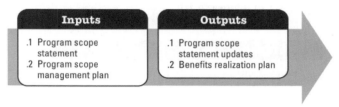

Figure 3-7. Define Program Goals and Objectives: Inputs and Outputs

3.4.3　Plan and Establish Program Governance Structure

The Plan and Establish Program Governance process identifies the governance goals, defines the necessary governance structure, roles, and responsibilities for the governance bodies, and ensures alignment of the governance goals (Figure 3-8).

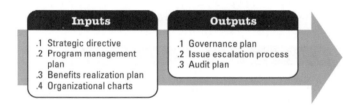

Figure 3-8. Plan and Establish Program Governance Structure: Inputs and Outputs

3.4.4　Identify Program Stakeholders

The Identify Program Stakeholders process addresses the formal identification of the stakeholders in the program and creates the stakeholder register. The register serves as the primary input for the Plan Program Stakeholder Management process (Section 14.1), as well as for the distribution of program reports and other communications (Figure 3-9).

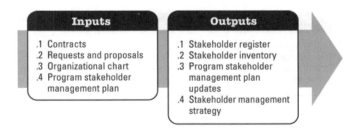

Figure 3-9. Identify Program Stakeholders: Inputs and Outputs

3.4.5   Develop Program Management Plan

The Develop Program Management Plan process consolidates the outputs of the other planning processes, including strategic planning, to create a consistent, coherent set of documents that can be used to guide both program execution and program control (Figure 3-10).

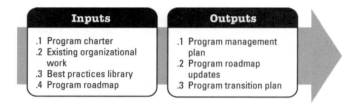

Figure 3-10. Develop Program Management Plan: Inputs and Outputs

3.4.6   Develop Program Infrastructure

The Develop Program Infrastructure process helps the program manager define and establish the organizational structure in which work will occur, along with the technical infrastructure to support that work (Figure 3-11).

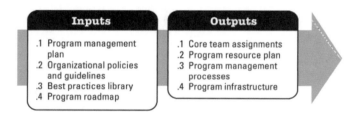

Figure 3-11. Develop Program Infrastructure: Inputs and Outputs

3.4.7   Develop Program Requirements

The Develop Program Requirements process facilitates the development and formal identification of the program requirements and specifications to deliver the program goals and objectives (Figure 3-12).

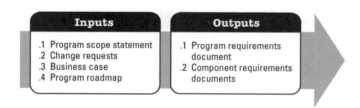

Figure 3-12. Develop Program Requirements: Inputs and Outputs

3.4.8 Develop Program Architecture

The Develop Program Architecture process defines the structure of the program components and identifies the interrelationships between all the program components (Figure 3-13).

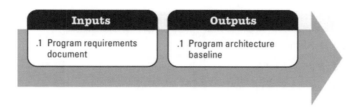

Figure 3-13. Develop Program Architecture: Inputs and Outputs

3.4.9 Develop Program WBS

The Develop Program Work Breakdown Structure (PWBS) process produces a PWBS that communicates from the program-level perspective a clear understanding and statement of the technical objectives and the end item(s) or end product(s), service(s), or result(s) of the work to be performed (Figure 3-14).

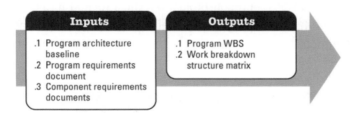

Figure 3-14. Develop Program WBS: Inputs and Outputs

3.4.10 Develop Program Schedule

The Develop Program Schedule process determines the order and timing in which the components needed to produce the program deliverables should be executed, estimates the amount of time required to accomplish each one, identifies significant milestones during the performance period of the program, and documents the outcome (Figure 3-15).

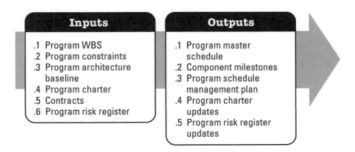

Figure 3-15. Develop Program Schedule: Inputs and Outputs

3.4.11 Develop Program Financial Plan

The Develop Program Financial Plan process facilitates the development and management of the program budget and the payment schedules of the components (Figure 3-16).

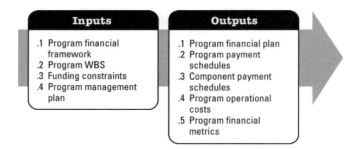

Figure 3-16. Develop Program Financial Plan: Inputs and Outputs

3.4.12 Estimate Program Costs

The Estimate Program Costs process aggregates all costs at the program level into a program cost. It includes all program activities, project activities, and non-project activities related to the program. The estimates are made by the program team for the entire program or combined based on individual estimates of projects and work packages. The program cost estimates are presented to the decision makers for approval and further funding (Figure 3-17).

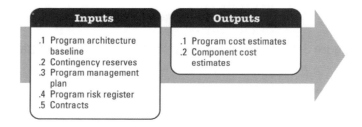

Figure 3-17. Estimate Program Costs: Inputs and Outputs

3.4.13 Budget Program Costs

The Budget Program Costs process establishes the financial plan for the program based on the budgets of the individual projects, non-project activities, and any other financial constraints that impose monetary boundaries. The latter may be a consequence of fiscal year budgetary planning cycles or funding limits for particular periods. Since programs can span multiple planning periods, the program team may use different budget techniques over the program life cycle (Figure 3-18).

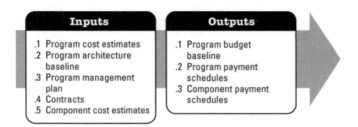

Figure 3-18. Budget Program Costs: Inputs and Outputs

3.4.14 Plan Program Procurements

The Plan Program Procurements process determines what to acquire and when, validates product requirements, and develops procurement strategies. This process precedes the contracts planning process and generates several outputs that become inputs to contracts planning updates (Figure 3-19).

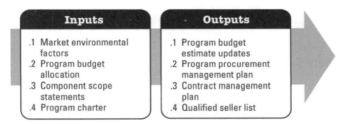

Figure 3-19. Plan Program Procurements: Inputs and Outputs

3.4.15 Plan Program Stakeholder Management

The Plan Program Stakeholder Management process covers planning how stakeholders will be identified, analyzed, engaged, and managed throughout the life of the program. It outlines the processes, tools and techniques, and resources to be used in the other processes in this Knowledge Area (Figure 3-20).

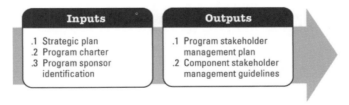

Figure 3-20. Plan Program Stakeholder Management: Inputs and Outputs

3.4.16 Plan Communications

The Plan Communications process determines the information and communication needs of the program stakeholders: who need what information, when they need it, how it will be given to them, and by whom. Adequate communications requirements must be conveyed as input to the projects in order to facilitate information capture from the projects to be fed back into the program (Figure 3-21).

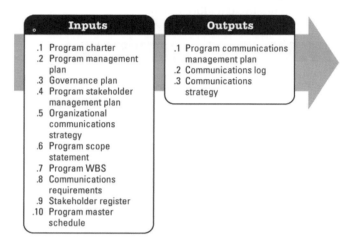

Inputs

.1 Program charter
.2 Program management plan
.3 Governance plan
.4 Program stakeholder management plan
.5 Organizational communications strategy
.6 Program scope statement
.7 Program WBS
.8 Communications requirements
.9 Stakeholder register
.10 Program master schedule

Outputs

.1 Program communications management plan
.2 Communications log
.3 Communications strategy

Figure 3-21. Plan Communications: Inputs and Outputs

3.4.17 Plan for Audits

The Plan for Audits process ensures that the program is prepared for both external and internal audits of finances, processes and documents; and demonstrates compliance with approved organizational program management processes (Figure 3-22).

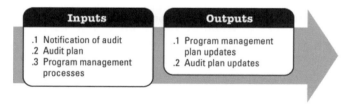

Inputs

.1 Notification of audit
.2 Audit plan
.3 Program management processes

Outputs

.1 Program management plan updates
.2 Audit plan updates

Figure 3-22. Plan for Audits: Inputs and Outputs

3.4.18 Plan Program Quality

The Plan Program Quality process identifies the quality standards that are relevant to the program and specifies how to satisfy them. Quality planning and preparation must happen early in the program to ensure that the competency is available during the planning stages of critical program activities and processes. Quality planning should take advantage of existing quality expertise and methodologies within the program domain. If the latter are required but do not exist, then they should be implemented within the program (Figure 3-23).

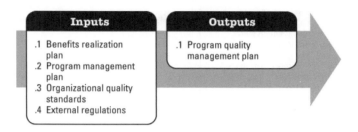

Figure 3-23. Plan Program Quality: Inputs and Outputs

3.4.19 Plan Program Risk Management

The Plan Program Risk Management process determines how to approach, plan, and analyze risk management activities for a program, including risks identified in the individual program components. It includes strategies, tools, methods, reviews and re-assessment processes, metrics gathering, standard assessment parameters, and reporting requirements to be used by each project in the program (Figure 3-24).

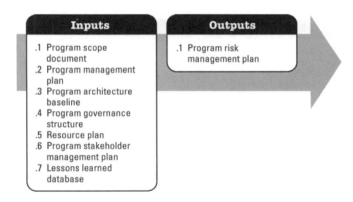

Figure 3-24. Plan Program Risk Management: Inputs and Outputs

3.4.20 Identify Program Risks

The Identify Program Risks process determines which risks might affect the program and its components. It also helps document the risk characteristics (Figure 3-25).

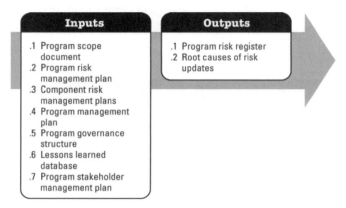

Figure 3-25. Identify Program Risks: Inputs and Outputs

3.4.21 Analyze Program Risks

The Analyze Program Risks process prioritizes risks for further analysis or action by assessing their probability of occurrence and impact. This process analyzes risks quantitatively and qualitatively to determine the effect of these risks on the overall program, its constituent components, and management of the interdependencies of those components (Figure 3-26).

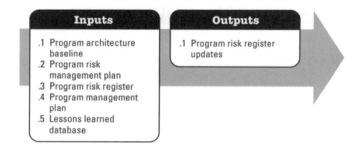

Figure 3-26. Analyze Program Risk: Inputs and Outputs

3.4.22 Plan Program Risk Responses

The Plan Program Risk Responses process serves as a decision-making tool for developing options and actions to enhance opportunities, and to reduce threats to program objectives and the realization of the program benefits (Figure 3-27).

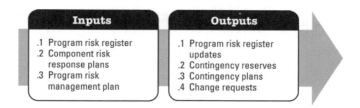

Inputs	Outputs
.1 Program risk register	.1 Program risk register updates
.2 Component risk response plans	.2 Contingency reserves
.3 Program risk management plan	.3 Contingency plans
	.4 Change requests

Figure 3-27. Plan Program Risk Responses: Inputs and Outputs

3.5 Executing Process Group

The Executing Process Group contains the processes that drive the program work in accordance with the program management plan and its subsidiary plans (Figure 3-28). These processes ensure that benefits management, stakeholder management, and program governance are executed in accordance with established policies and plans.

By using these processes, the program team acquires and marshals the resources needed to accomplish the goals and benefits of the program, including internal program staff, contractors, and suppliers.

The Executing Process Group involves managing the cost, quality, and schedule plans, often as an integrated plan; and providing status information and change requests to the program Monitoring and Controlling Process Group through approved change requests, corrective actions, and preventive actions.

The Executing Process Group ensures that all stakeholders receive the information they need in a timely manner. This includes administering all the program's communications channels and providing information such as status updates, notifications of change requests, and approvals and responses to governmental and regulatory agencies.

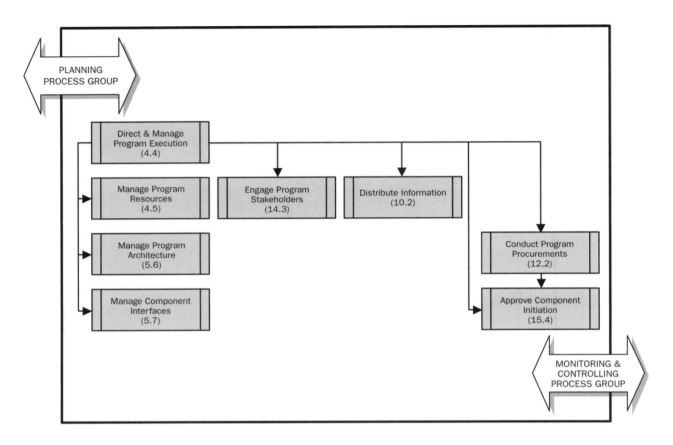

Figure 3-28. Executing Process Group

3.5.1 Direct and Manage Program Execution

The Direct and Manage Program Execution process delivers the program's intended benefits. This process focuses specifically on those projects and program work packages currently in progress, and integrates other executing processes (Figure 3-29). Its purpose is to produce the cumulative deliverables and other work products of the program. It also facilitates and resolves inter-project issues, risks, and constraints.

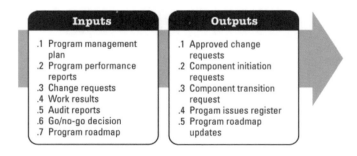

Inputs	Outputs
.1 Program management plan	.1 Approved change requests
.2 Program performance reports	.2 Component initiation requests
.3 Change requests	.3 Component transition request
.4 Work results	.4 Progam issues register
.5 Audit reports	.5 Program roadmap updates
.6 Go/no-go decision	
.7 Program roadmap	

Figure 3-29. Direct and Manage Program Execution: Inputs and Outputs

3.5.2 Manage Program Resources

As the program progresses, the Manage Program Resources process allows for the adjustment and reallocation of resources as required to meet the needs of the overall program (Figure 3-30). Change requests approved by the governance bodies are managed through this process across the program.

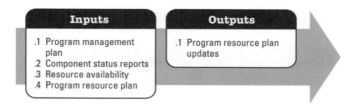

Inputs
.1 Program management plan
.2 Component status reports
.3 Resource availability
.4 Program resource plan

Outputs
.1 Program resource plan updates

Figure 3-30. Manage Program Resources: Inputs and Outputs

3.5.3 Manage Program Architecture

The Manage Program Architecture process manages the relationships across all program components to ensure that the program architecture remains consistent across all deliverables (Figure 3-31).

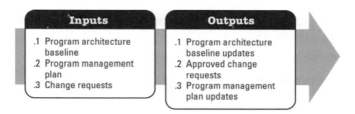

Inputs
.1 Program architecture baseline
.2 Program management plan
.3 Change requests

Outputs
.1 Program architecture baseline updates
.2 Approved change requests
.3 Program management plan updates

Figure 3-31. Manage Program Architecture: Inputs and Outputs

3.5.4 Manage Component Interfaces

The Manage Component Interfaces process maintains the integrity of program delivery and manages the interrelationships among the program's components (Figure 3-32).

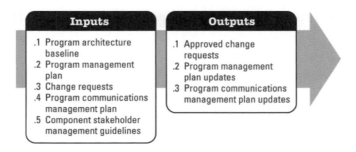

Inputs
.1 Program architecture baseline
.2 Program management plan
.3 Change requests
.4 Program communications management plan
.5 Component stakeholder management guidelines

Outputs
.1 Approved change requests
.2 Program management plan updates
.3 Program communications management plan updates

Figure 3-32. Manage Component Interfaces: Inputs and Outputs

3.5.5   Engage Program Stakeholders

The Engage Program Stakeholders process helps the program management team ensure that the correct stakeholders are involved in the program (Figure 3-33). Effective stakeholder engagement requires thorough knowledge of stakeholders' needs and expectations as well as the potential impact and issues to and from various stakeholders. It also requires interacting effectively with stakeholders to communicate strategic objectives and status, influence expectations, and resolve conflicts.

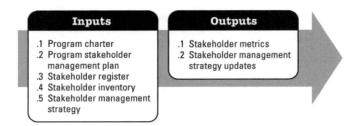

Figure 3-33. Engage Program Stakeholders: Inputs and Outputs

3.5.6   Distribute Information

The Distribute Information process provides timely and accurate information to program stakeholders in useful formats and appropriate media (Figure 3-34). It includes administration of three major communications channels: the clients, the sponsors, and the component management.

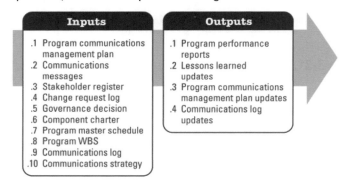

Figure 3-34. Distribute Information: Inputs and Outputs

3.5.7   Conduct Program Procurements

The Conduct Program Procurements process details how to conduct the procurement activities of a program (Figure 3-35). It includes strategies, tools, methods, metrics gathering, reviews and update mechanisms, standard assessment parameters, and reporting requirements to be used by each component of the program in conducting the procurement activities for the program.

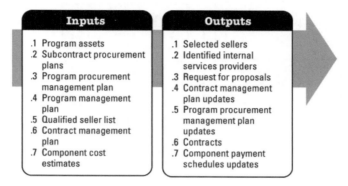

Inputs	Outputs
.1 Program assets .2 Subcontract procurement plans .3 Program procurement management plan .4 Program management plan .5 Qualified seller list .6 Contract management plan .7 Component cost estimates	.1 Selected sellers .2 Identified internal services providers .3 Request for proposals .4 Contract management plan updates .5 Program procurement management plan updates .6 Contracts .7 Component payment schedules updates

Figure 3-35. Conduct Program Procurements: Inputs and Outputs

3.5.8   Approve Component Initiation

The Approve Component Initiation process provides the appropriate processes and decision-making structure for initiating and changing the overall program and components within the program (Figure 3-36).

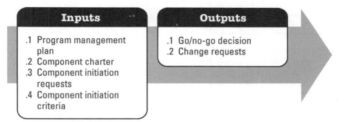

Inputs	Outputs
.1 Program management plan .2 Component charter .3 Component initiation requests .4 Component initiation criteria	.1 Go/no-go decision .2 Change requests

Figure 3-36. Approve Component Initiation: Inputs and Outputs

3.6 Monitoring and Controlling Process Group

At the program level, monitoring and measurement involves obtaining and consolidating data on status and progress from individual projects or program packages (i.e., non-project tasks) (Figure 3-37). Monitoring also entails interfacing with the program governance structure to ensure the organization has a clear picture of the current benefit delivery and expected future benefits.

Effective program performance reporting supports appropriate preventive and corrective actions at the program level, especially during the delivering benefits phase of the program life cycle. In addition, these corrective actions could also be a result of governance oversight, especially when programs require statutory compliance with external and governmental agencies.

For programs, integrated change control involves redirecting or modifying the program as needed, based on feedback from individual projects or work packages. In addition, changes could originate from interfaces with other subsystems of the program or factors external to the program. The latter could be due to government regulations, market changes, economic fluctuations, or political issues.

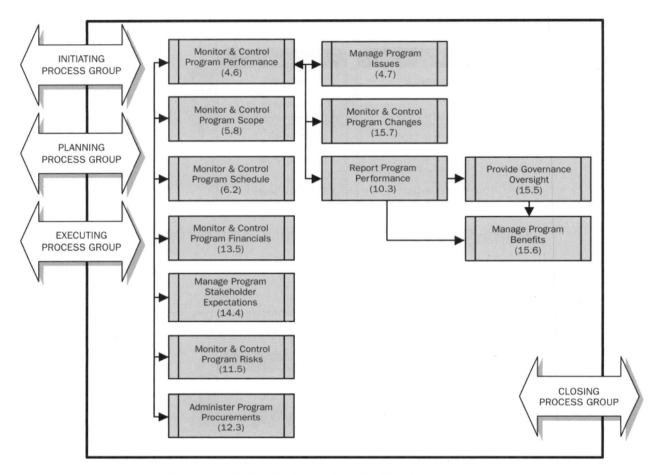

Figure 3-37. Monitoring and Controlling Process Group

3.6.1   Monitor and Control Program Performance

The Monitor and Control Program Performance process monitors activities in all Program Management Process Groups and ensures that program execution occurs according to the approved program management plan (Figure 3-38).

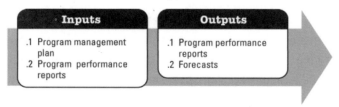

Figure 3-38. Monitor and Control Program Performance: Inputs and Outputs

3.6.2   Monitor and Control Program Scope

The Monitor and Control Program Scope process controls changes to the program scope (Figure 3-39).

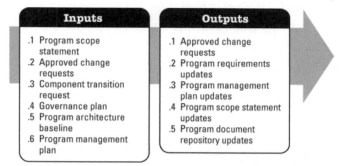

Figure 3-39. Monitor and Control Program Scope: Inputs and Outputs

3.6.3   Monitor and Control Program Schedule

The Monitor and Control Program Schedule process ensures that the program produces its required deliverables and solutions on time (Figure 3-40). The activities in this process include tracking the actual start and finish of activities and milestones against the planned timeline, and updating the plan so that the comparison to the plan is always current. Schedule control must work closely with the other program and portfolio control processes. It involves identifying not only slippages but also opportunities.

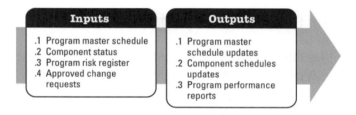

Figure 3-40. Monitor and Control Program Schedule: Inputs and Outputs

3.6.4 Monitor and Control Program Financials

The Monitor and Control Program Financials process entails controlling changes to, and producing information from, the program budget (Figure 3-41). Cost control is proactive—it analyzes actual cost as incurred against the plan to identify variances from the plan, and, where possible, conducts trend analysis to predict problem areas early. Cost control is also reactive because it deals with unanticipated events or necessary but unplanned activities that affect the budget. Cost control is frequently thought of as merely holding down cost so that the program remains on budget, or bringing it back to budget when there is an overrun. However, of equal importance, cost control involves identifying opportunities to return funding from the program to the enterprise wherever possible.

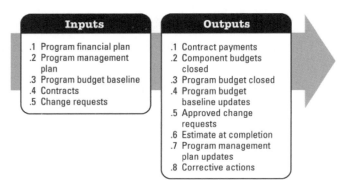

Figure 3-41. Monitor and Control Program Financials: Inputs and Outputs

3.6.5 Manage Program Stakeholder Expectations

The Manage Program Stakeholder Expectations process ensures that stakeholders' expectations are identified and that they are kept informed as to program status and any information of interest to them (Figure 3-42). Because of the greater impact of programs than of projects, the scope and extent of the stakeholder management process is much greater at the program level than at the project level. Furthermore, since programs tend to be of larger size, greater cost, and much longer in duration, for some programs proactive communication is required with the community at large. Such external communications will not only include addressing issues specific to a program (such as environmental issues), but also managing public and media relations at the social and political level as may be appropriate to the program.

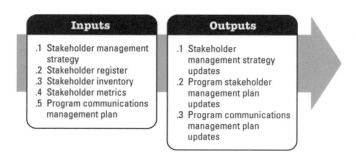

Figure 3-42. Manage Program Stakeholder Expectations: Inputs and Outputs

3.6.6 Monitor and Control Program Risks

The Monitor and Control Program Risks process tracks known program risks, identifies new risks to the program, executes risk response plans, and evaluates their effectiveness in reducing risk through the program life cycle (Figure 3-43). They include oversight of risks and responses at the project level within the program. Risk monitoring and control are ongoing processes.

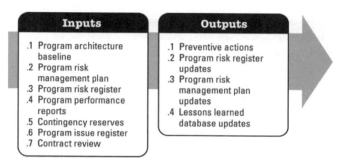

Figure 3-43. Monitor and Control Program Risks: Inputs and Outputs

3.6.7 Administer Program Procurements

The Administer Program Procurements process includes strategies, tools, methods, metrics gathering, reviews and update mechanisms, standard assessment parameters, and reporting requirements to be used by each component in the program and in the administration of the procurement activities for the program (Figure 3-44).

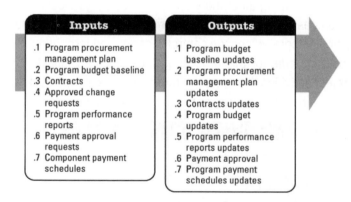

Figure 3-44. Administer Program Procurements: Inputs and Outputs

3.6.8 Manage Program Issues

The Manage Program Issues process identifies, tracks, and closes issues effectively to ensure that stakeholder expectations are aligned with program activities and deliverables (Figure 3-45). This alignment can be accomplished by several approaches, including modifying requirements or the program scope, adjusting organizational policies, or changing stakeholder expectations.

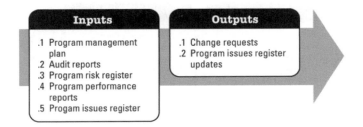

Figure 3-45. Manage Program Issues: Inputs and Outputs

3.6.9 Monitor and Control Program Changes

The Monitor and Control Program Changes process coordinates changes across the entire program, including changes to cost, quality, schedule and scope (Figure 3-46). This process controls the approval and refusal of requests for change, escalates requests in line with authority thresholds, determines when changes have occurred, influences factors that create changes, makes sure those changes are beneficial and agreed-upon, and manages how and when the approved changes are applied. Analysis of the change request involves identifying, documenting and estimating all of the work that the change would entail, including a list of all of the program management processes that need to be carried out again (such as updating the PWBS, revising the program risk register, etc.). Integrated change control is performed throughout the entire program life cycle from initiation through closure. Inputs for this process include change requests from components and from program-level and non-project activities. The outputs from this process feed back to the component level and as such, the process is iterative between the program and component domains.

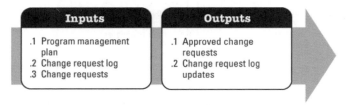

Figure 3-46. Monitor and Control Program Changes: Inputs and Outputs

3.6.10 Report Program Performance

The Report Program Performance process consolidates performance data to provide stakeholders with information about how resources are being used to deliver program benefits (Figure 3-47). Performance reporting aggregates all performance information across projects and non-project activities to provide a clear picture of the program as a whole. This information is conveyed to the stakeholders by means of the Information Distribution process to provide them with status and deliverable information. Additionally, this information is provided to stakeholders of the program and its constituent projects to provide them with information about the program's performance.

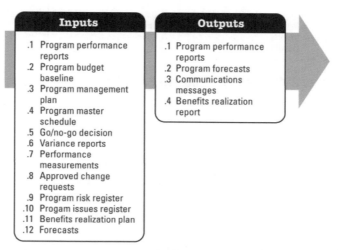

Inputs	Outputs
.1 Program performance reports	.1 Program performance reports
.2 Program budget baseline	.2 Program forecasts
.3 Program management plan	.3 Communications messages
.4 Program master schedule	.4 Benefits realization report
.5 Go/no-go decision	
.6 Variance reports	
.7 Performance measurements	
.8 Approved change requests	
.9 Program risk register	
.10 Progam issues register	
.11 Benefits realization plan	
.12 Forecasts	

Figure 3-47. Report Program Performance: Inputs and Outputs

3.6.11 Provide Governance Oversight

Governance is defined as the process of developing, communicating, implementing, monitoring, and assuring the policies, procedures, organizational structures, and practices associated with a given program (Figure 3-48). Governance is oversight and control.

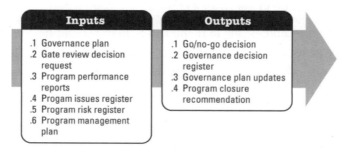

Inputs	Outputs
.1 Governance plan	.1 Go/no-go decision
.2 Gate review decision request	.2 Governance decision register
.3 Program performance reports	.3 Governance plan updates
.4 Progam issues register	.4 Program closure recommendation
.5 Program risk register	
.6 Program management plan	

Figure 3-48. Provide Governance Oversight: Inputs and Outputs

3.6.12 Manage Program Benefits

The Manage Program Benefits process ensures there is a defined set of reports or metrics reported to the program management office, program stakeholders, governance committee, and/or sponsors (Figure 3-49). By consistently monitoring and reporting benefits metrics, stakeholders can assess the overall health of the program, and take action as required to ensure successful benefit delivery.

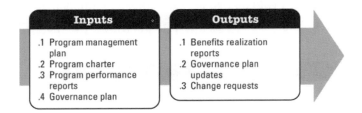

Inputs	Outputs
.1 Program management plan	.1 Benefits realization reports
.2 Program charter	.2 Governance plan updates
.3 Program performance reports	.3 Change requests
.4 Governance plan	

Figure 3-49. Manage Program Benefits: Inputs and Output

3.7 Closing Process Group

The Closing Process Group formalizes acceptance of products, services, or results that bring the program, or a project within a program, to completion (Figure 3-50). The closing Process Group includes the processes required to formally terminate all of the program activities, finalize closure of a project within the program and hand-off the completed product to others, or to close a cancelled program or project within the program.

The purposes of the closing processes include the following:

- To demonstrate that all program benefits have been delivered and that the scope of work has been fulfilled, or to document the current state in the case of early termination;

- To demonstrate that contractual obligations with the seller and/or the customer have been met, or to document the current state in the case of early termination;

- To demonstrate that all payments to the seller or from the customer have been delivered, or to document the current state in the case of early termination;

- To release all human resources and to demonstrate that all other resources have either been made available to other activities, sold, discarded, returned to the owner, transferred to the organization maintaining the product or service or transferred to the customer, or otherwise disposed;

- To demonstrate that all required documentation has been archived in the manner prescribed by the program management plan;

- To demonstrate that any intellectual property developed during the course of the program has been captured and documented for future use, in a manner which ensures legal protection of this valuable asset;

- To transition ongoing activities such as product support, service management or customer support from a project or the program to an operational support function;

- To leave in place a legacy of operational benefit sustainment, deriving optimum value from the work accomplished by the program; and

- To provide a program lessons learned knowledge base that can be incorporated into the organizational process asset library.

Program closure activities occur throughout the program; not just at program completion. As specific components are completed, closing activities must occur.

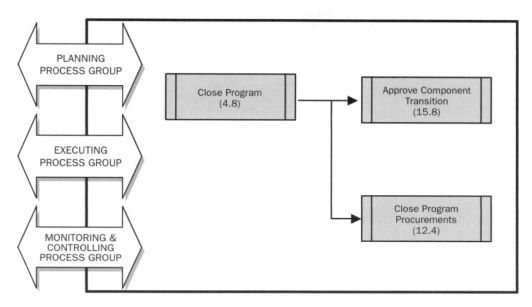

Figure 3-50. Closing Process Group

3.7.1   Close Program

The Close Program process belongs to the Closing Process Group (Figure 3-51). The Close Program process establishes processes to formally terminate program activities. The program is shut down and its artifacts stored for future reference.

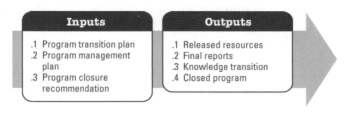

Figure 3-51. Close Program: Inputs and Outputs

3.7.2   Approve Component Transition

The Approve Component Transition process ensures that the program has completed the handover of knowledge, responsibilities, and benefit realization to ongoing operations (Figure 3-52). The resources that become available as a result of approving program transition may be reallocated to other programs or program components that are either active or awaiting activation. Program records must be closed and archived as transitioning occurs.

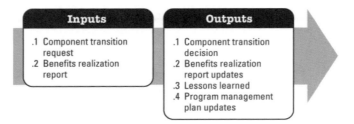

Figure 3-52. Approve Component Transition: Inputs and Outputs

3.7.3   Close Program Procurements

The Close Program Procurements process addresses how to shut down the procurement activities within a program (Figure 3-53). Such shutdown may include performing reviews on suppliers and reconciling the budget allocation. It also includes strategies, tools, methods, metrics gathering, reviews and update mechanisms, standard assessment parameters, and reporting requirements to be used by each component of the program and in the closing of the procurement activities for the whole program.

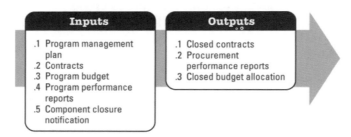

Figure 3-53. Close Program Procurements: Inputs and Outputs

SECTION III

THE PROGRAM MANAGEMENT KNOWLEDGE AREAS

Chapter 4

- Program Integration Management

Chapter 5

- Program Scope Management

Chapter 6

- Program Time Management

Chapter 7

- Program Cost Management

Chapter 8

- Program Quality Management

Chapter 9

- Program Human Resource Management

Chapter 10

- Program Communication Management

Chapter 11

- Program Risk Management

Chapter 12

- Program Procurement Management

Chapter 13

- Program Financial Management

Chapter 14

- Program Stakeholder Management

Chapter 15

- Program Governance

CHAPTER 4

PROGRAM INTEGRATION MANAGEMENT

The Program Integration Management Knowledge Area includes the processes and activities needed to identify, define, combine, unify, and coordinate multiple components within the program as well as coordinate the various processes and program management activities within the Program Management Process Groups (Figure 4-1). In the program management context, integration includes characteristics of unification, consolidation, articulation, and integrative actions that are crucial for completing the program, managing stakeholder expectations, and delivering program benefits. Integration requires making choices as to where to concentrate resources and effort, anticipating issues and dealing with them before they become critical, and coordinating work for the overall success of the program. Integration also involves making trade-offs among competing objectives and alternatives. The program management processes are usually presented as discrete processes with defined interfaces that, in practice, overlap and interact in ways that cannot be completely defined in this standard.

Program management integration is most valuable where program components interact. The program deliverables should be integrated, if appropriate, with ongoing operations of either the performing organization or the customer's organization, and with the long-term strategic planning that takes future problems and opportunities into consideration.

In large part, most of the planning that will integrate upwards into the program management plan will be developed in other processes. The program manager and program team must address every process to determine the most appropriate level of implementation. The team will use existing organizational and program guidelines, and established practices to determine which processes to employ and in what order they should be employed. Program management processes and their requisite skills and knowledge are applied in varying degrees but generally match the intrinsic complexity of the program.

The integrative nature of programs and program management is best understood if it is considered in light of other types of activities that are performed while completing a program. For example, some of the integrative activities performed by the program management team include:

- Transform the program's strategic directives and business case into a program management plan, and an initial program roadmap, by leveraging the team's knowledge and skills, the organization's accepted best practices, and the structured approach described in this standard;

- Employ program management planning processes to create the requisite program and high-level component management plans that will make up the program management plan, and roll the overall plan up into an updated program roadmap. This includes program objectives, program benefits, infrastructure plans, various financial assumptions and constraints, schedule criteria, component characteristics and artifacts, risk, communications, stakeholders, and other influences related to the program and the organization sponsoring it and/or funding it;

- Identify, define, and document critical success factors;

- Manage program resources. This includes financial, material, and manpower resources, whether internal or external to the organization;

- Develop and manage the governance structure to ensure the program performs to a proper set of policies and guidelines;

- Monitor, correct, forecast, and report program progress, issues, and risks; and

- Understand the program's defined goals and success criteria, what it will take to reach it according to plan, and then close the program either by delivering the final product to the client, by transitioning the program into operations, or by canceling the program.

The integrative program management processes are:

4.1 Initiate Program—The starting point for a program may be nothing more than a concept and a business case. Initiating a program begins with determining the need for a program, and initially defining the program's expected outcomes.

The Initiate Program process may end with an approved charter or the decision not to continue. Either decision is documented in the charter and stored for future reference.

Considerable preliminary work must be completed before the program execution. This is because of the size, cost, duration, and inherent risks in a program. This may be a preliminary pilot program, it may take place during the initiation phase or before the program charter is officially approved.

The purpose of Initiate Program is to produce the information needed to begin effective program planning as a basis for efficient execution and obtain the authorization for this work approval of the program charter.

4.2 Develop Program Management Plan—The process of consolidating and coordinating all subsidiary plans into a program management plan as well as updating the program roadmap. This plan will serve as the consolidated plan for executing, monitoring, and closing the program.

4.3 Develop Program Infrastructure—The process of identifying, assessing, and developing the infrastructure required to support the program.

4.4 Direct and Manage Program Execution—The process of managing the execution of the program management plan to achieve program objectives.

4.5 Manage Program Resources—The process of tracking, assessing, and adapting to the use of resources throughout the program's life cycle.

4.6 Monitor and Control Program Performance—The process of monitoring and controlling the program's execution to meet performance objectives as defined in the program management plan.

4.7 Manage Program Issues—The process of addressing unplanned risks and events that may impact the program's planned directives. Issues are assessed and, if necessary, a change request is issued to address the issue or referred to the Risk Management process, for example, for further analysis and planning.

4.8 Close Program—The process of finalizing all activities across all of the Program Management Process Groups to formally close the program.

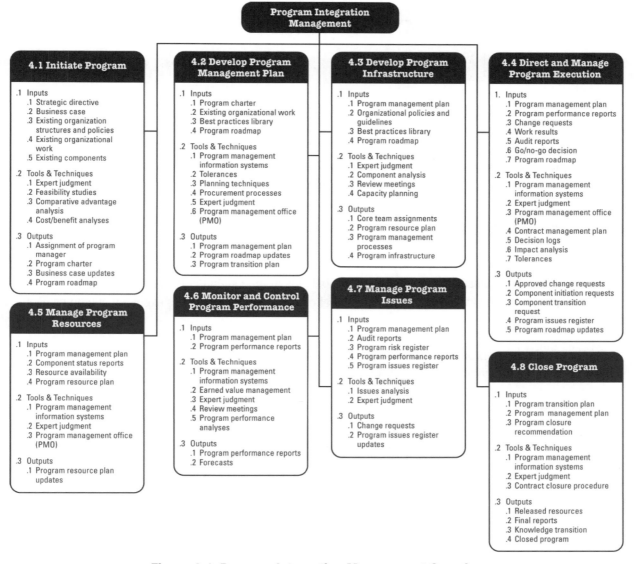

Figure 4-1. Program Integration Management Overview

There is a close link between Program Integration and Program Governance, particularly in the areas of change and issue management and the initiation and transition of components. The authority to approve or reject changes in scope or cost within a defined range of tolerances is often delegated to the program manager, while changes identified within a particular component may require action by the program board or steering group. Figure 4-2 illustrates how Program Integration and Program Governance are linked through the change control process.

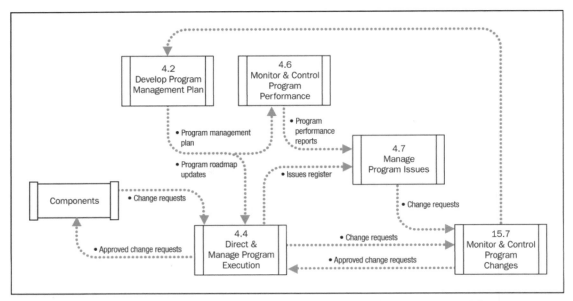

Figure 4-2. Change Control Process Links Between Components, Program Management, and Program Governance

4.1 Initiate Program

The starting point for a program may be nothing more than a concept or a mandate from organizational management and a business case. Initiate Program belongs to the Initiating Process Group and begins with a determination of the need for a program, and an initial definition of the program's expected outcomes (Figures 4-3 and 4-4).

The Initiate Program process ends with either an approved charter or the decision not to continue. Either decision is documented in the charter and stored for future reference.

The purpose of Initiate Program is to produce the information needed to begin effective program planning as well as to define the cost and risks associated with establishing a program and its technical feasibility. For example, this process may produce results that cause the organization to decide not to approve the program charter. This may occur, for example, where analysis suggests that forming a program to satisfy the business objectives is not necessary, inefficient, or too risky or that the program as defined in the program charter is not technically feasible.

This process typically occurs as follows (and not necessarily in this order):

- Assess the feasibility of forming a program to achieve intended objectives;
- Clarify the benefits, objectives, and critical success factors that the program is expected to deliver;
- Define the program end-state;
- Establish the mission, vision, and constraints within which the program will operate;
- Authorize the program;

- Assign a program manager;

- Link the program to the organization's ongoing work and strategic priorities;

- Develop the cost vs. benefits analysis;

- Authorize the program manager to utilize organizational resources per charter guidelines; and

- Develop an initial high-level program roadmap.

The approved program may also include the designation of other key resources and a preliminary outline of the program's organizational structure.

Included in a program are one or more components, typically projects, which may include some portion of ongoing operations. In some instances, initiating the program may entail configuring or grouping proposed and existing projects into a program based on specific benefits or other strategic criteria.

The Initiate Program process takes into account the organization's strategic goals, the program's business case and risks, and the extent to which the program satisfies organizational needs.

The business case and strategic directive are developed external to the program and prior to the program's approval. Initiate Program generally calls for order-of-magnitude estimates, feasibility studies, pilot programs, or concept development efforts. During the life span of the program, changes will occur in the program's architecture, the financial environment, and the organization's strategic goals. The business case should be revisited on a regular basis to ensure the program continues to meet the planned goals.

Programs are typically chartered and authorized at the organizational executive level, by a steering committee, a portfolio management body, or an external funding organization.

The key output of this process is the program charter, which may be approved or rejected.

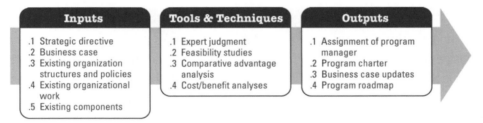

Figure 4-3. Initiate Program: Inputs, Tools & Techniques, and Outputs

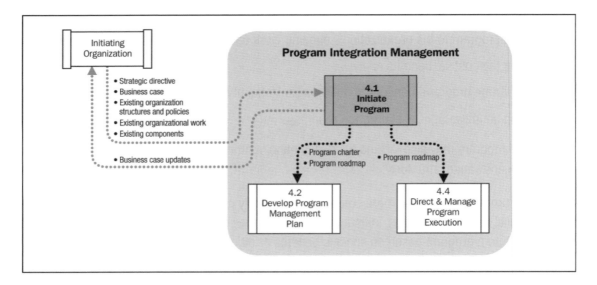

Figure 4-4. Initiate Program: Data Flow Diagram

4.1.1   Initiate Program: Inputs

.1 Strategic Directive

The strategic directive formally expresses the organization's concept, vision, and mission for the program, intended benefits, and/or program benefits. It includes high-level program goals and objectives. It may be as detailed as the organization desires. It may identify any strategic core resources or competencies believed essential to the successful planning, execution, monitoring, or closing of the program's directives.

.2 Business Case

For most programs, a business case is developed to assess the program's cost/benefit justification. The business case may be basic and high-level or detailed and comprehensive. Implied or explicit in its content is the justification for the effort required to perform the Initiate Program process. The business case, if provided, includes key parameters used to assess the objectives and constraints for the intended program. The business case may include the following parameters, among others, financial analyses, benefits, market demand and/or barriers, potential profits, technical risk assessments, time to market data, constraints, and the extent to which the program satisfies the organization's strategic objectives.

.3 Existing Organization Structures and Policies

For some programs, such as in the major construction industry, an organization is newly created to plan, develop, and manage the program. In programs where the parent organization is already established, knowledge of the present and planned structure is important when assessing the organization's capacity to apply the resources necessary to engage the intended program.

.4 Existing Organizational Work

Existing programs and other work compete for organizational resources. A new program initiation effort should be aware of all the organizational entities with which it will be competing and integrating.

.5 Existing Components

Some programs may incorporate one or more existing projects and other components. In general, if components already exist, they contain risks and issues that are inherited by the parent program. Initial assessments and feasibility studies consider the external characteristics of existing components that may affect outcomes at the program level.

4.1.2 Initiate Program: Tools and Techniques

.1 Expert Judgment

Expert judgment is expertise based on knowledge and experience in the area. Such expertise may be provided by any group or person with specialized education, knowledge, skills, or experience applicable to the area under analysis. It is available from multiple sources including other units within the organization, consultants, professional and technical organizations, industry groups, and others.

.2 Feasibility Studies

Consulting the business case, the strategic directive, organizational goals, and other existing initiatives, this process assesses and recommends the feasibility of creating a program to achieve the desired objectives. An analysis of the strengths, weaknesses, opportunities and threats (SWOT) of the endeavor provides information for developing a viable program charter.

.3 Comparative Advantage Analysis

When conducting comparative analysis against a strategic initiative and/or business case, it is important to consider that competing efforts may reside within or external to the organization. A typical business case includes some level of analysis and comparison against real or imagined alternative efforts. Where appropriate, this technique may also include conducting a what-if analysis to consider how the strategic directive and its intended benefits might be achieved by other means.

.4 Cost/Benefit Analyses

Cost/benefit analyses seek to define the benefits that will be provided by the program and compare it to the costs of the program. Benefits may be financial, such as increased profits, but may also be non-financial such as increased market share or a new capability. The cost/benefit analysis should be tracked and re-evaluated as required during the program, as the program changes or as the financial or competitive environment changes.

4.1.3   Initiate Program: Outputs

.1   Assignment of Program Manager

It is generally considered good practice to assign the program manager, and define his/her role and organizational interfaces, as early in the Program Initiation process as is possible. A skilled and knowledgeable program manager effectively guides the initiation process, ensuring that the program charter and business case contain the parameters needed for effective execution and management of subsequent processes.

.2   Program Charter

The program charter is the key output of this process. Once approved, it formally authorizes the program, provides the program manager with the authority to apply organizational resources to program activities, and links the program to the organization's ongoing work and strategic priorities. If the program is not authorized (failing at any point in this process) the event should be recorded in the program charter and stored in lessons learned.

.3   Business Case Updates

The process of assessing the feasibility of forming a program to achieve intended benefits and objectives may result in updates to the business case. The business case is revised and updated accordingly, regardless of whether the program charter is approved or rejected.

.4   Program Roadmap

The program roadmap is a chronological representation of a program's intended direction. It depicts key dependencies between major milestones, communicates the linkage between the business strategy and the planned and prioritized work, reveals and explains gaps, and provides a high level view of key milestones and decision points. The program roadmap summarizes key end-point objectives, key challenges and risks, comments on evolving aspects of the program, and a high-level snapshot of the supporting infrastructure and component plans.

The program roadmap can be a valuable tool for managing the execution of the program and for assessing the program's progress toward achieving its expected benefits. To better enable effective governance of the program, the program roadmap can be used to show how components are organized within major stages or blocks. In a large construction program, for example, these may be stages of construction. In a system development and production program, the program roadmap may depict how the capability is delivered through incremental releases or a series of models.

A program roadmap communicates, in a chronological fashion, the high-level overall scope and execution of the program. It accomplishes this by building a bridge between program activities and expected benefits.

Initiate Program creates the initial, high-level, roadmap based on the program's business case and strategic directive. In the Develop Program Management Plan process, the initial roadmap is further refined in a rolling wave fashion, culminating with the final roadmap.

4.2 Develop Program Management Plan

The Develop Program Management Plan process belongs to the Planning Process Group. This process includes the tools and techniques used to integrate all subsidiary program plans, and other inputs, into a cohesive overall program management plan and update the program roadmap (Figures 4-5 and 4-6).

The Develop Program Management Plan process integrates the program's subsidiary plans and establishes the starting point for the plans to be developed by the program's individual components. This set of plans includes the following subsidiary plans:

- Program roadmap,

- Program schedule,

- Program governance plan,

- Governance metrics and critical success factors,

- Benefits realization plan,

- Program stakeholder management plan,

- Program communications management plan,

- Program financial plan,

- Contracts management plan,

- Scope management plan,

- Procurement management plan,

- Quality management plan,

- Program risk response plan,

- Program risk management plan, and

- Schedule management plan.

Program management plan development is an iterative process (along with all of the other planning processes) as competing priorities, assumptions, and constraints are resolved to address critical factors, such as business goals, deliverables, benefits, time, and cost.

Each planning process in the program Planning Process Group produces, at a minimum, a plan addressing a specific aspect of the program, such as communications or risks, as well as a set of supporting documents and details. These other plans may be incorporated into the program management plan or they may serve as subsidiary plans to the program management plan.

Updates and revisions to the program management plan, its subsidiary plans, and the program roadmap are approved or rejected through Program Governance (Chapter 15).

Figure 4-5. Develop Program Management Plan: Inputs, Tools & Techniques, and Outputs

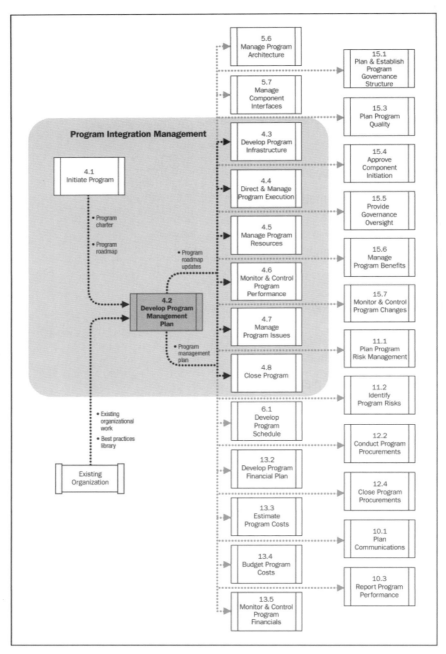

Figure 4-6. Develop Program Management Plan: Data Flow Diagram

4.2.1 Develop Program Management Plan: Inputs

.1 Program Charter

Described in Section 4.1.3.2.

.2 Existing Organizational Work

Programs compete for resources with existing work such as operations or other programs/projects. Some programs may be initiated where some or all of their components already exist. Since all project plans under its auspices are subsidiary to this program, it is essential that existing project plans and their influences are considered when planning program outcomes.

.3 Best Practices Library

Organizations adopt and/or develop and apply best practices to achieve economies of scale and other efficiencies. This applies to assessing, planning, and managing a supporting infrastructure.

The best practices library is not a best practice by itself; it is a repository for retrieval and management of best practices. Defining or specifying best practices is outside the intent of this standard. The library includes applicable methodologies, such as quality assurance, cost estimation, and program management.

A program management methodology is a system of practices, techniques, procedures, and rules used for managing programs within an organization or industry. Program management methodologies reduce program risk, achieve program benefits, complete the program as planned, improve stakeholder and customer satisfaction, and reduce conflict and unplanned change. Program management methodologies are adopted and approved at an organizational level and must complement (not conflict with) project management methodologies.

Best practices, like lessons learned, must be communicated effectively and appropriately—often with limited or controlled access by select stakeholders. Best practices must be properly evaluated, accepted by the organization, appropriately stored for retrieval, and demoted as their usefulness expires—or a superior practice is adopted by the organization.

Example 1: An organization adopted the practice of organizing programs under the auspices of a program management office (PMO). The templates, guidelines, and policies and procedures for organizing a PMO are retrieved from the best practices library. This practice becomes a critical part of planning and managing the program under the guidance of a PMO.

Example 2: An organization developed a reduced-risk, low cost means for delivering and dispensing fuel to a remote region of the country where the program will construct a communications facility. This proprietary method is a best practice and also guarded as a company secret.

.4 Program Roadmap

Described in Section 4.1.3.4.

4.2.2 Develop Program Management Plan: Tools and Techniques

.1 Program Management Information Systems

Program management information systems collect and manage schedules, costs, earned value data, risk information, changes in component status and issues, and other information needed to manage and control the program. They provide methods by which internal consistency can be observed and program metrics collected, monitored, and controlled. They can also support performance-improvement initiatives.

A program management information system provides a technology-based method of capturing and managing all program related data and information. An effective program management information system enables the program to define, analyze, design, generate/produce, construct, and manage information systems to ensure a successful program. This system incorporates such tools and processes as:

- Software tools,
- Document repository and document version control system,
- Change management system,
- Risk database and analysis tools,
- Financial management systems,
- Earned value management processes and tools,
- Requirements management processes and tools, and
- Other tools and processes as required.

.2 Tolerances

Tolerances, also referred to as margins or envelopes, are ranges set for aspects of programs and components such as cost, schedule, scope, and risk that are associated with a particular level of responsibility. The component project manager can control variations that fall within a defined tolerance range for a component without the need to obtain the approval of the program manager. Variations that fall outside this range, such as an excessive cost overrun, require corrective action by the program manager.

Without defined tolerances, there is the potential for conflicts over boundaries of authority between component and program managers or between the program manager and the program governance function. Too restrictive tolerances can slow down program execution over minor changes. Too large tolerances can prevent the program manager from anticipating and resolving potential problems before they occur.

The effective use of tolerances can directly enable the efficient execution of a program. The program management plan and its subsidiary plans may define tolerance ranges for variations in cost, schedule, scope, risk, or other factors, and their associated levels of management, to effectively manage the program in accordance with the stakeholders' expectations and the governance board.

.3 Planning Techniques

Each part of the program requires thorough planning: the program's schedule, its financing and budget, the resources it requires, the risks that may occur, the quality standards and plans, procurement, and all other aspects. The specific planning techniques utilized depend on which area is being planned. Planning for resources requires different planning techniques than does planning the overall schedule, but both are required to be planned. Developing the most efficient means of planning each part of the program is a critical requirement for the program management team.

.4 Procurement Processes

Described in Section 12.

.5 Expert Judgment

Described in Section 4.1.2.1.

.6 Program Management Office (PMO)

Described in Section 4.4.2.3.

4.2.3 Develop Program Management Plan: Outputs

.1 Program Management Plan

The program management plan integrates and incorporates all program and component plans. It includes the component milestones, benefit deliverables, and component dependencies.

The program management plan outlines the key elements of program direction and management. It also identifies how decisions should be presented and recorded, and describes how performance reports will be prepared and distributed.

.2 Program Roadmap Updates

A high-level program roadmap, initially created in the Initiate Program process, was based on preliminary information provided in the business case and strategic initiative (see 4.1.3.4). During the program's established planning processes, the program roadmap may be further refined in a rolling wave fashion. When all plans have been developed the program roadmap is updated.

.3 Program Transition Plan

This plan outlines the steps needed to move the program from a development state to an operational state pending approval that the program has satisfied all requirements and is ready to turn over to the client or into operations.

4.3 Develop Program Infrastructure

The Develop Program Infrastructure process belongs to the Planning Process Group and investigates, assesses, and plans the support structure that will enable the program to successfully achieve its goals (Figures 4-7 and 4-8). This process is typically invoked after the program has been initiated and may be invoked again at any time during the program in order to update or modify the infrastructure to support the program. Changes to the infrastructure must however be approved by the governance change control process.

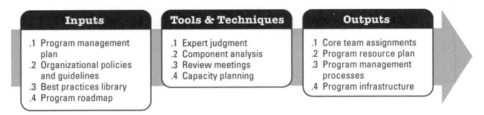

Figure 4-7. Develop Program Infrastructure: Inputs, Tools & Techniques, and Outputs

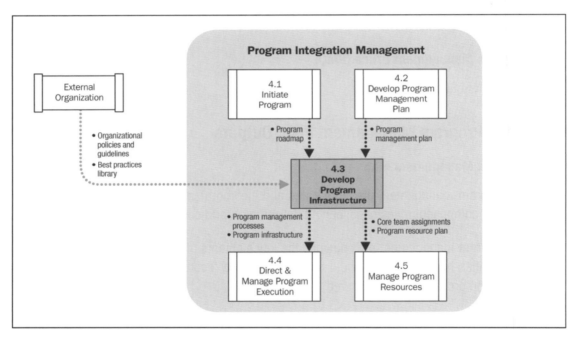

Figure 4-8. Develop Program Infrastructure: Data Flow Diagram

4.3.1   Develop Program Infrastructure: Inputs

.1 Program Management Plan

The program management plan contains information about finances, required resources, schedules, scope, communications, stakeholder needs, risks, and other factors essential to understanding the demands of the program. Virtually every subsidiary plan will be used to assess, plan, and implement the program infrastructure.

.2 Organizational Policies and Guidelines

Policies and guidelines are established standards of behavior that provide governance on appropriate courses of action toward an organization's mission and vision. Policies and guidelines may be detailed or general in language.

Generally, the program management team has the authority to establish policies at the program level. Program level policies must not conflict with policies at the organizational level unless expressed otherwise and approved at the organizational level. It is important that the program management team is aware of, and kept abreast of, organizational policies and guidelines and any changes made to them. Unless otherwise defined, program infrastructures conform to organizational policies first, and program policies second.

.3 Best Practices Library

Described in Section 4.2.1.3.

.4 Program Roadmap

Described in Section 4.1.3.4.

4.3.2   Develop Program Infrastructure: Tools and Techniques

.1 Expert Judgment

Described in Section 4.1.2.1.

.2 Component Analysis

Overall program objectives are successively decomposed into self-contained and clearly defined components. Component analysis may also be used to further decompose components to form benefits packages. Each component may be a project, a set of projects and sub-project, and non-project activities that, together, provide a measurable contribution to the planned benefits of the program.

.3 Review Meetings

Program level review meetings are typically held with executive management to discuss individual project reports with project managers in attendance. These meetings keep program managers and executives informed of the program's progress.

.4 Capacity Planning

Program infrastructure development is concerned with necessary resources such as staff, information, expertise, funds, facilities, and production capabilities. Limitations in these resources are addressed as capacity constraints and alternatives or mitigations.

4.3.3   Develop Program Infrastructure: Outputs

.1   Core Team Assignments

Although the program manager is assigned in the Initiate Program process, the core program management and governance team (including the program management office, steering committees, governance body members, key consultants, and boards of advisors) is designated in this process, as part of establishing the program infrastructure. Although not necessarily assigned full time to the program, these key stakeholders will be instrumental in determining and developing the program's infrastructure requirements. The governance team, unless employed full-time by the program, may not be included in the program resource plan.

.2   Program Resource Plan

The program requires resources to manage the program such as personnel, tools, facilities, and finances that will be used to manage the program. These are separate and distinct from the resources required to manage the individual components within the program. The majority of the resources and costs of the program will be managed at the component level (see program capacity plan described in Section 4.3.3.4). The program resource plan covers only those resources substantially or fully employed in program management or governance functions.

.3   Program Management Processes

The specific list of selected program management processes required for implementing and managing the defined program infrastructure.

.4   Program Infrastructure

Program infrastructure defines the required support structure and capabilities, including human and material resources, and also considers the unique challenges and needs of the program and how components interface. For most programs, the program management office forms the core of the program infrastructure.

4.4 Direct and Manage Program Execution

Direct and Manage Program Execution is the process of managing the execution of the program management plan (Figures 4-9 and 4-10). This process is part of the Executing Process Group. This process ensures that components remain aligned with the program's strategic directives and business case. Its overall purpose is to deliver the aggregate output of all program components to the organization according to the approved program management plan.

Component initiation requests are created based on the timing of components indicated in the program roadmap. As program components close or transition from one component to another, this process receives component initiation, closure, or transition requests, provides an integrated assessment, and forwards the request to the Governance process for decision.

All measured activities at the program level generate requests to initiate or transition components, entries in an issues log, change requests, or entries in lessons learned.

Program management plan execution becomes the primary responsibility of the program manager and the program team once the initial planning activities are completed and execution of the program has begun (although the other Process Groups remain active, particularly planning and monitoring and controlling). Progress of the work is tracked regularly by means of updates on individual projects, and is forwarded to the performance reporting process.

As components execute, they may generate change requests. These change requests are assessed in this process and forwarded to the Program Governance process, which serves to authorize the program to implement the change. Other change requests may come from the stakeholders, identification of missing requirements or technical issues, or from external sources. The analysis of the change request should identify impacts to:

- **Program finances.** Proposed changes to the program architecture may have an adverse impact on the program financial status. It is important to analyze whether modifications to the program financial components are necessary.

- **Program schedule.** Proposed changes to the program architecture may affect the program timelines and schedules commitments. Existing schedules are analyzed to determine critical path variations or changes to agreed-upon scheduled activities. It is important to ensure that long lead time components, resources, equipment, or activities are not adversely affected or that the program is suddenly delinquent in meeting requirements.

- **Program requirements.** Proposed changes may impact requirements at the program and at the component level. Changes requested by one component may impact other components.

- **Program architecture baseline.** Proposed changes may change the architecture of the delivered product. Any changes to the overall architecture need to be incorporated at the component level where there are identified impacts.

- **Interfaces among components.** Any change to one component has a potential impact on other components. Identification and analysis of these impacts are part of the change management process.

- **Documentation.** All approved change requests are incorporated into the program documentation. Version control of these documents ensures that the most current documents are identified and made available to all program participants.

- **Risk.** Proposed changes may have impacts to the program's risk universe and these new or changed risks should be identified and managed in accordance with the program risk management plan.

Inputs	Tools & Techniques	Outputs
.1 Program management plan .2 Program performance reports .3 Change requests .4 Work results .5 Audit reports .6 Go/no-go decision .7 Program roadmap	.1 Program management information systems .2 Expert judgment .3 Program management office (PMO) .4 Contract management plan .5 Decision logs .6 Impact analysis .7 Tolerances	.1 Approved change requests .2 Component initiation requests .3 Component transition request .4 Progam issues register .5 Program roadmap updates

Figure 4-9. Direct and Manage Program Execution: Inputs, Tools & Techniques, and Outputs

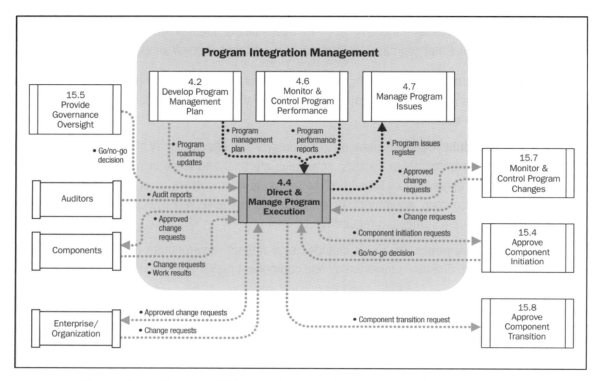

Figure 4-10. Direct and Manage Program Execution: Data Flow Diagram

4.4.1 Direct and Manage Program Execution: Inputs

.1 Program Management Plan

The Direct and Manage Program Execution process concerns itself with every artifact of this consolidated plan. It is the program manager's responsibility to ensure that all activities within the program execute only to the requirements, expectations, guidelines, parameters, and constraints outlined in the program management plan. If the program is not executing to the program management plan, it is likely doing so outside the scope and charter of the program.

.2 Program Performance Reports

Other processes, especially monitoring processes, generate program performance information, which is compiled by the report program performance process into a program performance report. The program performance report is available where necessary to highlight the progress and pitfalls of each process in order to effectively direct and manage the program's execution.

.3 Change Requests

Change requests are addressed through the change control process. They are considered by the appropriate authority in the program management team and approved, rejected or modified for further consideration. Proposed changes must go through a formal change request process for an analysis of the impact to scope, schedule, cost, and risk to both the overall program and to any components within the program.

.4 Work Results

This process monitors the delivery of work results from components to track progress toward component completion or transition.

.5 Audit Reports

Audits are increasingly performed on programs of all types. The audit is an independent, objective assessment of program status and whether identified program management processes are being followed.

.6 Go/No-Go Decision

Described in Sections 15.4.3.1 and 15.5.3.1.

.7 Program Roadmap

Described in Section 4.2.3.2. The program roadmap is used by this process to determine when new components should be initiated and component initiation requests produced.

4.4.2 Direct and Manage Program Execution: Tools and Techniques

.1 Program Management Information Systems

Described in Section 4.2.2.1.

.2 Expert Judgment

Described in Section 4.1.2.1.

.3 Program Management Office (PMO)

For most programs, the program management office is a core part of the program infrastructure. The program management office supports the management and coordination of the program and component work. The program manager heads the program management office and structures it to manage the unique needs of the program and the reporting and governance needs of the larger organization. The program management office performs many of the tasks in this process, such as preparing and coordinating change request assessments.

.4 Contract Management Plan

Described in Section 12.1.3.3.

.5 Decision Logs

The program manager keeps the decision log, which documents all major decisions made in managing the program including the background information supporting the decision. Decision logs are significant especially in long-term programs where it may be necessary to look up, sometimes years later, why a particular technical or management decision was made.

.6 Impact Analysis

Change requests received from components must be analyzed to determine their impacts on scope, schedule, cost, risk, and other considerations, both to the overall program and to any components within the program.

.7 Tolerances

Described in Section 4.2.2.2.

4.4.3 Direct and Manage Program Execution: Outputs

.1 Approved Change Requests

Change requests that fall within the program manager's scope of authority are approved or rejected in this process.

.2 Component Initiation Requests

Described in Section 15.4.1.3.

.3 Component Transition Request

As program components reach the end of their respective life cycles and/or planned program-level milestones are reached, this formal request is sent to governance for gate transition approval.

.4 Program Issues Register

Issues are resolved either through acceptance (where no action is taken) or through changes to the program's plan. The log of resolved issues should be included in the impact reports and checklists and stored for future reference by all stakeholders on an ongoing basis. These assets may also be used to support ongoing and post-program audit inquiries.

This log is used by other processes, such as Program Risk Management, as input for the incidental and ongoing management of risk. Entries in the issues register describe the effect that issues had or will have within the program and possibly to the greater organization. This log may contain assessments of risk but is not intended to replace the risk register or other Program Risk Management outputs.

.5 Program Roadmap Updates

The program roadmap is updated to reflect both go/no go decisions and approved change requests affecting high-level milestones, the scope or timing of major stages or blocks of the program.

4.5 Manage Program Resources

Manage Program Resources is the process of tracking and adapting the use of program resources throughout the program's life cycle (see Figures 4-11 and 4-12). This process is part of the Executing Process Group. During the execution of the program, the need for staff, facilities, funds, and other resources change. This process monitors program-level resource allocation and recognizes that the majority of the program's resources are located in, and managed at, the component level. This separates the provision of resources—a program-level responsibility—from the day-to-day management of these resources, which is the component manager's responsibility.

This process also monitors the expenditure or use of resources to ensure compliance with organizational guidelines. To this end, guidance on the appropriate use of program resources may be issued to project managers and program staff through this process. Such guidance may relate to the depreciation or release of purchased equipment or the recurring costs of leased facilities or services.

Finally, this process provides inputs to strategic planning and budgeting processes to reflect any changes required to support execution according to the program management plan.

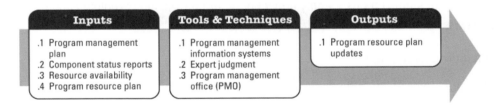

Figure 4-11. Manage Program Resources: Inputs, Tools & Techniques, and Outputs

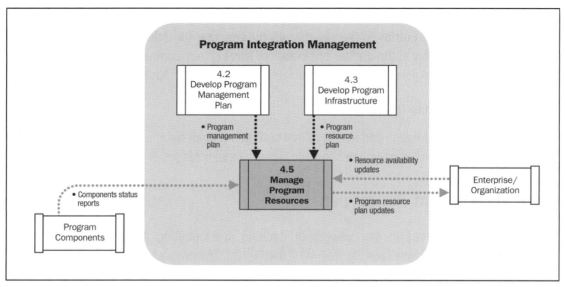

Figure 4-12. Manage Program Resources: Data Flow Diagram

4.5.1   Manage Program Resources: Inputs

.1   Program Management Plan

The program management plan guides the allocation and use of program resources throughout program execution. While Manage Program Resources primarily concerns itself with the program resources plan, the risk management plan, communications plan, stakeholder management plan, and other plans are important to the effective management of resources.

.2   Component Status Reports

Component status reports identify project or program execution problems that stem from resource allocation issues that should be addressed by this process.

.3   Resource Availability

Resource availability indicates the availability of a person, **asset, material, or capital which is required to be used to accomplish the program's goal/deliverable.**

.4   Program Resource Plan

Described in 4.3.3.2.

4.5.2   Manage Program Resources: Tools and Techniques

.1   Program Management Information Systems

Program management information systems collect program and project status and performance data to assist in the early identification and assessment of program resource issues.

.2 Expert Judgment

Described in Section 4.1.2.1.

.3 Program Management Office (PMO)

The program management office (PMO) manages program level resources. The office calls upon the larger organization when resources outside the program, but available within the organization, are required.

4.5.3 Manage Program Resources: Outputs

.1 Program Resource Plan Updates

The program resource plan identifies how the program-level resources will be identified, obtained, and managed. Changes in the assignment of program staff are reflected as updates to the program resource plan.

The resources obtained or provided for the execution of the program may include equipment or facilities purchased with capital funds, services leased through an operating budget, or facilities shared with other elements of the strategic organization.

4.6 Monitor and Control Program Performance

The Monitor and Control Program Performance process belongs to the Monitoring and Controlling Process Group (Figures 4-13 and 4-14). It monitors activities in all Program Management Process Groups, phases, and components and ensures that program execution occurs according to the approved program management plan.

Monitoring is performed throughout a program's life cycle, which includes collecting, measuring and disseminating performance information, and assessing overall program trends. This process provides program management with the data necessary to determine the program's state and trends, which may point to areas in need of correction. Requests for corrective or preventive action are taken to Program Governance for approval.

Figure 4-13. Monitor and Control Program Performance: Inputs, Tools & Techniques, and Outputs

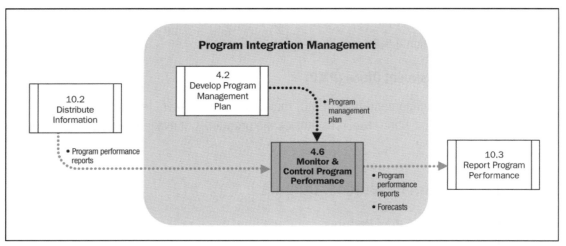

Figure 4-14. Monitor and Control Program Performance: Data Flow Diagram

4.6.1 Monitor and Control Program Performance: Inputs

.1 Program Management Plan

The program management plan contains all subsidiary program and component plans as well as other information needed to monitor and control the program. The program management plan includes schedule milestones and budget goals for the program's components. The components receive schedule and cost goals and decompose them into sufficient detail to manage the component. If a component cannot achieve the planned program-level goals, this information is fed back into the program management plan and the plan is adjusted accordingly.

.2 Program Performance Reports

This includes program and component performance reports on schedule and budget status, issues and risks, significant resource issues, contract issues, architectural and technical issues, and earned value status.

4.6.2 Monitor and Control Program Performance: Tools and Techniques

.1 Program Management Information Systems

Described in Section 4.2.2.1.

.2 Earned Value Management

Earned value information is compiled for the entire program and weighed against baselines and benefits measurements to assist in tracking the program's progress. This data determines whether current trends indicate the program will deliver its chartered objectives according to plan.

.3 Expert Judgment

Described in Section 4.1.2.1.

.4 Review Meetings

Described in Section 4.3.2.3.

.5 Program Performance Analyses

Program performance analyses include:

- **Gap analysis.** Program metrics may be used to assess and report gaps in the program's cost, schedule, or anticipated benefits.

- **Risk analysis.** Real-time monitoring and assessment of program risk is crucial for success. Continuous monitoring and control of program risk registers ensure that risk response plans have the desired effect.

- **Issues analysis.** Program-level issues are prioritized and assigned to an owner. All issues must be recorded, impacts analyzed, and the root cause identified and dispositioned.

- **Trend and probability analysis.** Program metrics and other tools and sources (CV, SV, and aggregated risk probability scores) predict the likelihood of program success or failure (e.g., early measures of realized project benefits that might contribute to the ongoing calibration of achievable end-state benefits and serve to manage stakeholder expectations).

4.6.3 Monitor and Control Program Performance: Outputs

.1 Program Performance Reports

Performance status reports at the program level include a summation of the progress of its components. At a minimum, this report contains high-level statements about what work has been accomplished (especially milestones and gates), earned value status, remaining work, and any risks, issues, and changes being considered.

.2 Forecasts

Forecasts are based on the combined results of program and earned value analysis and expert judgment. Their objective is to assist executives in predicting the likelihood of achieving planned outcomes.

4.7 Manage Program Issues

As part of the Monitoring and Controlling Process Group, the Manage Program Issues process assesses issues and escalates where necessary (see Figures 4-15 and 4-16). An issue is an unplanned event, concern or dispute that may have an impact to cost, schedule, technical architecture, or other program area.

Issue management and control at the program level can also include addressing the issues escalated from the constituent projects that could not be resolved at the project level. These unresolved project issues can impact the overall progress of the program and must be tracked.

When an issue is identified, it is recorded in an issues register and analyzed by a reviewing authority or body. Issue reviews should be conducted on a regular schedule to track the status of all open issues. It is essential that each issue be associated with an owner who has the authority and means to resolve and close the issue. When an issue is unresolved, it is then escalated progressively higher on the authority scale until resolution can be achieved. Program Governance processes and procedures should be in place to selectively allow issues to receive appropriate visibility for possible impact across other portfolios within the organization.

The process of issue management and control is carried out in parallel with controlling risks, especially those risks which do not get resolved at the project level. Issues may be sent to Program Risk Management for further analysis and planning, to Program Governance for high-level oversight or change control, or to Program Scope Management to determine whether the program's scope has been or will be impacted, or whether the issue needs further scope analysis and planning. Issue resolution or acceptance is decided by program management, the program steering committee, or others identified in Direct and Manage Program or Manage and Control Program Changes processes. Program management refers an issue to the appropriate process and management resources for decision by comparing the potential impact of the issue to the tolerances established within the program management plan.

When an issue is addressed, the process addressing the issue communicates its actions by means of the issue register. This process ensures that the issue has been appropriately reflected and, if necessary, invokes an appropriate process (such as Stakeholder Management) assigned for further action.

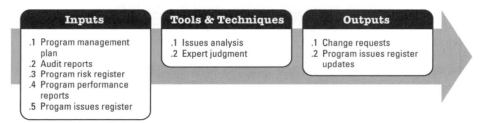

Figure 4-15. Manage Program Issues: Inputs, Tools & Techniques, and Outputs

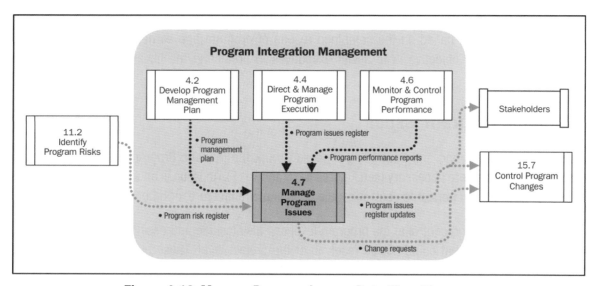

Figure 4-16. Manage Program Issues: Data Flow Diagram

4.7.1 Manage Program Issues: Inputs

.1 Program Management Plan

This process is concerned with the program risk management plan and the communications management plan, which provides the guidelines for assessing and reporting program risks. Risk assessment is an integral part of issues management.

.2 Audit Reports

Described in Section 4.4.1.5.

.3 Program Risk Register

Described in Section 11.2.3.1.

The program risk register assists with decision-making. By maintaining awareness of the likelihood, impact, and status of program risks, decision makers can more effectively weigh the pros and cons of their decisions.

.4 Program Performance Reports

Described in Section 4.6.3.1.

.5 Program Issues Register

Described in Section 4.4.3.4.

4.7.2 Manage Program Issues: Tools and Techniques

.1 Issues Analysis

The analysis of issues may utilize any number of organizationally accepted methodologies for assessing the impact and severity of an issue, its origin (root cause), and possible remedies. However, in some cases issues may require the assistance of a process better equipped to make these determinations. Issues may be escalated to a higher level for consideration by a governance board or steering committee, for example.

.2 Expert Judgment

Described in Section 4.1.2.1.

4.7.3 Manage Program Issues: Outputs

.1 Change Requests

Described in Section 4.4.3.2.

.2 Program Issues Register Updates

Issues are resolved either through acceptance (where no action is taken) or through changes to the program's plan. The log of resolved issues should be included in the impact reports and checklists and stored for future reference by all stakeholders on an ongoing basis. These assets may also be used to support ongoing and post-program audit inquiries.

This log is used by other processes, such as Program Risk Management, as input for the incidental and ongoing management of risk. Entries in the issues register describe the effect that issues had or will have within the program and possibly to the greater organization. This log may contain assessments of risk but is not intended to replace the program risk register or other Program Risk Management outputs.

4.8 Close Program

The Close Program process formalizes the acceptance of the program's outcome by the sponsor or customer (Figures 4-17 and 4-18). However, administrative closure should not wait until the program has completed the execution process. Projects under the program need to be closed before the program is closed. As each project or each non-project activity closes, program closure should be done to capture information and records, archive them, communicate the closure event and status, and obtain sponsor or customer sign-off.

Formal acceptance of the program is achieved by reviewing, with the sponsor or customer, the program scope and the closure documents of the program's constituent projects and non-project activities. These closure documents include the sponsor's or customer's sign-off of the projects or non-project activities, and the results of any verification of deliverables against requirements. Once the review is complete, the sponsor or customer is asked to acknowledge a final acceptance by signing the closure documents.

During this process, the lessons learned are input from other program management processes that created them as outputs. In this process, they are analyzed, significant lessons learned are incorporated into the closure report output, and all lessons learned are included in the program archives.

A program itself comes to an end either because its charter has been fulfilled or conditions arise that bring the program to an early close. When a program has fulfilled its charter, its benefits may have been fully realized or benefits may continue to be realized and managed as part of organizational operations. In the latter case, the Close Program process ensures a smooth transition to operations.

A program may also be terminated with no transition to operations. This may occur because the charter has been fulfilled and operations are not necessary to continue realization of ongoing benefits, or its charter is no longer useful to the organization, In any case, program closure must include justification and approvals for closure, all program and component documentation (whether hardcopy or soft), resource releases, and final reports stored for future reference.

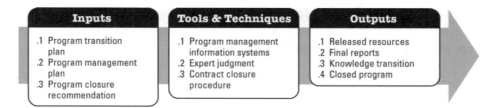

Figure 4-17. Close Program: Inputs, Tools & Techniques, and Outputs

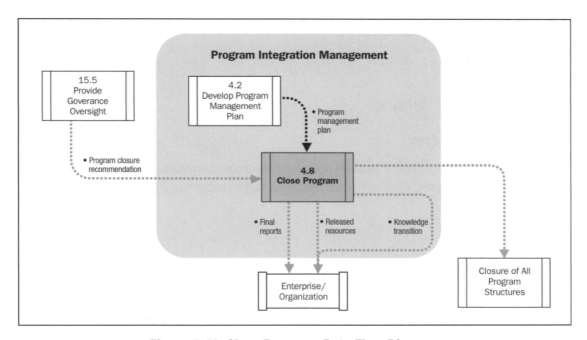

Figure 4-18. Close Program: Data Flow Diagram

4.8.1 Close Program: Inputs

.1 Program Transition Plan

Described in Section 4.2.3.3.

.2 Program Management Plan

Every subsidiary program plan is evaluated to ensure that its requirements have been met, final updates made, and any outstanding or active components are brought to an orderly close.

.3 Program Closure Recommendation

Program Governance recommends the closure of the program based on evaluation of the program benefits and program management plan to ensure all aspects of the program have been realized. Part of the program closure recommendation is to close out the component budgets and the program budget. These recommendations are outputs of Section 13.5.3 on Monitor and Control Program Financials.

4.8.2   Close Program: Tools and Techniques

.1   Program Management Information Systems

Described in Section 4.2.2.1.

.2   Expert Judgment

Described in Section 4.1.2.1.

.3   Contract Closure Procedure

Described in Section 12.4.2.1.

4.8.3   Close Program: Outputs

.1   Released Resources

Efficient and appropriate release of program resources is an essential activity of program closure. At the component level, Program Governance releases resources through the Approve Component Transition process.

.2   Final Reports

A final program report documents critical information that may be used towards the success of future programs and projects, as well as data that senior management requires to perform corporate governance. Items that may be included in the final report are:

- Financial and earned value assessments,
- Program lessons learned,
- Successes and failures,
- Areas for improvement,
- Risk management outcomes,
- Unforeseen risks,
- Scope verification summary and customer buy-off,
- Reason for contract termination (cause, convenience, or completion),
- Technical and programmatic baseline history, and
- Program documentation archive plan.

.3   Knowledge Transition

Upon program completion, the program manager assesses the program's performance and shares lessons learned with all team members. If additional lessons learned are reported during this meeting, this information should be added to the final program report.

.4 Closed Program

The program itself is formally closed out by either canceling the program, delivering the program to the customer, or by transitioning the program into operations. The program may be cancelled due to poor performance or by changes in the business case that obviate the program. Successful completion of the program is judged against the business case and the original goals of the program or the last approved baseline. Before the program is closed, all components should be successfully completed and all contracts formally closed.

Careful consideration must be brought to the systematic shutdown of the all program structures by ensuring that critical personnel remain available to work closeout activities, as required. While most individuals will be released to pursue new positions on other projects and programs, some will be required to stay on the program in a part or full-time capacity until all contractual obligations are met.

A full scope verification audit and accounting of all financial records is required in order to request final payment of amounts due. Planning for the systematic shutdown of the governance structure is similar in scope to the staffing plan, and may be included in the staffing management plan. It is essential to ensure that critical members of the team remain accessible, after they have been released from the team. It is difficult to forecast every situation that may arise during the closeout process. Having the ability to reach back to former team members may be required to answer certain contract compliance questions that may arise during a contract closeout audit.

CHAPTER 5

PROGRAM SCOPE MANAGEMENT

Program Scope Management identifies the deliverables, estimates the major risks, and establishes the relationship between product scope and program scope, while setting standards for clear achievable objectives (Figure 5-1).

5.1 Plan Program Scope—The process of identifying and developing activities to produce deliverables and benefits that meet the program goals and objectives.

5.2 Define Program Goals and Objectives—The process for establishing the overall goals and objectives of the program and ultimately what is to be delivered.

5.3 Develop Program Requirements—The process for development and formal identification of the program requirements and specifications to deliver the program goals and objectives.

5.4 Develop Program Architecture—The process of defining the structure of the programs components and identifies the interrelationships between all of the program components.

5.5 Develop Program WBS—The process for subdividing the program into its constituent parts (components, deliverables, and activities). It provides a deliverable orientated hierarchical decomposition of the work to be executed and accomplished by each component of the program.

5.6 Manage Program Architecture—The process for managing the relationships between all of the program components to ensure the program architecture remains up to date.

5.7 Manage Component Interfaces—The process for maintaining the adherence of program delivery and its constituent parts and managing interrelationships between the program components.

5.8 Monitor and Control Program Scope—The process for ensuring the program's scope is controlled to meet the agreed-upon goals and realize the agreed program objectives and benefits identified in the program charter.

These processes interact with each other and with processes in the other Knowledge Areas. Each process can involve effort from one or more persons or groups of persons, based on the needs of the program. Each process occurs at least once in every program and occurs in one or more program phases, if the program is divided into phases. Although the processes are presented here as discrete components with well-defined interfaces, in practice they can overlap and interact in ways too complex to address in detail here. Process interactions are detailed in Chapter 3.

©2008 Project Management Institute. *The Standard for Program Management* — Second Edition

In the program context, the term scope can refer to:

- **Product Scope**—The features and functions that characterize a product, service, or result.
- **Program Scope**—The work required to deliver a major product, service, or benefit result with the specified features and functions at the program level.

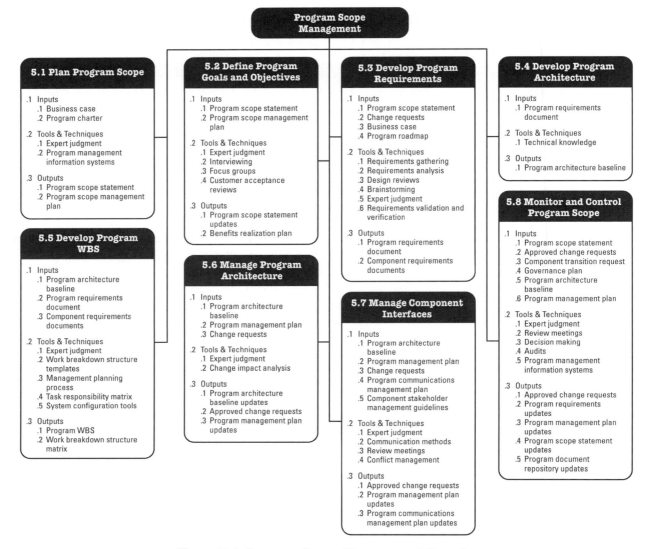

Figure 5-1. Program Scope Management Overview

5.1 Plan Program Scope

Scope planning is the process of identifying and developing activities to produce deliverables and benefits that meet the program goals and objectives (Figures 5-2 and 5-3). Elements that are considered in this activity include:

- Stakeholder analysis,
- Defining acceptance criteria,

- Defining and prioritizing stakeholder requirements,

- Developing the scope description,

- Defining the scope boundaries, and

- Defining stakeholder acceptance criteria.

This section establishes the criteria for identifying and understanding the program deliverables.

Inputs	Tools & Techniques	Outputs
.1 Business case .2 Program charter	.1 Expert judgment .2 Program management information systems	.1 Program scope statement .2 Program scope management plan

Figure 5-2. Plan Program Scope: Inputs, Tools & Techniques, and Outputs

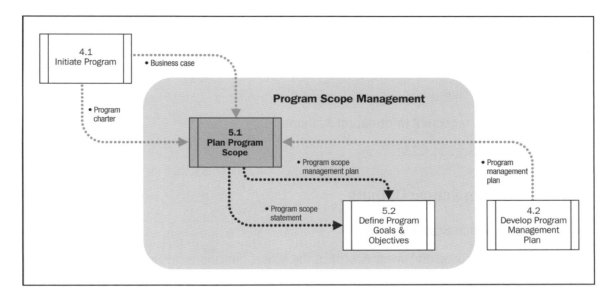

Figure 5-3. Plan Program Scope Process Data Flow

5.1.1   Plan Program Scope: Inputs

.1   Business Case

The business case establishes the authority, intent, and philosophy of the business need. This document provides direction for structure, guiding principles, and organization.

.2   Program Charter

The program charter is a high-level document developed by the program manager and the program team to assist in documenting and capturing the framework of the overall program. This document is a

---

source of high-level information that can assist in charting the program direction, developing program deliverables, and developing schedule requirements.

5.1.2 Plan Program Scope: Tools and Techniques

.1 Expert Judgment

Expert judgment comprises the decisions, opinions, and estimates made by individuals possessing skills, knowledge, understanding, and experience in a particular field, endeavor or occupation and are recognized by their peers as being knowledgeable. This is often used to assess inputs and outputs of other activities to make decisions and to develop current process. Individuals possessing expert judgment skills are available from many sources, such as:

- Other units within the organization,
- Project managers,
- Consultants,
- Stakeholders, including customers or sponsors,
- Professional and technical associations, and
- Industry groups.

.2 Program Management Information Systems

Described in Section 4.2.2.1.

5.1.3 Plan Program Scope: Outputs

.1 Program Scope Statement

The program scope statement describes the scope, limitations, expectations, and the business impact of the program as well as a description of each project and its resources The scope statement should address the following topics:

- Organizational needs and requirements,
- Initial, high-level product requirements,
- Vision of the solution, and
- Assumptions and constraints.

.2 Program Scope Management Plan

The program scope management plan is a subsidiary element of the overall program plan. It should include an assessment of the expected stability of the program scope. The plan describes how scope changes will be identified and classified, how scope will be managed and how scope changes will be integrated into the overall program.

5.2 Define Program Goals and Objectives

Defining the program goals and objectives are accomplished by understanding and identifying the program scope statement, identifying the scope management plan, and implementing expectations (Figures 5-4 and 5-5). The level of detail needed to accomplish the endeavor is determined by the technical complexity, speed or duration in which the activity must be accomplished, and resource availability. The program background summarizes the problem that the program is solving. It provides a brief history of the problem and provides the justification for the approach taken to solve the problem. Inclusion of this information in a program scope statement will depend on stakeholders' preferences, maturity of the organization, and the time available.

The objectives of this section are to:

- Identify the broad outcomes that are expected of the program,

- Clarify what is to be accomplished, and

- Communicate planned outcomes to all stakeholders.

Figure 5-4. Define Program Goals and Objectives: Inputs, Tools & Techniques, and Outputs

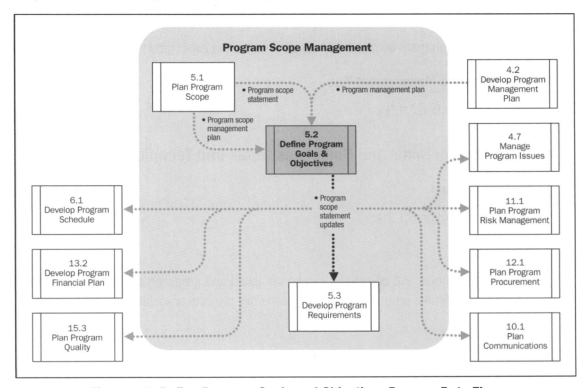

Figure 5-5. Define Program Goals and Objectives Process Data Flow

5.2.1 Define Program Goals and Objectives: Inputs

.1 Program Scope Statement

The program scope statement is the responsibility of the program manager. It addresses the vision, range, capacity, and extent of the program endeavor. At the start of the program, the program manager ensures that the context and framework of the program endeavor is properly defined and assessed. This is accomplished through the program scope statement. The program scope statement establishes the direction taken and identifies the essential aspects that must be accomplished. The intent of this document is to ensure that each stakeholder shares a common understand of the nature, purpose, and needs which must be addressed by the program. The program scope statement addresses:

- Business requirements,
- Vision of the solution,
- Scope and limitations,
- Program business context,
- Potential risks,
- Criteria for success,
- Program boundaries,
- Program benefits, and
- Program deliverables.

In essence, the program scope statement establishes the expectations of the endeavor.

.2 Program Scope Management Plan

Described in Section 5.1.3.2.

5.2.2 Define Program Goals and Objectives: Tools and Techniques

.1 Expert Judgment

Described in Section 5.1.2.1.

.2 Interviewing

The program's goals and objectives can be compiled and assessed by interviewing participants who are familiar with the program and/or the interactive projects associated with the program.

.3 Focus Groups

A focus group is a group of individuals assembled to address specific questions about their attitude towards a product, service, or concept. These questions are asked in an interactive group setting where participants are free to talk with other group members. Focus groups may solve problems and/or find solutions to the case at hand.

.4 Customer Acceptance Reviews

Goals and objectives may be enhanced and fine tuned by conducting customer acceptance reviews. Acceptance management is the process of reviewing deliverables within the program and gaining the customer's acceptance that they are 100% complete. Obtaining customer acceptance for each deliverable can mitigate customer dissatisfaction by:

- Identifying customer acceptance issues early in the project,

- Improving deliverables to meet a customer's requirements,

- Maximizing customer confidence in the delivery of the project, and

- Keeping customers happy increases the chances of success.

5.2.3 Define Program Goals and Objectives: Outputs

.1 Program Scope Statement Updates

The program scope statement should be updated to include any approved change requests resulting from the Develop Program WBS process. Updates should be formally recorded using a configuration management system. The revision history should be well documented and listed in the document's revision history log or version control log.

.2 Benefits Realization Plan

The benefits realization plan identifies the business benefits and documents the plan for realizing the benefits. This enables the team to monitor the agreed upon benefits through to the conclusion of the program. This benefit plan is generated in much the same way as other documents — through interviewing, brainstorming, and review sessions. Additionally, the benefits realization plan identifies the organizational processes and systems needed for the transformation, the required changes to the processes and systems, and how and when the transition to the new arrangements will occur. The benefits realization plan should,

- Ensure that all stages of the program are managed in a way that will satisfy the utilization of the program's outputs,

- Link the outputs to the planned program outcomes,

- Assess the program's outputs,

- Perform corrective action if required, and

- Ensure the planned program outcomes are achieved prior to formal program closure.

5.3 Develop Program Requirements

Develop Program Requirements identifies and details program specifications and outcomes for implementation (Figures 5-6 and 5-7). A considerable amount of detail is needed at the program level to ensure that all internal components and external entities are adequately addressed. The performing organization must have a robust process for managing requirements including high-level requirements covering the business, customer, industry, and other program enterprise-related areas.

The objective of this section is to develop and identify requirements and specifications that will lead to the successful implementation of the program.

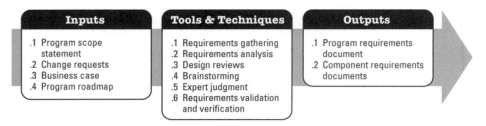

Figure 5-6. Develop Program Requirements: Inputs, Tools & Techniques, and Outputs

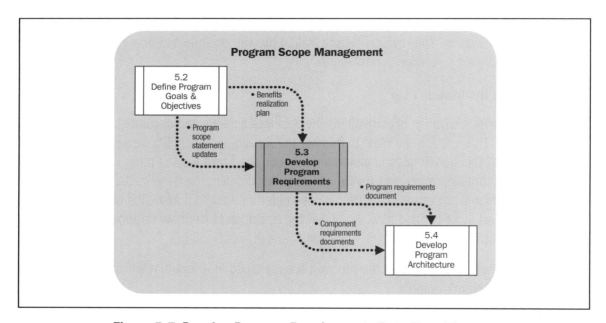

Figure 5-7. Develop Program Requirements Data Flow Diagram

5.3.1 Develop Program Requirements: Inputs

.1 Program Scope Statement

Described in Section 5.1.3.1 and 5.2.1.1.

.2 Change Requests

Change requests may arise from components, program level and non-project activities or factors external to the program.

.3 Business Case

Described in Section 4.1.1.2.

.4 Program Roadmap

Described in Section 4.1.3.4.

5.3.2 Develop Program Requirements: Tools and Techniques

.1 Requirements Gathering

This is the process of collecting the requirements from the various sources: stakeholders, architects, existing documentation, process analysis, or other sources. Methods of gathering requirements include, but are not limited to, the following:

- **Interviews.** Interviewing techniques are one of the many methods used in requirements gathering. Interviewing experienced project participants, stakeholders, and subject matter experts help identify program requirements influencing the program.

- **Focus Groups.** Described in Section 5.2.2.3.

- **Questionnaires and Surveys.** These can be used to obtain requirements by gathering representative information from stakeholders and others.

.2 Requirements Analysis

The requirements analysis process takes the requirements that have been gathered, ensures they are thorough, consistent, and complete, and begins the process of decomposing the top-level requirements into more detailed requirements.

.3 Design Reviews

There are several levels of design reviews, such as in-process reviews, internal reviews, and formal design reviews. A major program may incorporate any of the different types of design reviews. In-process reviews usually involve peer groups and are typically performed periodically within the program to evaluate program activity and to make recommendations. Internal reviews are more formal than in-process reviews but less formal than formal design reviews. In general, internal reviews determine compliance to best practices of the given subject matter by peers and subject matter experts. In formal design reviews, the design (in this case, requirements), is presented to and assessed by the customer. Specialists and senior level management attend formal design reviews.

.4 Brainstorming

Brainstorming is a general management technique used to stimulate the thought process and thinking surrounding program requirements. Through brainstorming, the team obtains a comprehension of the requirements and strives to identify the requirements that might affect the outcome of the program. During a brainstorming session, ideas are discussed, shared, and recorded. Afterwards, those ideas are analyzed as they pertain to the subject at hand.

.5 Expert Judgment

Described in Section 5.1.2.1.

.6 Requirements Validation and Verification

Once the initial requirements are gathered and decomposed to a sufficient level of detail, the program undertakes an on-going process of validating that the requirements are accurate and complete. As the program evolves and changes occur, the requirements must be continually reassessed for impacts.

As the program develops into the later stages of development and construction, the products being produced must be verified against the requirements to ensure that they satisfy the requested requirements. This verification process can entail testing, at both a detailed and at a systems level, inspection, analysis, or other methods of ensuring that the requirements have been met.

5.3.3 Develop Program Requirements: Outputs

.1 Program Requirements Document

The program requirements document describes the high-level requirements that will deliver the program benefits. It details a range of topics including the business, the environment, and technical and legal issues. These are different than technical design specifications. For instance, a program to develop a new airplane might include requirements related to the maximum passenger seat capacity, cargo capacity, and take off/landing parameters.

.2 Component Requirements Documents

The requirements documentation developed at the program level describe the high-level requirements. These are decomposed in increasing levels of detail until they are sufficiently detailed that they can be written into contracts that are provided to the component-level contractors. The components then take these requirements and continue the decomposition process until the component's schedule can be accurately estimated and the final component product designed.

5.4 Develop Program Architecture

The Develop Program Architecture process produces the structure of the program components by identifying the relationships among components and the rules that govern their inclusion (Figures 5-8 and 5-9). Care should be taken to ensure that the scope of each project in the program is consistent with the program architecture.

The objectives of this section are to:

- Define the structure of the program's or systems' components,

- Identify the interrelationships among the components, and

- Establish a set of rules that govern the interaction and evolution of the program or system.

Figure 5-8. Develop Program Architecture: Inputs, Tools & Techniques, and Outputs

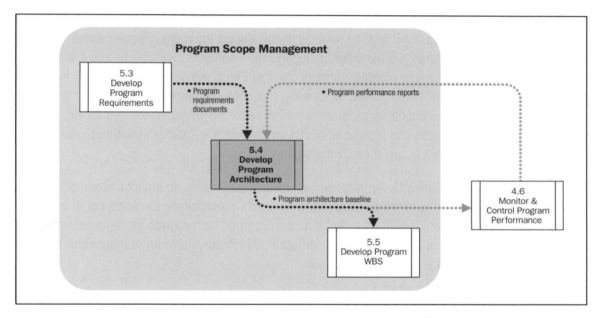

Figure 5-9. Develop Program Architecture Process Data Flow

5.4.1 Develop Program Architecture: Inputs

.1 Program Requirements Document

Described in Section 5.3.3.1.

5.4.2 Develop Program Architecture: Tools and Techniques

.1 Technical Knowledge

Architects skilled and experienced in developing solutions that satisfy the requirements are the core of the work done during this process. The optimal solution architectures are designed by designers/

---

architects that have the training and experience in the program area, whether aerospace engineers, construction architects, civil engineers, software/database architects, or other resources skilled in the type of program.

5.4.3 Develop Program Architecture: Outputs

.1 Program Architecture Baseline

The program architecture baseline is the set of program components, which outlines their characteristics, capabilities, deliverables, timing, and external interfaces. It also describes how the components contribute to the specified program benefits.

5.5 Develop Program WBS

Developing the Program WBS (PWBS) is the process of subdividing the major program deliverables, project activities, and implementation phases of the program (Figures 5-10 and 5-11). It is the process of breaking down all the work activities into more manageable components. The PWBS provides the framework for organizing and managing the work. It is an essential tool for building realistic schedules, developing cost estimates and organizing work. In addition, it is critical for program or project reporting, tracking, and controlling. The PWBS is developed and used for all projects and programs. It is important that the PWBS is structured in such a manner so that future activities and work scope is easily managed.

A PWBS is a deliverable-oriented hierarchical decomposition encompassing the total scope of the program, and it includes the deliverables to be produced by the constituent components. Elements not in the PWBS are outside the scope of the program. The PWBS includes, but is not limited to, program management artifacts such as plans, procedures, standards, processes, major program milestones, program management deliverables, and program management office support deliverables.

The PWBS is a key to effective control and communication between the program manager and the managers of component projects—the PWBS provides an overview of the program and shows how each project fits in. Decomposition stops at the level of control required by the program manager. Typically, this corresponds to the first one or two levels of the WBS of each component project. Given this, the PWBS serves as the controlling framework for developing the program schedule, and defines the program manager's management control points that will be used for earned value management, as well as other purposes.

The PWBS components at the lowest level of the PWBS are known as program packages. The complete description of the PWBS components and any additional relevant information is documented in the PWBS Dictionary, which is an integral part of the PWBS. The PWBS does not replace the WBS required of each project within the program. Instead, it is used to clarify the scope of the program, help identify logical groupings of work for components, identify the interface with operations or products, and clarify the program's conclusion. It is also the place to capture all non-project work within the program. This includes program management artifacts developed for use within the program management office, external deliverables such as public communications, and end-solution deliverables overarching the projects, such as facilities and infrastructure.

The objectives of this section are to:

- Identify and define specific work tasks that are assigned to each PWBS element,

- Define the solution to the problem in terms of a product, and

- Provide the complete definition of the work to be performed.

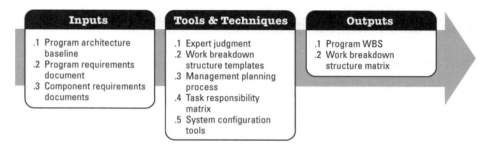

Figure 5-10. Develop Program WBS: Inputs, Tools & Techniques, and Outputs

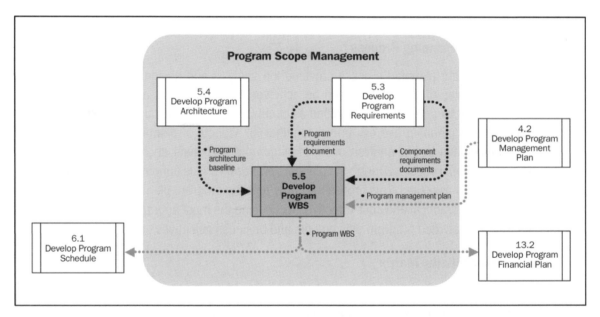

Figure 5-11. Develop Program WBS Data Flow Diagram

5.5.1   Develop Program WBS: Inputs

.1   Program Architecture Baseline

The program architecture is the starting point for developing the WBS as it contains the necessary elements. Large, complex projects are organized and understood by breaking them into progressively smaller pieces until they are a collection of defined "work packages" that may be further broken down into tasks.

.2 Program Requirements Document

Described in Section 5.3.3.1.

.3 Component Requirements Documents

Described in Section 5.3.3.2.

5.5.2 Develop Program WBS: Tools and Techniques

.1 Expert Judgment

Described in Section 5.1.2.1.

.2 Work Breakdown Structure Templates

Any WBS templates that are available for this type of program should be utilized whenever possible. These templates might be available from organizational internal sources, from professional organizations, or from external commercial sources such as consulting organizations.

.3 Management Planning Process

The management planning process provides the analysis and design effort to map out how the goals and objectives of the program will be achieved. A plan delivers a fixed starting point and a direction that may be subsequently modified as circumstances change during the life of the program. The management planning process brings together all aspects of planning into a coherent, unified process that includes careful analysis of the management objectives, and possible sources of conflict among organizational policies. During the planning process, various options for managing the program are developed and assessed. This process ensures that the program plans are fully considered, well-focused, resilient, practical and cost-effective. In choosing the most appropriate option, the intent is to reach a balance between program deliverables and business objectives.

.4 Task Responsibility Matrix

The task responsibility matrix is a tool to help document and communicate the roles and level of involvement each team member and/or different functional groups will exercise in the ownership of specific tasks.

.5 System Configuration Tools

System configuration tools provide consistent documentation of product versions for use throughout the program. These tools help to provide change control for design documents, scope, requirements, processes and the myriad of items that will be modified during the life of the program. Knowing which version is the most current is invaluable and critical throughout the life of the program. Incorporating system configuration tools provides the ability to monitor change control while enhancing organizational control.

5.5.3 Develop Program WBS: Outputs

.1 Program WBS

The program work breakdown structure (PWBS) provides deliverable-oriented hierarchical decomposition of the work to be executed and accomplished by each project of the program. It depicts the program's statement of work. The output is a deliverable or product-oriented grouping of the program work elements, depicted graphically, which organizes and subdivides the total work scope of the program. The WBS outlines the program's scope baseline, which is necessary for achieving the technical objectives of the work described.

.2 Work Breakdown Structure Matrix

The program or project work breakdown structure matrix is a deliverable or product-oriented grouping of project work elements depicted graphically to organize and subdivide the total work scope of a project.

5.6 Manage Program Architecture

Manage Program Architecture ensures the relationships among the program's elements are well structured and adhere to the set of governing rules as defined in the program architecture (Figures 5-12 and 5-13). During the program life cycle, changes to the program architecture may be necessary. For example, this may be due to a failure to adhere to the major scope elements such as a project-related WBS and the overall program architecture.

Figure 5-12. Manage Program Architecture: Inputs, Tools & Techniques, and Outputs

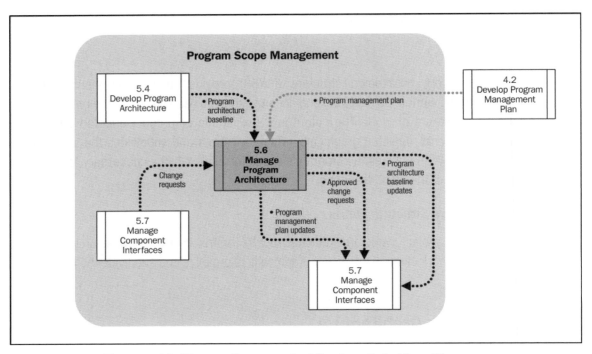

Figure 5-13. Manage Program Architecture Data Flow Diagram

5.6.1 Manage Program Architecture: Inputs

.1 Program Architecture Baseline

The program architecture document is described in Section 5.4.3.1.

.2 Program Management Plan

Program management plan is described in Section 4.2.3.1.

.3 Change Requests

Described in Section 4.4.1.3.

5.6.2 Manage Program Architecture: Tools and Techniques

.1 Expert Judgment

Described in Section 5.1.2.1.

.2 Change Impact Analysis

Described in Section 4.4. Architectural change analysis analyzes the integrity and influence the impacts have on the architectural elements and its components outlined in the program architecture document, which supports the overall program management plan.

5.6.3   Manage Program Architecture: Outputs

.1   Program Architecture Baseline Updates

Managing the program architecture may require updating the program-related documents to reflect any relevant alterations.

.2   Approved Change Requests

Approved change requests are incorporated into the program plan and associated components, or rejected if the change would be detrimental to the program goals and objectives. Formal governance processes surround the change request processes to support consistent decision making.

.3   Program Management Plan Updates

Formal updates to the program management plan are made upon approval of change requests made in the Manage Program Architecture process.

5.7 Manage Component Interfaces

Program management interfaces with both operational and projects activities as well as those distinctive work components, which are part of the program overall scope (Figures 5-14 and 5-15). Transparent management of the component interfaces is crucial for scope adherence within the program. Interrelated project scope parts may need to be reviewed, together with elements of program architecture. Outputs from other planning processes are updated accordingly.

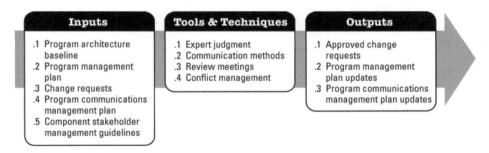

Figure 5-14. Manage Component Interfaces: Inputs, Tools & Techniques, and Outputs

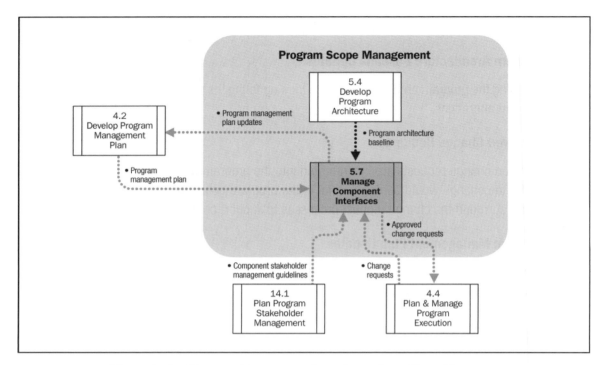

Figure 5-15. Manage Component Interfaces Data Flow Diagram

5.7.1 Manage Component Interfaces: Inputs

.1 Program Architecture Baseline

Described in Section 5.4.3.1.

.2 Program Management Plan

Described in Section 4.2.3.1.

.3 Change Requests

Described in Section 4.4.1.3.

.4 Program Communications Management Plan

Described in Section 10.1.3.1.

.5 Component Stakeholder Management Guidelines

Described in Section 14.1.3.2.

5.7.2 Manage Component Interfaces: Tools and Techniques

.1 Expert Judgment

Described in Section 5.1.2.1.

.2 Communication Methods

Described in Section 10.1.2.3.

.3 Review Meetings

Described in Section 4.6.2.4.

.4 Conflict Management

Described in Section 14.4.2.2.

5.7.3 Manage Component Interfaces: Outputs

.1 Approved Change Requests

Described in Section 5.6.3.2.

.2 Program Management Plan Updates

Change requests at the project level may be reflected in the various program interfaces. These changes are used to update the program management plan.

.3 Program Communications Management Plan Updates

Updates to the program communications management plan ensure that any modifications requiring additional communications deliverables from the interfaces communication needs are gathered and supported.

5.8 Monitor and Control Program Scope

Because of the size, complexity, and duration of many programs, it is critical to manage the scope as the program develops in order to ensure successful completion (Figures 5-16 and 5-17). Scope changes that can have significant impact to a component and/or to the program may originate from stakeholders, from components within the program, from previously unidentified requirements or architecture issues, or from external sources. Each potential change needs to be analyzed and impacts identified.

The change control process on a program is often hierarchical. The program has a change control board (CCB) that analyzes changes at the program level. If the program CCB identifies an impact to a component, the change is sent to the component-level CCB for a more detailed impact analysis. The results of that analysis are returned to the program CCB and any impacts to other components or to component interfaces are identified.

Figure 5-16. Monitor and Control Program Scope: Inputs, Tools & Techniques, and Outputs

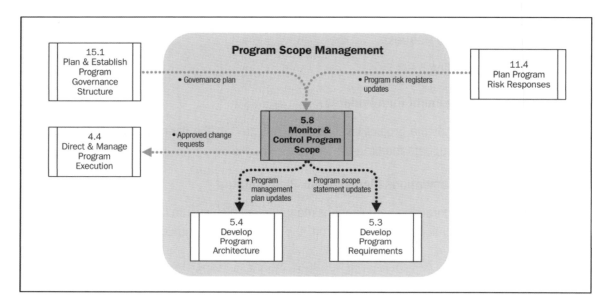

Figure 5-17. Monitor and Control Program Scope Process Data Flow Diagram

5.8.1 Monitor and Control Program Scope: Inputs

.1 Program Scope Statement

Described in Section 5.1.3.1.

.2 Approved Change Requests

Described in Section 5.6.3.2.

.3 Component Transition Request

The component closure decision is recommended to the program manager who makes the decision based on input from the Governance function.

.4 Governance Plan

Described in Section 15.1.3.1.

.5 Program Architecture Baseline

Described in Section 5.4.3.1.

.6 Program Management Plan

Described in Section 4.2.3.1.

5.8.2 Monitor and Control Program Scope: Tools and Techniques

.1 Expert Judgment

Described in Section 5.1.2.1.

.2 Review Meetings

Described in Sections 4.3.2.3 and 4.6.2.4.

.3 Decision Making

Decision making encompasses a wide variety of techniques to arrive at a reasonable approach or a reasonable resolution of an issue or a change request. Decision making requires good information and experienced personnel to arrive at appropriate conclusions.

.4 Audits

Described in Section 15.1.3.3.

.5 Program Management Information Systems

Described in Section 4.2.2.1.

5.8.3 Monitor and Control Program Scope: Outputs

.1 Approved Change Requests

Described in Sections 4.4.3.1 and others.

.2 Program Requirements Updates

Described in Sections 5.3.3.1.

.3 Program Management Plan Updates

Described in Sections 4.3.3.1.

.4 Program Scope Statement Updates

Described in Sections 5.2.3.1.

.5 Program Document Repository Updates

Described in Section 4.2.2.1.

CHAPTER 6

PROGRAM TIME MANAGEMENT

Program Time Management involves processes for scheduling the defined program components and entities necessary to produce the final program deliverables (Figures 6-1 and 6-2). It includes determining the order in which the individual components are executed, the critical path for the program, and the milestones to be measured to keep the overall program on track and within the defined constraints.

Program Time Management processes include:

6.1 Develop Program Schedule—Schedule development is the process of defining the program components needed to produce the program deliverables, determine the order in which the components must be executed, estimate the amount of time required to accomplish each component, and identify the major program level milestones during the performance period.

6.2 Monitor and Control Program Schedule—Schedule control is the process of ensuring the program produces the required deliverables and solutions on time. Activities include tracking the start and finish dates as well as significant intermediate milestones against the planned timelines. Updating the schedule and reporting the impact of missed dates is part of this process.

While project managers concentrate on managing their project's deliverables to a pre-planned schedule, program managers concentrate on coordinating all of the component schedules within the program and integrating them to ensure the program itself completes on schedule.

The dependencies among the various components have a significant impact on the overall schedule. A late completion of one component may impact other components or integration activities that depend upon its completion. Rather than manage the details of any single component, the program manager concentrates on the integration of each component into the overall program schedule.

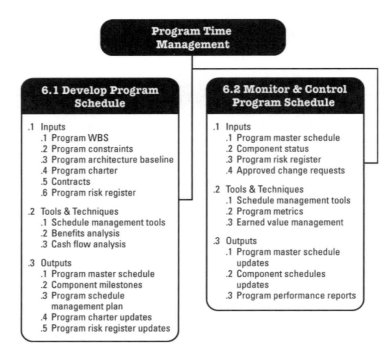

Figure 6-1. Program Time Management Overview

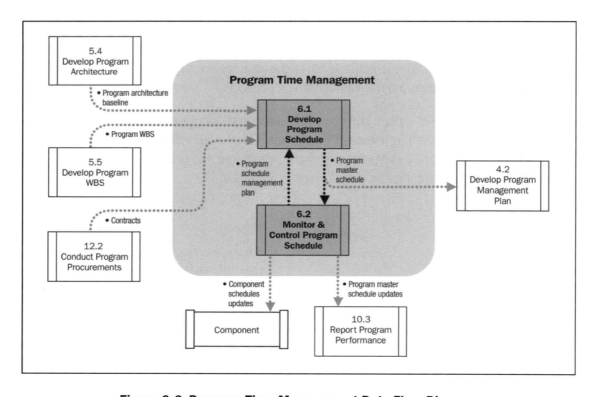

Figure 6-2. Program Time Management Data Flow Diagram

6.1 Develop Program Schedule

The initial program schedule is often created before the detailed schedules of the individual components are available. The program's delivery date and major milestones are developed using the business case and, if available, the program charter. As the program architecture is created, more detailed schedule information is made available. As more detailed analysis is performed, and feedback from the individual components is received, the schedule is developed in greater detail (Figures 6-3 and 6-4).

The schedule at program level should only include those component milestones that represent an output to the program or share an interdependency with other components. The first draft of a program schedule often has the character of a roadmap—it identifies the order and start and end dates of components. Later, this is enriched with more intermediate component results as the component schedules are developed. The detailed component schedules are written into contracts as well as being used to create the overall program master schedule.

When planning a component's schedule, it is often adequate for the planning to be done centrally by the program manager and the program management team. By contrast, on a program there may be so many different components, each managed by a different contractor and involving radically different types of work, therefore centralized planning can only be done at a very high level. Detailed planning must be done at the component level. It is often advisable to have the contractors meet with each other and work through any conflicts or constraints in their respective schedules. If there are subcontractors involved, the prime contractor can coordinate their schedule constraints. The resolved schedule is reported to the program management office and incorporated into the program master schedule.

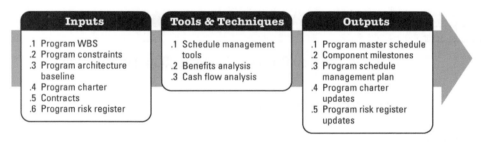

Figure 6-3. Develop Program Schedule: Inputs, Tools & Techniques, and Outputs

Once the overall program schedule is determined, the dates for each individual component are identified and are used to develop the component's schedule. The program need dates act as a constraint on individual component scheduling. If a component has multiple deliverables to which other components rely upon, those deliverables and interdependencies should be reflected in the overall program master schedule.

A program schedule is typically created using the program work breakdown structure (PWBS) as the starting point. The individual project managers build the details for their specific project which are then rolled up at the management control points into program packages for the PWBS. The interdependencies between the constituent projects must also be reflected and managed in the program schedule. The schedule includes all of the program packages in the PWBS that produce the deliverables. The program schedule comprises timelines of various program packages and non-project program activities, and indicates significant milestones.

An essential element of schedule development is timing the program packages, which allows the scheduler to forecast the date on which the program will finish, as well as finish dates for the milestones within the program (e.g., key deliverables within each constituent project).

In addition to producing the program schedule, this process normally creates a plan by which the schedule will be managed over the life of the program. This schedule management plan becomes part of the program management plan.

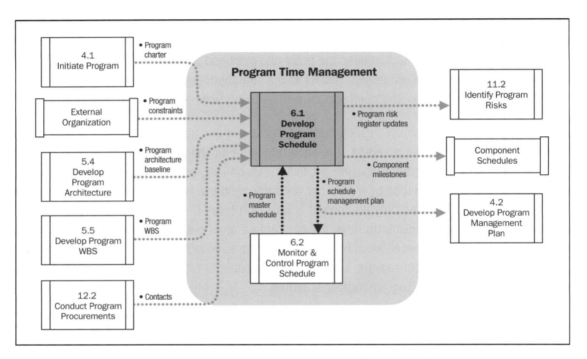

Figure 6-4. Develop Program Schedule: Data Flow Diagram

6.1.1   Develop Program Schedule—Inputs

.1   Program WBS

Described in 5.5.3.1. The Develop Program Work Breakdown Structure (Section 5.5) takes the components described in the Develop Program Architecture process (Section 5.4) and breaks them down into phases and program-level deliverables. Besides projects, the components typically include program management and program support activity groups.

.2   Program Constraints

When developing the program master schedule, due attention needs to be paid to the constraints posed by various factors both within and external to the program. These might include:

- Funding constraints,
- Resource availability,

- Technical constraints,

- Contracts,

- Hard deadlines,

- Labor laws,

- Environmental constraints,

- Other external dependencies, and

- Other factors in the program's environment.

.3 Program Architecture Baseline

Described in Section 5.4.3.1.

.4 Program Charter

The program charter provides the mandate to execute the program within a certain timeline. It could also present milestones for the delivery of products or incremental benefits.

.5 Contracts

The detailed schedules developed by the component contractors feed into the program master plan. Any single contractor may potentially affect the overall program schedule if they cannot deliver a key component within the initially expected timeline.

.6 Program Risk Register

Described in Section 11.2.3.1.

6.1.2 Develop Program Schedule: Tools and Techniques

.1 Schedule Management Tools

A primary tool used in developing the program schedule is schedule management software. The overall program schedule is entered into the tool as well as the milestones for each individual component. These milestones are then provided to the procurement processes and the contractors provide responses against the due dates for their proposed component. Once the work begins at the component level, the tool is used to manage and control the schedule during the execution of the program.

The automated tool can be very simple or it can be highly advanced and capable of handling a program costing billions of euros, dollars, or other local currency, and taking five or ten years or longer. The tool should be appropriate to the type of project and to its scale. Although the contractor manages each component in detail at the component level (for programs where contractors are involved), the program tool should have sufficient component-level detail to allow the program manager to understand the status of the entire program. If all of the program work is being done internally without the use of contractors, the tool should have every component and resource in its database and allow the program manager to drill down to the lowest level of detail.

When there are multiple contractors involved, there is a significant benefit to having all contractors use tools that are technologically compatible. This allows the component schedule management tools to output status reports in a format that can be readily inputted to the program-level tool rather than having to be re-entered.

.2 Benefits Analysis

Benefits analysis is the process of looking at any incremental benefits the program provides and making adjustments to the schedule to enhance the delivery of those benefits. Many programs do not provide incremental benefits (all the benefits may come at the end). The program manager may still perform a benefits analysis in order to improve decisions made during the execution of the program.

.3 Cash Flow Analysis

Cash flow analysis examines the funding schedule for the program's revenues and expenses. Money payable to contractors or for other program expenses cannot be paid out unless the money is available to the program. Scheduling of component activities may be done with consideration of when money to pay for the activity is available.

For example, in the construction industry funds are not always available on a continuous basis, but paid when milestones are met. Scheduling activities may be done at the latest possible start in order to defer expenses until as close as possible to when the funds will be available to pay for them. Component contractors must pay attention to their own cash flow with regard to retainage or other funds held back until the full contract is completed.

6.1.3   Develop Program Schedule: Outputs

.1 Program Master Schedule

The program master schedule is the top level program document, which defines the individual component schedules and dependencies between program components (individual projects and other work) to achieve the program goal. The program master schedule determines the timing of individual components and enables the program manager to determine when benefits will be delivered by the program. The program master schedule also identifies external dependencies to the program.

.2 Component Milestones

The component milestones identify all program deliverables. This enables program benefits to be realized and identifies milestones for transitioning component deliverables into the program. In addition, component milestones are utilized to indicate internal program dependencies.

.3 Program Schedule Management Plan

This process produces the program schedule management plan. The plan identifies the agreed sequence of component deliveries to enable the individual component deliveries to be planned and managed. It provides the program team/stakeholders with the plan on how the program is going to be managed throughout the life of the program. It is a living document, enabling the program manager the means of identifying risks and escalated component issues that may affect the program goals.

.4 Program Charter Updates

This process may generate updates to the program charter, where the development of the program schedule identifies a need to alter the charter to realize the program goals or amend the program goals as a result of schedule development.

.5 Program Risk Register Updates

Any risks identified as part of the schedule development should be incorporated into the program risk register, as they are identified through the development of the program schedule. These risks may be a result of component dependencies within the schedule or on external factors identified as a result of the agreed program schedule management plan.

6.2 Monitor and Control Program Schedule

Program schedule control includes the processes of ensuring that the program produces the required deliverables and solutions on time and within budget and specifications (Figures 6-5 and 6-6). The processes include tracking and monitoring the start and finish of all high-level component and program activities and milestones against the planned timelines. Updating the program master schedules and directing changes to individual project schedules is required to maintain an accurate and up-to-date program master schedule. Monitor and Control Program Schedule works closely with other program processes to identify variances to the schedules and direct corrective action when necessary to bring the program back to the schedule baseline. Identification of both slippages and early deliveries are necessary as part of the overall program management function. Identification of early deliveries may provide opportunities for program acceleration.

Figure 6-5. Monitor and Control Program Schedule: Inputs, Tools & Techniques, and Outputs

---

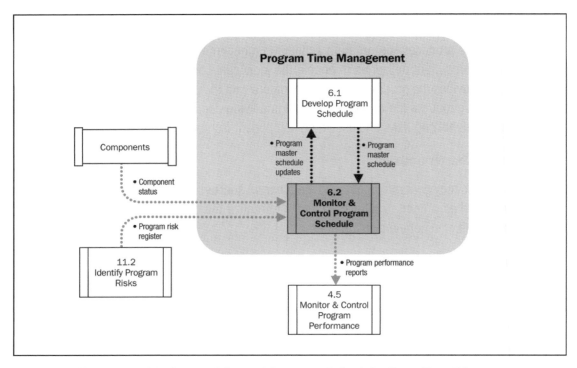

Figure 6-6. Monitor and Control Program Schedule: Data Flow Diagram

6.2.1　Monitor and Control Program Schedule: Inputs

.1　Program Master Schedule

The program master schedule is the key input for monitoring and controlling the individual component schedules. The program manager maintains a delicate balance between giving guidance to and monitoring the progress of the components on the one hand and giving the component leaders with the freedom to develop their respective schedules.

.2　Component Status

For all component project and non-project related work, this input should include the actual start and completion times for the top level planning elements based on predefined measurement techniques (measurable milestones, weighted percent complete, level of effort (LOE), etc). The template for the component status reports should provide the program management function with ample warning if a program level milestone is in danger of changing. Typically, these program level milestones point to inter-component dependencies. A delay in the delivery of a component product might have a cascading or adverse effect on the schedules of other components of the program. The component status reports come from Section 10.2 on Distribute Information.

.3 Program Risk Register

A large portion of the risks identified will have an impact on the timeline. At the program level, the buffer time built into the schedule needs to be analyzed and compared to the risk tolerance of the sponsoring organization.

.4 Approved Change Requests

Once program governance accepts a change request, the schedule of the impacted component(s) needs to be adjusted. The impact of a change request can range from adding or removing tasks at the component level to introducing new components or stopping/removing existing components.

6.2.2 Monitor and Control Program Schedule: Tools and Techniques

.1 Schedule Management Tools

Described in Section 6.1.2.1.

.2 Program Metrics

Program metrics identify the specific numbers to which the program schedule progress is measured. For example, if a program is 10% behind schedule—is the status red, yellow, or green? The metrics identify what will be measured and how the status will be reported against those metrics.

.3 Earned Value Management

Earned value management is an approach that integrates scope, schedule, and resources to provide an accurate and objective measurement of program and component status. A number of studies indicate that it is the most accurate way of measuring status and is particularly useful for large programs where individual activities may be measured in weeks or months.

EVM requires that the program requirements be identified 100% for near-term activities, and that well-defined metrics be created for measuring progress. EVM uses the values of:

- **Planned value (PV).** PV is the amount of money that was budgeted for the work that is scheduled to be completed on any WBS activity.

- **Actual cost (AC).** AC is the cost for the activity that has been completed or is in progress.

- **Earned value (EV).** EV is the amount of money that was budgeted for work that has already been completed.

EVM uses these measurement methods or standards to calculate program status to date by measuring the cost variance (CV is the earned value minus the actual cost) and the schedule variance (SV is the earned value minus the planned value).

EVM techniques involve developing estimate to completion (ETC) forecasts as well as estimate at completion (EAC) forecasts.

6.2.3 Monitor and Control Program Schedule: Outputs

.1 Program Master Schedule Updates

Updates to the program master schedule are included as a result of delivery performance of the program against the agreed schedule. These updates include changes to the master schedule in response to risks identified during the life of the program or changes to component statuses.

Due to the complex nature and duration of programs, some spanning global boundaries and operating for many years, these updates are included to achieve delivery of the program goals or revised program goals as a result of the accepted change requests.

The program master schedule is updated to include new components identified as a result of accepted change requests or additional activity required to meet the program goals, as a result of component statuses. As the status of individual components change, the program master schedule must be reviewed to assess the impact of component-level changes on other components and on the program itself. Such things as purchased items, which experience unexpectedly long lead-time can have a significant effect on the overall schedule performance of the program.

.2 Component Schedules Updates

Deviations to agreed components may be required as a result of current delivery performance. These changes are requested to maintain realization of the agreed program benefits and goals. The changes to component schedules provide the necessary direction to the individual components to correct negative deviations to the individual component schedules that affect the over-all program master schedule.

There may be a need to accelerate or decelerate components within the schedule to achieve program goals. In addition, opportunities for realizing benefits early may be presented as result of early component delivery.

.3 Program Performance Reports

Updates to the program delivery status are made against the agreed upon schedule to provide performance monitoring status for communicating the performance of the program to program stakeholders (see Section 10.3 on Report Program Performance).

Clear definition on the metrics to be used to define the program's schedule status must be provided at the beginning of performance. Generally, a program will have multiple components, each in a different phase. For example, one project may be in the initiation phase and is on time, one in the execution phase that is 20% over schedule, one in the testing and integration phase that is 5% early. What is the status of the program at that point? While no universally acceptable answer can be given, the program manager and the governance organization or body must come to a common understanding of how to clearly define the schedule status of the overall program.

CHAPTER 7

PROGRAM COST MANAGEMENT

This section not included in this standard, but is provided so as to be aligned with the *PMBOK® Guide –* Fourth Edition.

CHAPTER 8

PROGRAM QUALITY MANAGEMENT

This section not included in this standard, but is provided so as to be aligned with the *PMBOK® Guide –* Fourth Edition.

CHAPTER 9

PROGRAM HUMAN RESOURCE MANAGEMENT

This section not included in this standard, but is provided so as to be aligned with the *PMBOK® Guide –* Fourth Edition.

CHAPTER 10

PROGRAM COMMUNICATION MANAGEMENT

Program Communication Management is the Knowledge Area that includes the processes for ensuring timely and appropriate generation, collection, distribution, storage, retrieval, and ultimate disposition of program information. The Program Communication Management processes provide the critical links between people and information that are necessary for successful communications. Program managers can spend a significant amount of time communicating with the program team, project teams, project managers, stakeholders, customer, and sponsor. Everyone involved in the program should understand how communications affect the program as a whole. Managing communications on the program, both internal and external communications, is an area that cannot be underestimated or overlooked. Significant problems can occur if a sufficient effort is not committed to communications.

Program Communication Management is different from the project communications. Since it affects a wider array of stakeholders, different communications tools and marketing are required.

Figure 10-1 provides an overview of the Program Communication Management processes, with inputs, tools and techniques, and outputs. The Program Communication Management processes include the following:

10.1 Plan Communications—Determining the information and communications needs of the program stakeholders.

10.2 Distribute Information—Making needed information available to program stakeholders in a timely manner.

10.3 Report Program Performance—Collecting and distributing performance information. This includes status reporting, progress measurement, and forecasting.

These processes interact with each other and with the processes in other Knowledge Areas. Program Communication Management and Program Stakeholder Management are closely related Knowledge Areas. Each process can involve effort from one or more persons or groups based on the needs of the program. Each process occurs at least once in every program and occurs in one or more program phases. Although the processes are presented here as discrete elements with well-defined interfaces, in practice they may overlap and interact in ways not detailed here.

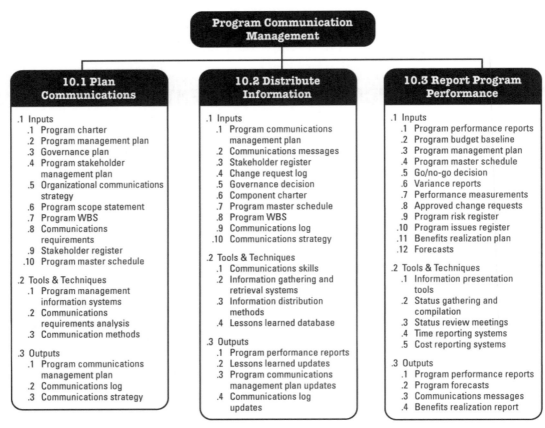

Figure 10-1. Program Communication Management Overview

10.1 Plan Communications

Plan Communications is the process of determining the information and communication needs of the program stakeholders based on who needs what information, when they need it, how it will be given to them and by whom. Communications requirements must be clearly defined to ensure the transfer of information from the projects to the program (Figures 10-2 and 10-3).

As compared to projects, programs generally take longer to complete and are more complex. This distinction must be addressed when planning communications. Since programs generally take longer to complete, team members, project sponsors, project managers, and program managers often leave programs before they are completed. When multiple vendors are part of a program team the number of stakeholders is increased. Cultural and language differences, time zones, and other factors associated with globalization must be considered when developing the communications plan. Although complex, communications planning is vital to the success of any program.

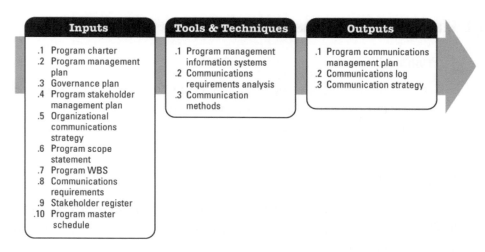

Figure 10-2. Plan Communications: Inputs, Tools & Techniques, and Outputs

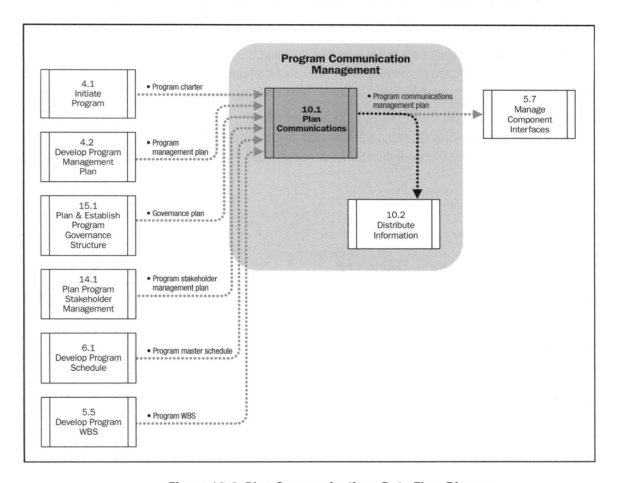

Figure 10-3. Plan Communications Data Flow Diagram

10.1.1 Plan Communications: Inputs

.1 Program Charter

The program charter is a key input to the Plan Communications process. It helps determine the communications requirements by providing information about the program's requirements, business needs, purpose, as well as other high-level information. The program charter is further discussed in Section 4.1.3.2.

.2 Program Management Plan

The program management plan provides background information about the program. It includes details related to scope, risks, quality requirements, schedule, and other information relevant to communications planning.

The program team needs to give special attention to the assumptions and the constraints, which may require additional communications planning.

- **Constraints**—Constraints are factors that can limit the program management team's options. Examples of constraints include team members situated in different geographic locations, incompatible communication software versions, or limited communications technical capabilities.

- **Assumptions**—Specific assumptions that affect Plan Communications depend upon the particular program, confidentiality clauses in contracts, and governmental or organizational regulations.

.3 Governance Plan

Described in Section 15.1.3.1.

.4 Program Stakeholder Management Plan

Described in Section 14.1.3.1. Communications is the primary tool for managing stakeholder expectations.

.5 Organizational Communications Strategy

The organization's communications strategy, if one exists, should be reviewed as part of this process. This will ensure that program communications are consistent with any guidelines and policies already in place and that it follows the organization's processes.

.6 Program Scope Statement

Described in Section 5.1.3.1. By analyzing the program scope statement, communications can be more thorough.

.7 Program WBS

Described in Section 5.5.3.1.

.8 Communications Requirements

Communications requirements can vary depending on the specific program needs. Many factors must be considered when gathering communications requirements including the size and complexity of the program. Information typically required to determine program communications requirements include:

- Organizational charts;

- Program organization and role and responsibility matrices;

- Disciplines, departments, and specialties involved in the project;

- Logistics of how many persons will be involved with the program and at which locations;

- Internal information needs (e.g., communications within the organization and communications within the program and among the components of the program);

- External information needs (e.g., communications with the media, with contractors, or with government agencies); and

- Stakeholder information, that is, who needs to be communicated with, how frequently, what information will be communicated, and the formats of the communications.

.9 Stakeholder Register

Described in Section 14.2.3.1. This is a critical input to communications planning as it provides a description of the stakeholders and helps guide decisions about the best ways to communicate with the various stakeholders to ensure optimal exchange of information.

.10 Program Master Schedule

Described in Section 6.1.3.1. The program master schedule outlines the individual component schedules and dependencies between program components including individual projects and other work. The program master schedule determines the timing of individual component milestones.

10.1.2 Plan Communications: Tools and Techniques

.1 Program Management Information Systems

Described in Section 4.2.2.1. Program management information systems provide the means for program reporting and communicating with program stakeholders. These systems are used frequently during the life of the program for communicating status, changes, and performance.

.2 Communications Requirements Analysis

An analysis of the communications requirements results in the sum of the information needs of the program stakeholders. This involves determining the type and format of information needed and analyzing the value of that information. Program resources are expended only on communicating information that contributes to success, or where a lack of communication can lead to failure. This does not mean that "bad news" should not be shared; rather, the intent is to prevent overwhelming stakeholders with minutiae.

The program manager should consider the number of potential communication channels or paths as an indicator of the complexity of a program's communications. A key component of communications planning is deciding who will communicate what information to whom.

.3 Communication Methods

The methodologies used to transfer information among program stakeholders can vary significantly. For example, a program management team may engage in brief conversations or extended meetings. Information may be communicated through simple written documents or more complex material such as schedules and databases.

Communications factors that can affect the program include:

- **Urgent need for information.** Is program success dependent upon having frequently updated information available on a moment's notice, or would regularly issued written reports suffice?

- **Availability of technology.** Are the systems in place appropriate, or do program needs warrant change?

- **Expected program staffing.** Are the proposed communications systems compatible with the experience and expertise of the project participants, or is extensive training required?

- **Length of the program.** Is the available technology likely to change before the program is concluded?

- **Program environment.** Does the team meet and operate on a face-to-face basis or in a virtual environment?

10.1.3 Plan Communications: Outputs

.1 Program Communications Management Plan

The program communications management plan is contained in, or is a subsidiary plan of, the program management plan (Section 4.2.3.1). The program communications management plan outlines:

- Stakeholder communication requirements;

- Information to be communicated, including format, content, and level of detail;

- Person responsible for communicating the information;

- Person or groups who will receive the information;

- Methods or technologies used to convey the information, such as memoranda, e-mail, and/or press releases;

- Frequency of the communication;

- Escalation process for identifying time frames and the management personnel responsible for escalation of issues that cannot be resolved at a lower staff level;

- Method for updating and refining the communications management plan as the program progresses and develops; and

- Glossary of common terminology.

The program communications management plan can also include guidelines for program status meetings, program team meetings, e-meetings, and e-mail. The program communications management plan can be formal or informal, highly detailed or broadly framed, and based on the needs of the program.

Communications planning often entails creating additional deliverables that, in turn, require additional time and effort. Thus, the program's work breakdown structure, program schedule, and program budget are updated accordingly.

.2 Communications Log

The program manager or program communications leader should maintain a comprehensive log of stakeholder meetings and communications. The log should identify the who, what, when, how, and why for each form of communication, including stakeholder meetings, published reports and memos, presentations, announcements, etc.

.3 Communications Strategy

A documented communications strategy will help ensure that communication with stakeholders is timely and relevant. The communications strategy incorporates the stakeholder register, stakeholder engagement log and the program communications management plan. It ensures that all stakeholders are communicated with and have their issues and concerns thoroughly addressed.

10.2 Distribute Information

Distribute Information is the process of providing timely and accurate information to program stakeholders in useful formats and appropriate media (Figures 10-4 and 10-5). Information is distributed to three major receiving parties: the clients, the sponsors, and the component managers. Distributed information can include the following:

- Status information on the program and projects, including progress, cost information, risk analysis, and other information relevant to internal or external audiences;

- Notification of change requests to the program and project teams, and the corresponding response to the change requests;

- Internal budgetary information;

- External filings with government and regulatory bodies as prescribed by laws and regulations; and

- Public announcements communicating information useful to the general public.

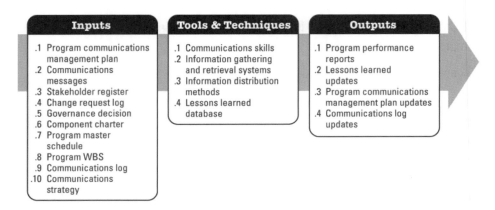

Inputs	Tools & Techniques	Outputs
.1 Program communications management plan .2 Communications messages .3 Stakeholder register .4 Change request log .5 Governance decision .6 Component charter .7 Program master schedule .8 Program WBS .9 Communications log .10 Communications strategy	.1 Communications skills .2 Information gathering and retrieval systems .3 Information distribution methods .4 Lessons learned database	.1 Program performance reports .2 Lessons learned updates .3 Program communications management plan updates .4 Communications log updates

Figure 10-4. Distribute Information: Inputs, Tools & Techniques and Outputs

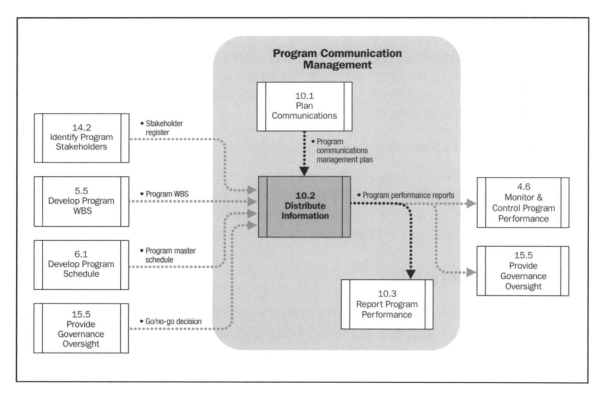

Figure 10-5. Distribute Information Data Flow Diagram

10.2.1 Distribute Information: Inputs

.1 Program Communications Management Plan

Described in Section 10.1.3.1.

.2 Communications Messages

These are the messages distributed to the stakeholders. Examples include: emails, performance reports, voice mails, and presentations.

During the life of the program, ad hoc requests for information will be frequent if the stakeholders feel that their needs for information are being unmet. If these ad hoc requests become burdensome, changes to the program communications management plan may be required.

.3 Stakeholder Register

Described in Section 14.2.3.1.

.4 Change Request Log

Described in Section 15.7.3.2.

.5 Governance Decision

Described in Section 15.5.3.1.

.6 Component Charter

Described in Section 15.4.1.2. The component charter may define the components stakeholders and deliverables, which will influence the program communications management plan.

.7 Program Master Schedule

Described in Section 6.1.3.1 and Section 10.1.1.10. The program master schedule should define the timing of the various program communications.

.8 Program WBS

The program work breakdown structure (PWBS) (described in Section 5.5.3.1.) is useful in communicating the size and complexity of the program. It allows the program team to refine its communications strategy and tactics.

The program communications management plan uses the program WBS in planning the various program communications.

.9 Communications Log

Described in Section 10.1.3.2.

.10 Communications Strategy

Described in Section 10.1.3.3.

10.2.2 Distribute Information: Tools and Techniques

.1 Communications Skills

Program managers must be highly skilled in communicating. The program manager must translate the program's strategic goals into day to day tactical activities. It is important that the program manager communicates well at all levels. Although a program manager generally communicates at a higher level than project managers, program managers must be able to communicate details to project team members as easily as concepts to executives. Given the wide range of communications scenarios that a program manager might experience, having excellent written and oral communication skills is important to a program's success. Program managers must also have good presentation skills to ensure that information is communicated accurately and is clearly understood by the stakeholders. The way the message can be interpreted by the recipients and the effects of the message should be carefully considered before communicating.

Communications skills are part of general management skills and are used to exchange information. General management skills related to communications include ensuring that the right persons get the right information at the right time, as defined in the communications management plan. General management skills also include the art of managing stakeholder requirements.

.2 Information Gathering and Retrieval Systems

Information can be gathered and retrieved through a variety of media including manual filing systems, electronic databases, project management software, and systems that allow access to technical documentation such as engineering drawings, design specifications, and test plans.

.3 Information Distribution Methods

Information distribution involves communicating information to program stakeholders in a timely manner across the program life cycle. Program information can be distributed using a variety of methods, including:

- Face to face meetings, hard-copy document distribution, manual filing systems, and shared-access electronic databases;

- Electronic communication and conferencing tools, such as e-mail, fax, voice mail, telephone, video and web conferencing, and web publishing;

- Electronic tools for program management, such as web interfaces to scheduling and project management software, meeting and virtual office support software, portals, and collaborative work management tools; and

- Informal communications can include emails, small group conversations, and staff meetings. These are the primary methods for communicating day-to-day activities but are not used to formally communicate the program's status.

.4 Lessons Learned Database

Lessons learned are a compilation of knowledge gained. This knowledge may be acquired from executing similar and relevant programs in the past, or it may reside in public domain databases. Lessons learned are critical assets to be reviewed when developing an effective communications management plan. The lessons learned database is updated at the end of components as well as at the end of the program.

10.2.3 Distribute Information: Outputs

.1 Program Performance Reports

There are a variety of ways to represent status reports: dashboards, memos, presentations to stakeholders, question and answer forums. These are the primary methods for communicating a program's status; there are many other formal communications methods.

.2 Lessons Learned Updates

Lessons learned focuses on identifying program and project successes and failures, and includes recommendations to improve future performance on programs and on other projects within the program. During the program life cycle, the program team and key stakeholders identify lessons learned concerning the technical, managerial, and process aspects of the program. The lessons learned are compiled, formalized, and stored through the program's duration.

The focus of lessons learned meetings vary. In some cases, the focus is on strong technical or product development processes, while in other cases the focus is on the processes that aided or hindered performance of the work. Teams can gather information more frequently if they feel that the increased quantity of data merits the additional investment of time and money. Lessons learned provide future program and project teams with the information that can increase effectiveness and efficiency of program management. In addition, phase-end lessons learned sessions provide a good team-building exercise. Program managers have a professional obligation to conduct lessons learned sessions for all programs with key internal and external stakeholders, particularly if the project yielded less than desirable results.

Some specific outputs of lessons learned activities include:

- Update of the lessons learned knowledge base;
- Input to knowledge management system;
- Updated corporate policies, procedures, and processes;
- Improved business skills;

- Overall product and service improvements; and

- Updates to the risk management plan.

.3 Program Communications Management Plan Updates

Changes to the Distribute Information process should trigger changes/updates to the program communications management plan.

.4 Communications Log Updates

Key communications and changes to the Distribute Information process should trigger changes/updates to the communications log created during the Plan Communications process.

10.3 Report Program Performance

Report Program Performance is the process of consolidating performance data to provide stakeholders with information about how resources are being used to deliver program benefits (Figures 10-6 and 10-7). Performance reporting aggregates all performance information across projects and non-project activity to provide a clear picture of the program performance as a whole.

This information is conveyed to the stakeholders by means of the Distribute Information process to provide them with needed status and deliverable information. Additionally, this information is communicated to team members of the program and its constituent projects to provide them with general and background information about the program's performance.

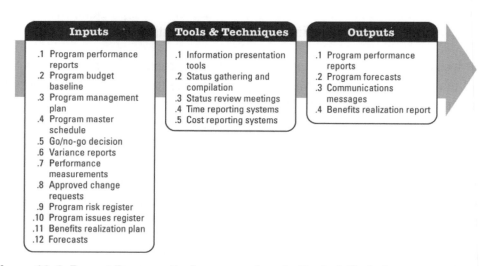

Inputs	Tools & Techniques	Outputs
.1 Program performance reports .2 Program budget baseline .3 Program management plan .4 Program master schedule .5 Go/no-go decision .6 Variance reports .7 Performance measurements .8 Approved change requests .9 Program risk register .10 Program issues register .11 Benefits realization plan .12 Forecasts	.1 Information presentation tools .2 Status gathering and compilation .3 Status review meetings .4 Time reporting systems .5 Cost reporting systems	.1 Program performance reports .2 Program forecasts .3 Communications messages .4 Benefits realization report

Figure 10-6. Report Program Performance: Inputs, Tools & Techniques, and Outputs

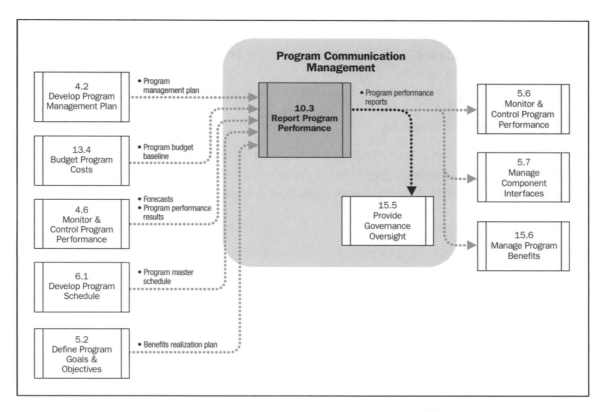

Figure 10-7. Report Program Performance Data Flow Diagram

10.3.1 Report Program Performance: Inputs

.1 Program Performance Reports

Described in Section 10.2.3.1. The program manager collects the performance and status report from each of the components. The program manager uses this information to build the program performance report that will be communicated to the program's stakeholders. These reports are the primary communication vehicle between the project managers and the program manager.

Work performance information on the completion status of the deliverables is collected as part of program execution, and is fed into the performance reporting process. Collecting the work performance information is discussed in further detail in the Direct and Manage Program Execution process (Section 4.4).

.2 Program Budget Baseline

Described in Section 13.4.3.1. The program manager reports the program's cost performance by comparing the actual money spent to the program budget. Earned value analysis is used when practical to assist with creating accurate performance reporting and projecting future performance. These results are reported to the stakeholders as part of the communications process.

.3 Program Management Plan

Described in Section 4.2.3.1. By frequently referring back to the program management plan, the program manager can compare the plan to the program's current execution performance. Differences between the actual execution and the plan will require corrective action.

.4 Program Master Schedule

Described in Section 6.1.3.1. The program manager reports the program's schedule performance by comparing the actual work completed to the program's schedule. Earned value analysis is used when practical to assist with creating accurate performance reporting and projecting future performance.

.5 Go/No-Go Decision

Described in Section 15.5.3.1.

.6 Variance Reports

When the actual result differs from the expected result, a variance is present. Variances can be positive or negative. Metrics that are measured and can be included on variance reports include cost variances, schedule variances, quality variances, number of issues generated variances, variances in stakeholder satisfaction levels, etc. Corrective action will likely be required for all variances.

.7 Performance Measurements

Described in Section 4.6.

.8 Approved Change Requests

Approved change requests (Section 15.7.3.1.) are requested changes to expand or contract program scope, to modify the estimated cost, or to revise activity duration estimates that have been approved and are ready for implementation by the program team.

.9 Program Risk Register

Described in Section 11.5.3.2.

.10 Program Issues Register

Described in Section 4.7.3.2.

.11 Benefits Realization Plan

Described in Section 5.2.3.2.

.12 Forecasts

Forecasts are based on the combined results of program and earned value analysis and expert judgment. Their objective is to assist executives in predicting the likelihood of achieving planned outcomes.

10.3.2 Report Program Performance: Tools and Techniques

.1 Information Presentation Tools

Software packages that include table reporting, spreadsheet analysis, presentations, or graphic capabilities can be used to create presentation-quality images of program performance data. Since program managers are often required to give presentations to various stakeholders, being familiar with these tools can be important to the success of a program.

.2 Status Gathering and Compilation

Information can be gathered and compiled from a variety of media including manual filing systems, electronic databases, project management software, and systems that allow access to technical documentation such as engineering drawings, design specifications, and test plans, to produce forecasts as well as performance, status, and progress reports.

- **Program records.** Program records can include correspondence, memos, and documents describing the program. This information should, to the extent possible and appropriate, be maintained in an organized fashion. Program team members can also maintain records in a program notebook.

- **Program reports.** Formal and informal program reports detail program status and include lessons learned, issues logs, program closure reports, and outputs from the other Knowledge Areas.

- **Program presentations.** The program team provides information formally or informally to the program stakeholders. The information provided needs to be relevant for the targeted audience, and the method of presentation needs to be appropriate.

- **Feedback from stakeholders.** Information received from stakeholders concerning program operations can be distributed and used to modify or improve future performance of the program.

- **Stakeholder notifications.** Information may be provided to stakeholders about resolved issues, approved changes, and general program status.

.3 Status Review Meetings

Status review meetings are regularly scheduled events to exchange information about the program. On most programs, status review meetings are held at various frequencies and on different levels. For example, the program management team can meet weekly by itself and monthly with the customer.

.4 Time Reporting Systems

Time reporting systems record and provide time expended for the program.

.5 Cost Reporting Systems

Cost reporting systems record and provide the cost expended for the program.

10.3.3 Report Program Performance: Outputs

.1 Program Performance Reports

The program manager reports the program's performance through performance reports and program dashboards. Performance reports organize and summarize the information gathered and present the results of any analysis as compared to the performance measurement baseline. Reports typically provide the status and progress information at the level of detail required by various stakeholders as documented in the communications management plan. Common formats for performance reports include bar charts, S-curves, histograms, and tables. Earned value analysis data is often included as part of performance reporting.

.2 Program Forecasts

As the program is executed, forecasts are updated and reissued based on work performance information. This information relates to how the program's past performance could impact the program in the future. Examples of forecasts include estimate at completion and estimate to complete.

.3 Communications Messages

These are the messages that are distributed to the stakeholders. Examples include: emails, performance reports, voice mails, and presentations.

.4 Benefits Realization Report

Benefits may occasionally be realized before the formal work of the program has completely ended.

Programs that deliver incremental benefits must be quantified so that their realization may be measured. This includes the dimensions of the benefit (e.g., the date when realization must start) and a quantification of the benefit (e.g., hours saved, profit increased, market share increased, competitor strength reduced, or incremental productivity improvements).

Governance must determine whether this is taking place within the required parameters so that changes to the component projects or the program as a whole can be proposed.

The benefit report measures the component against the benefits realization plan. The report, which is analyzed by the program team and reported to the enterprise executives, may cause the component to be realigned, terminated, or started early. See Section 15.6.3.1 for more discussion about benefits.

CHAPTER 11

PROGRAM RISK MANAGEMENT

Program risk is an event, or series of events or conditions that, if they occur, may affect the success criteria of the program. Positive risks are often referred to as opportunities and negative risks as threats. These risks arise from the program components and their interactions with each other, from technical complexity, schedule and/or cost constraints, and with the broader environment in which the program is managed.

Program risk categories include:

- **Environment-level risks**—The external environment in which the organization operates and the internal organizational climates in which programs are run create this type of risk. It is important to consider the organization's other initiatives and programs: how it reacts to the external environment and the organizational strategic issue. New initiatives may arise and changes to resource allocation and priorities may alter the relative importance between programs. The political environment and stakeholders competing for the limited organizational resources also should be considered.

- **Program-level risks**—These risks are associated with the program definition, governance, and management arrangements needed to deliver the program. The way in which the program is subdivided into components and the potential interactions between these components contribute to program-level risks.

- **Project risks**—Projects are the primary method of delivering programs; therefore, a considerable amount of program risk management is focused at the project level. In order to ensure effective separation of responsibilities, the program manager should not manage project risks but rather focus on program risks. Any risks outside the authority of the project manager should be escalated to the program manager, and vice versa. Risks should be reported in accordance with the program risk management plan. The program manager evaluates the corresponding effect on the success criteria of the program.

- **Operational-level risks**—These risks are associated with not only the effective transference of program results to normal business operations but also the acceptance and integration of changes to ways of working, including processes and procedures, and the availability of new systems and tools within the organization. This allows new capabilities to be enabled and benefits to be realized by the organization.

- **Portfolio-related risks**—These risks arise from interactions between a program and the set of programs, projects, and other related work grouped in a portfolio. One obvious category of threats and opportunities in this area is associated with resource availability.

- **Benefits-related risks**—Program benefits risks are more than just the sum of the benefits risk from program components. The overall effect of interlinked component risks on benefits delivery should be evaluated.

Risk monitoring involves tracking program-level risks currently identified in the program risk register and identifying new risks that emerge during the execution of the program, for example, unresolved project-level risks that demand resolution at the program level. It includes determining if new risks have developed, current risks have changed, risks have been triggered, risk responses are in effect where necessary and are effective, and if program assumptions are still valid.

Risk control focuses on risks that threaten to develop into actual problems or issues. Risk control involves implementing the mitigation actions and contingency plans contained in the risk response plan.

When risks remain unresolved, the program manager ensures that these risks are escalated progressively higher on the authority scale until resolution can be achieved. Governance process and procedures should be in place to allow risks to be assessed as necessary for possible impact across the organization.

Program risk situations, plans, and the status and effectiveness of ongoing or completed risk responses should be included in program management reviews. All modifications resulting from reviews and other changes in risks should be entered in the risk response plan.

The Program Risk Management processes include (see Figure 11-1):

11.1 Plan Program Risk Management—Deciding how to approach, plan, and execute the risk management activities for a program, including risks identified in the individual program components.

11.2 Identify Program Risks—Determining which risks might affect the program and documenting their characteristics.

11.3 Analyze Program Risks—Prioritizing risks for further analysis or action by assessing and tabulating their probability of occurrence and impact, analyzing the effect on the overall program and its components, and managing interdependencies.

11.4 Plan Program Risk Responses—Developing options and actions to enhance opportunities, and to reduce threats to program objectives.

11.5 Monitor and Control Program Risks—Tracking identified risks, monitoring residual risks, identifying new risks, executing risk response plans, and evaluating their effectiveness throughout program life cycle.

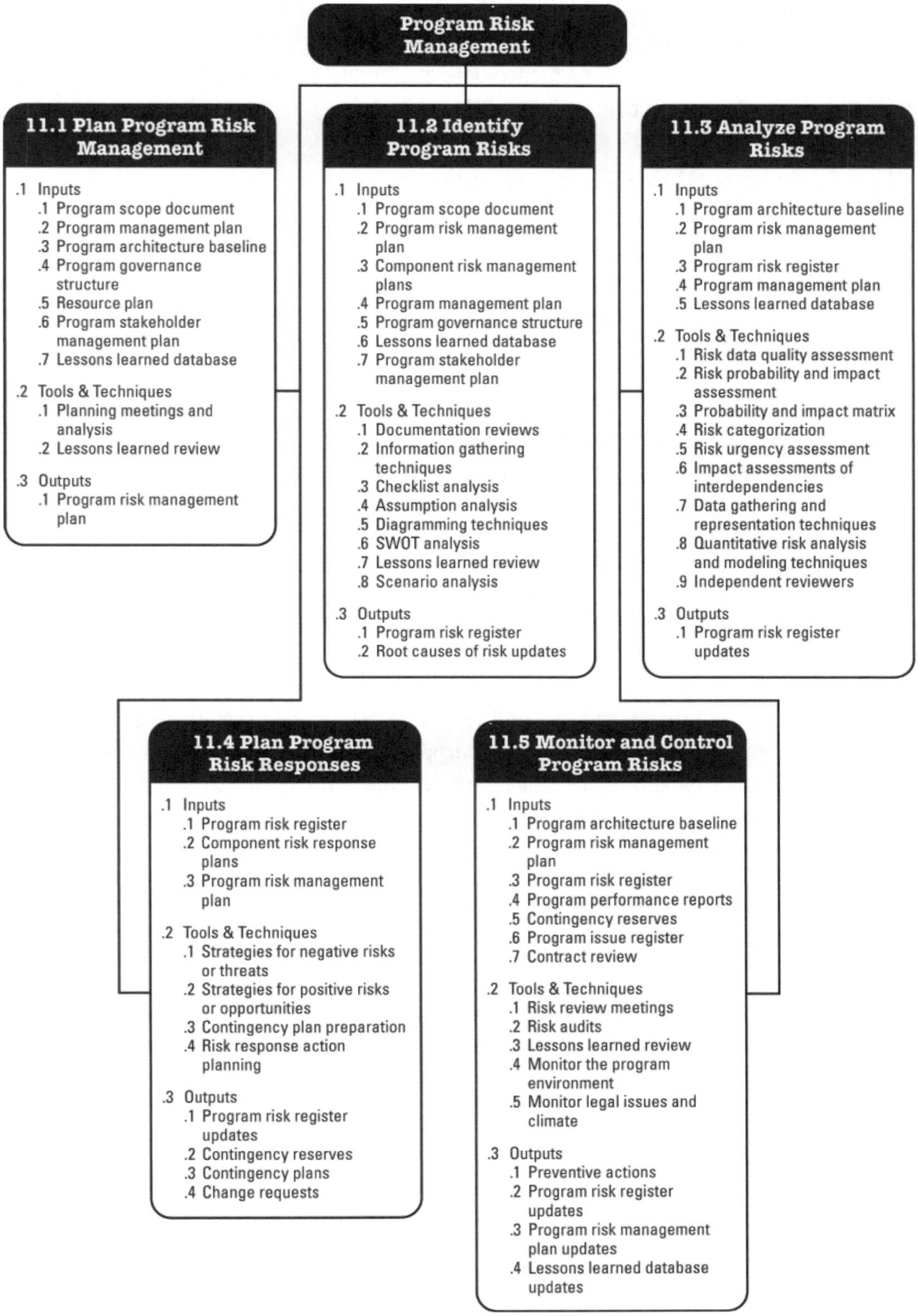

Program Risk Management

11.1 Plan Program Risk Management

.1 Inputs
  .1 Program scope document
  .2 Program management plan
  .3 Program architecture baseline
  .4 Program governance structure
  .5 Resource plan
  .6 Program stakeholder management plan
  .7 Lessons learned database

.2 Tools & Techniques
  .1 Planning meetings and analysis
  .2 Lessons learned review

.3 Outputs
  .1 Program risk management plan

11.2 Identify Program Risks

.1 Inputs
  .1 Program scope document
  .2 Program risk management plan
  .3 Component risk management plans
  .4 Program management plan
  .5 Program governance structure
  .6 Lessons learned database
  .7 Program stakeholder management plan

.2 Tools & Techniques
  .1 Documentation reviews
  .2 Information gathering techniques
  .3 Checklist analysis
  .4 Assumption analysis
  .5 Diagramming techniques
  .6 SWOT analysis
  .7 Lessons learned review
  .8 Scenario analysis

.3 Outputs
  .1 Program risk register
  .2 Root causes of risk updates

11.3 Analyze Program Risks

.1 Inputs
  .1 Program architecture baseline
  .2 Program risk management plan
  .3 Program risk register
  .4 Program management plan
  .5 Lessons learned database

.2 Tools & Techniques
  .1 Risk data quality assessment
  .2 Risk probability and impact assessment
  .3 Probability and impact matrix
  .4 Risk categorization
  .5 Risk urgency assessment
  .6 Impact assessments of interdependencies
  .7 Data gathering and representation techniques
  .8 Quantitative risk analysis and modeling techniques
  .9 Independent reviewers

.3 Outputs
  .1 Program risk register updates

11.4 Plan Program Risk Responses

.1 Inputs
  .1 Program risk register
  .2 Component risk response plans
  .3 Program risk management plan

.2 Tools & Techniques
  .1 Strategies for negative risks or threats
  .2 Strategies for positive risks or opportunities
  .3 Contingency plan preparation
  .4 Risk response action planning

.3 Outputs
  .1 Program risk register updates
  .2 Contingency reserves
  .3 Contingency plans
  .4 Change requests

11.5 Monitor and Control Program Risks

.1 Inputs
  .1 Program architecture baseline
  .2 Program risk management plan
  .3 Program risk register
  .4 Program performance reports
  .5 Contingency reserves
  .6 Program issue register
  .7 Contract review

.2 Tools & Techniques
  .1 Risk review meetings
  .2 Risk audits
  .3 Lessons learned review
  .4 Monitor the program environment
  .5 Monitor legal issues and climate

.3 Outputs
  .1 Preventive actions
  .2 Program risk register updates
  .3 Program risk management plan updates
  .4 Lessons learned database updates

Figure 11-1. Program Risk Management Overview

These processes interact with each other and with processes in the other Knowledge Areas. Each process can involve effort from one or more persons or groups of persons based on the needs of the program and its components. Although the processes are presented here as discrete elements with well-defined interfaces, in practice they may overlap and interact in ways not detailed here.

11.1 Plan Program Risk Management

Careful and explicit planning is crucial. Program Risk Management planning is the process of identifying how to approach and conduct risk management activities for a program by taking into account its components (Figures 11-2 and 11-3). The risk management plan, which is the output of this process, defines the approach to be used for managing risks.

Planning risk management processes is important. It ensures that the level, type, and visibility of risk management are appropriate for the risks and importance of the program to the organization. It identifies the resources and time required for risk management activities. In addition, it establishes an agreed-upon basis for evaluating risks.

The Plan Program Risk Management process should be conducted early in the planning process. It is crucial for the successful performance of other processes described in this chapter. It may need to be reiterated where major changes in the program occur.

It is essential to define risk profiles of organizations to construct the most suitable approach to managing program risks, adjust risk sensitivity, and risk criticality. Risk targets and risk limits influence the program management plan (Chapter 4). Risk profiles may be expressed in policy statements or revealed in actions. These actions may highlight organizational willingness to embrace high-threat situations or its reluctance to forego high opportunity choices. Market factors that apply to the program and to its components must be included as an environmental factor. Culture of the organization and stakeholders also plays a role in shaping the effectiveness of risk management.

Organizations may have predefined approaches to risk management such as risk categories, common definition of concepts and terms, risk statement formats, standard templates, roles and responsibilities, and authority levels for decision-making. Lessons learned from executing similar programs in the past are also critical assets to be reviewed as a component of establishing an effective risk management plan.

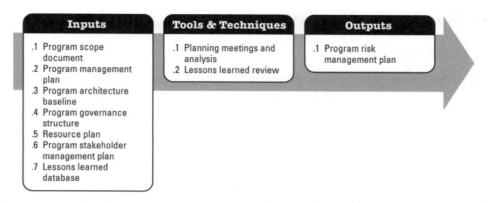

Figure 11-2. Plan Program Risk Management: Inputs, Tools & Techniques, and Outputs

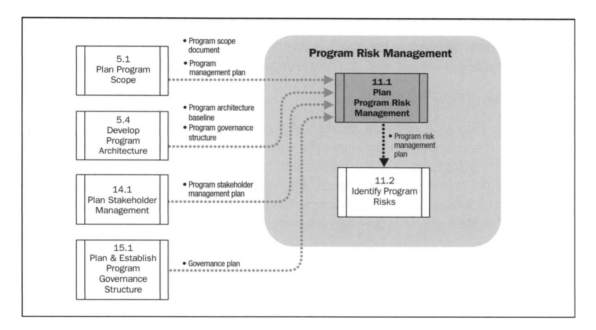

Figure 11-3. Plan Program Risk Management Data Flow Diagram

11.1.1 Plan Program Risk Management: Inputs

.1 Program Scope Document

The program scope document establishes the relative role for risk management among all the other program activities. It is the guiding document for establishing the scope of Program Risk Management.

.2 Program Management Plan

The program management plan establishes how risk management will be integrated and coordinated with all other parts of the program. It is the guiding document for designing Program Risk Management activities. See Section 4.2 (Develop Program Management Plan) for additional information.

.3 Program Architecture Baseline

The program architecture baseline is a plan that describes where the program will be at a given point in time, how it will get there, and how to determine if it was successful.

.4 Program Governance Structure

Effective program governance ensures that decision-making and delivery management activities focus on achieving program goals in a consistent manner, address appropriate risks, and fulfill stakeholder requirements. Programs are dynamic. When combined with a set of governance functions, it provides the means to identify, assess, and respond to internal and external events as well as changes by adjusting program components. The program governance plan establishes the role of Program Risk Management in governance activities and meetings.

.5 Resource Plan

A resource plan includes the set of people, materials, hardware, software, and equipment available to the organization, which is required to execute successfully the program and its components.

.6 Program Stakeholder Management Plan

Stakeholder analysis assists in the identification and assessment of key people, or institutions that may significantly influence program success. It identifies stakeholders' tolerance for risk as well as their potential influence in generating or responding to program risks.

.7 Lessons Learned Database

Lessons learned are a compilation of knowledge gained from executing similar, relevant programs within the organization or from public domain databases. They are critical assets to be reviewed when developing an effective risk management plan.

11.1.2 Plan Program Risk Management: Tools and Techniques

.1 Planning Meetings and Analysis

The program team holds planning meetings to develop the risk management plan. Attendees at these meetings may include the program manager, project managers, select program team members, stakeholders, persons with significant experience in similar programs and projects, and anyone in the organization with the responsibility to manage the risk planning and execution activities (risk manager). The meeting results should be shared with the component managers as part of an integrated Program Risk Management process for the entire program.

These meetings define the basic plans for conducting the risk management activities. Risk cost elements and schedule activities are included in the program budget and schedule, respectively. Risk responsibilities are assigned. General organizational templates for risk categories and definitions of terms, such as risk levels, probability by type of risk, impact by type of objectives, and the probability and impact matrix are tailored to the specific program and its components. The outputs of these activities are summarized in the risk management plan.

It is important to allow time to contact other program managers, vendors, companies, sources, and plant managers to discuss their lessons learned.

.2 Lessons Learned Review

Reviewing lessons learned may help identify additional program risks. It is advisable to exercise caution to ensure that the source of information is appropriate and relevant to the program under execution.

11.1.3 Plan Program Risk Management: Outputs

.1 Program Risk Management Plan

The program risk management plan describes how risk management will be structured and performed on the program. The plan documents the methodology, roles, responsibilities, standard processes, and tools and techniques for identifying, analyzing, planning, tracking (including metrics to measure the effectiveness), and controlling program risks.

- **Approach.** Defines the methodology, tools, and data sources that may be used to perform program risk management. It describes how the components and their outputs are linked to the program risk management process.

- **Roles and responsibilities.** Defines the lead, support, and risk management team membership for each activity in the risk management plan. It assigns people to these roles and clarifies their responsibilities. The plan addresses the following risks: inter-project, program level root causes, those escalated by component project managers, and those that may arise due to executing a risk response.

- **Budgeting.** Assigns resources, estimates risk management costs, and establishes protocol for application of contingency reserve. See Section 13.3 (Estimate Program Costs).

- **Timing.** Defines when and how often the risk management process is performed throughout the program life cycle, and identifies risk management activities to be included in the program schedule.

- **Risk categories.** Ensures a comprehensive process is in place to identify risks to a consistent level of detail and contributes to the effectiveness and quality of the Identify Program Risks process. A previously prepared categorization framework may be a simple list of categories, or might be structured into a risk breakdown structure (RBS). The RBS is a hierarchically organized depiction of causes of program risks arranged by risk category and subcategory. Risk categories from previous programs may need to be tailored, adjusted, or extended to new situations before being incorporated into the current program. The risk categories or RBS may be revisited during the Identify Program Risks process (Section 11.2).

- **Probability and impact matrix.**

- **Revised stakeholders' tolerances.** Stakeholders' tolerances may be revised in the scheduled iterations of the Plan Program Risk Management process.

- **Reporting formats.** Describes the content and format of the program risk register as well as any other required risk reports. Defines how the outcomes of the risk management process will be documented, analyzed, and communicated.

- **Tracking.** Documents how all facets of risk activities will be recorded for the benefit of the current program, future needs, and lessons learned. Documents how the risk management process will be audited.

- **Approval.** Program risk management plan must be reviewed and approved according to the program governance structure.

- **Input to enterprise Program Risk Management process.** Where a corporate risk management process is in place, program risk information is provided and consolidated according to corporate guidelines.

11.2 Identify Program Risks

The Identify Program Risks process determines which risks might affect the program, documents their characteristics, and prepares for their successful management (Figures 11-4 and 11-5). Participants in risk identification activities may include the program manager, program team members, risk management team, subject matter experts from outside the program team, customers, end users, project managers, managers of other program components, general stakeholders, risk management experts, and external reviewers as required.

Risk identification is an iterative process. New risks may evolve or become known as the program progresses through its life cycle. The frequency of iteration and involvement of participants may vary, but the format of the risk statements should be consistent. This allows for the comparison of risk events in the program. Each program staff member continually forecasts the outcomes of current strategies, plans, and activities, and exercises their best judgment to identify new risks. It is important to include contextual information that narrates how or why the risk may impact the program's success; the identification process must provide sufficient information to allow the risk to be analyzed and prioritized.

Risks may be identified by using published information, including commercial databases, academic studies, checklists, benchmarks, or other industry studies. The program team should also identify and manage risk attitudes and their influence on risk identification.

Program files from previous programs may be used to gather information. This includes actual data and lessons learned. These data may also include or lead to the generation of templates to document the risk statements.

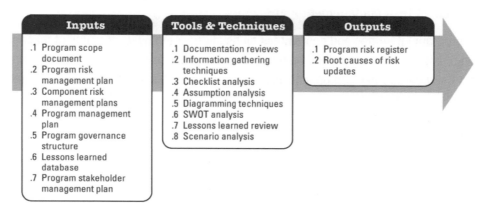

Figure 11-4. Identify Program Risks: Inputs, Tools & Techniques, and Outputs

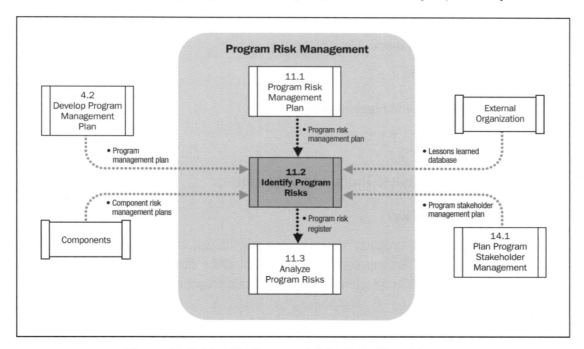

Figure 11-5. Identify Program Risks Data Flow Diagram

11.2.1 Identify Program Risks: Inputs

.1 Program Scope Document

Program assumptions and dependencies are described in the program scope document. Uncertainty in program assumptions and dependencies should be evaluated as potential causes of program risk.

.2 Program Risk Management Plan

Key inputs include the methodology, assignment of roles and responsibilities, provision of risk management activities in the budget and schedule, and categories of risk (see risk categories described in Section 11.1.3.1).

.3 Component Risk Management Plans

The program integrates and coordinates all risks escalated by its component managers. The list of prioritized risks and the corresponding responses from the component risk register identifies potential risk factors such as inter-component dependencies (e.g., responses to one component that would affect another component).

.4 Program Management Plan

Described in Section 4.2.3.1.

.5 Program Governance Structure

The program governance document describes the mechanism to monitor a program's compliance to standards or procedures.

.6 Lessons Learned Database

Described in Section 11.1.1.7.

.7 Program Stakeholder Management Plan

Described in Section 11.1.1.6.

11.2.2 Identify Program Risks: Tools and Techniques

.1 Documentation Reviews

A structured review of program documentation may be performed, including plans, assumptions and prior program files. The quality of the plans, as well as the consistency between those plans with the program requirements and assumptions, may indicate program risks.

.2 Information Gathering Techniques

Information gathering techniques used to identify risks include:

- **Brainstorming.** It is the most frequently used technique to generate new ideas or expand upon existing ideas in order to obtain a comprehensive list of program risks. The program team that performs brainstorming often includes a multidisciplinary set of experts. A facilitator oversees brainstorming. Brainstorming may be freeform with ideas contributed by participants, or structured using techniques such as nominal group technique or Crawford slip approach. Risk categories could be used as a framework.

- **Delphi technique.** The Delphi technique is an iterative process used to reach a consensus of experts and narrow down a potential range of values. Program risk experts participate in this technique anonymously. A facilitator uses a questionnaire to solicit ideas about the program risks. The responses are summarized and are then recirculated to the experts for further comment. Should the responses diverge, reviewing the wording of the questionnaire and the feedback is necessary. Consensus may be reached in a few rounds of this process. The Delphi technique helps reduce bias in the data and prevents any one person from having undue influence on the outcome.

- **Interviewing (internal and external).** Interviewing is an effective way to identify risk areas. Possible risks may be identified by interviewing experienced program participants, stakeholders, subject matter experts (internal and external). This technique is dependent on the effectiveness of the facilitator, the questions, and a well-defined terminology.

- **Root cause identification.** This is an inquiry into essential causes of a program's risks. It sharpens risk definition and allows grouping of risks by causes. Effective preemptive risk responses can be developed if the root cause of the risk is identified.

- **Business case analysis.** A more detailed and thorough analysis of the program's business case can provide additional sources of risk which lay outside the program itself, such as external financial risks.

.3 Checklist Analysis

Risk identification checklists are developed based on historical information and knowledge that has been accumulated from previous similar programs and from other sources of information. The lowest level of the RBS can also be used as a risk checklist. While a checklist can be quick and simple, it is impossible to build an exhaustive one. Care should be taken to explore items that fail to show up on the checklist. The checklist should be reviewed during program closure to improve it for use for future similar programs.

.4 Assumption Analysis

Every program is conceived and developed based on a set of hypotheses, scenarios, choices, or assumptions. Assumptions analysis is a tool that explores the validity of assumptions as they apply to the program. It identifies risk to the program from inaccuracy, inconsistency, or incompleteness of assumptions.

.5 Diagramming Techniques

Risk diagramming techniques may include:

- **Cause-and-effect diagrams.** These are known as Ishikawa or fishbone diagrams.

- **Program dependency analysis.** This analysis identifies the dependencies that the program may have on other program environment elements or vice versa. Money, people, services, information, and/or products are typical dependencies for consideration. Participants may include members from the core program team, internal customers, and any members outside the program who could add value.

- **Influence diagrams.** These are graphical representations of situations showing casual influences, time ordering of events, and other relationships among variables and outcomes.

- **Affinity diagrams.** A group decision-making technique designed to categorize sources of risk.

.6 SWOT (Strengths, Weaknesses, Opportunities, and Threats) Analysis

This technique identifies the internal strengths and weaknesses in relation to program risk using the information-gathering techniques listed earlier in this chapter. It further categorizes the lists into those that will have a direct impact on the program outcome. Further refinement is necessary to remove any duplicates and inconsistencies.

.7 Lessons Learned Review

Described in Section 11.1.2.2.

.8 Scenario Analysis

This technique involves constructing potential outcomes based on known facts, other risks, and current plans. It identifies the potential aggregated effect of multiple uncertain events. For programs, it should take into account two categories of risks:

Those escalated from the project level. These will need to be aggregated in order to identify their effect on program objectives

Those delegated from the strategic level. At the strategic level, senior management can provide considerable insight into potential events and outcomes.

11.2.3 Identify Program Risks: Outputs

.1 Program Risk Register

The program risk register lists the identified risks, their initial description, and potential effect. If potential responses are proposed at this stage, they should also be recorded.

.2 Root Causes of Risk Updates

These are the fundamental conditions or events that may give rise to one or more identified risks. They may be identified as a byproduct of the risk identification technique used or through analysis of risks documented in the program risk register. They should be recorded and used to support future risk identification in the program.

11.3 Analyze Program Risks

Risk analysis at the program level must integrate the program component risks. Managing the interdependencies among the component risks and the program can provide significant benefits to the program and the projects (Figures 11-6 and 11-7).

Both the qualitative and quantitative risk analysis techniques are useful to support program management decisions. This step in the risk management process produces the best information supporting the response contingency and management reserve that should be set aside to deal with risks that actually occur. The assessments should include costs, schedules, and performance outcomes for the complete life cycles of the component projects: this is necessary where the project objectives were not based on full cost estimates. Life cycles should include transition to operations, maintenance and other recurring costs during the utilization of project products, and closure activities. For programs, the life cycle over which risks are managed may include an entire product life cycle or the life cycle of a services group.

The impact of the negative (threats) and positive (opportunities) risks on the achievement of benefits and delivery of value to the organization should be considered at the program level (see Figure 11-8). One essential difference between programs and projects is the time scale: project level risks must be dealt with within a relatively short time frame (the end of a phase, or the project), while program risks may be applicable at a point in the potentially distant future.

The program management team should not assume the authority and responsibilities of the project level management team by managing risks that should be managed at the project level. If project level risks cannot be resolved by the project management team they are escalated to the program level. Risks are further analyzed at the project level to determine if they will have an impact outside of the project. Risks that are escalated to the program level may be managed at the project level, upon analysis by the program management team.

The program management team assists risk analysis by providing an environment conducive for effective risk management of its components. Four factors are crucial:

- **Availability of information.** Providing of an effective means of storing and retrieving information on the projects, stakeholders, environmental characteristics, and other information.

- **Availability of resources.** Maximizing and coordinating the effective use of resources. The program management team negotiates with the executives who control the funds and other resources, such as people, infrastructure, information, and applications.

- **Time and cost.** Providing the long-term view for effective project scheduling at a macro level and managing reserves to take into account the effects of individual project failures or shortfalls.

- **Control.** Devising mechanisms to keep apprised of work that is outside the direct control of project teams, to which they are dependent. This may include regular and effective communication, establishing command and control channels between components and with other programs.

The program management team and risk managers must continually be aware of, and manage, these four factors.

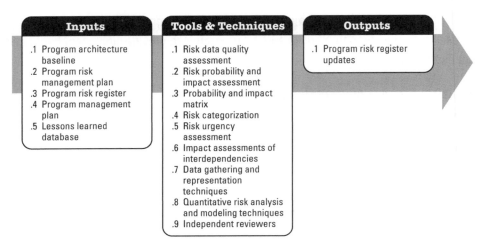

Figure 11-6. Analyze Program Risks: Inputs, Tools & Techniques, and Outputs

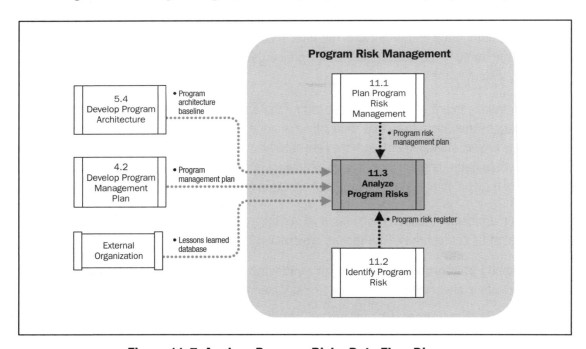

Figure 11-7. Analyze Program Risks Data Flow Diagram

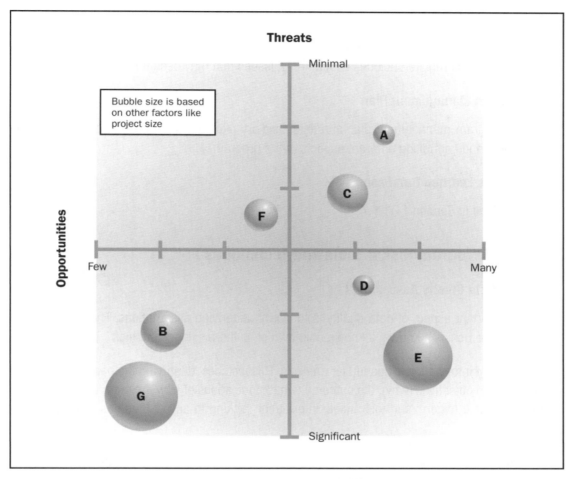

Figure 11-8. Threats and Opportunities

11.3.1 Analyze Program Risks: Inputs

.1 Program Architecture Baseline

Programs of a common or recurrent type tend to have more well-understood risks. Uncertainty is greater for unique or new programs. This can be evaluated by studying the program strategic structure (Section 5.4). The program strategic points to higher-level plans such as the organizational strategy, business, and operational plans.

.2 Program Risk Management Plan

Key elements of the program risk management plan for Analyze Program Risks include roles and responsibilities, budgets, and schedule activities, risk categories, the RBS, and stakeholders' risk tolerances.

.3 Program Risk Register

Key items from the program risk register include the list of identified risks grouped by categories. The program risk register includes watch items: issues that may become risks.

.4 Program Management Plan

The program management plan and its subsidiary plans set the format and establish criteria for developing and controlling different aspects of the program.

.5 Lessons Learned Database

Described in Section 11.1.1.7.

11.3.2 Analyze Program Risks: Tools and Techniques

.1 Risk Data Quality Assessment

An important aspect of data quality is to clarify underlying assumptions. These could include the nature of the risk: is it known, a known unknown or, is there evidence of bias?

Sufficient information is needed for analysis. This includes identifying the parties (who); their aims, motives, and objectives (why); the outcome (what); indications of how the team should proceed (how); the time frame (when); and tolerances. Information lacking in any of these aspects can be a risk in itself.

A lack of information (ambiguity, conflicting definitions, and insufficient data), resources (money, competent people), time, or control can cause risks. It may be necessary to describe how these root causes affect the specific risk, its description, and the accuracy of its impact and priority.

.2 Risk Probability and Impact Assessment

Risk probability is represented by the degree of uncertainty. The impact determines the effect it will have on the program objectives. In addition to probability and impact, the proximity of risks should also be evaluated. Questions to be asked include: the timing of the risk, does the risk disappear at some time in the future, is the risk strongest at particular times, does this happen in classes of component, do the probability and impact change over time? Are there particularly sensitive dates, and are there trigger conditions that may invoke action plans? Is it possible to identify a closure date beyond which the risk could no longer affect the program?

The effect on common objectives should be considered as a part of impact assessment at the program level. Factors that should be considered include manageability (how easy is it to control the risk), familiarity (how well can we describe the risk), frequency (is it one off, recurring, or continuous), proximity (near or in the future), locality (it affects us or is caused by us), and level of vulnerability.

In order to effectively understand and provide input to response planning, it may be useful to model the most severe threats and beneficial opportunities using diagrams, text charts, and mathematical models.

For maximum efficiency, the risk assessment team should ensure that the level of effort expended on the analysis is commensurate with the expected importance of the risk.

.3 Probability and Impact Matrix

This tool may be used for both communication and for prioritization. Risks escalated by component managers should be re-evaluated prior to inclusion in the program risk register. The program criteria for risk analysis is likely to be different from those used at component level.

.4 Risk Categorization

Categorization should be carried out on both threats and opportunities. This aids in analyzing the risks as well as in planning responses. These items should form part of the program RBS.

The categories usually depend on the corresponding industry but the following list is generally applicable:

- Strategic. Note that these may need to be escalated if not within the program manager's authority;
- Operational;
- Project-specific;
- Organizational: political or technical (e.g. infrastructure);
- Composite deliverable risks;
- Enterprise/commercial risks;
- Staff factors/change management risks;
- Economic/currency/financial/market risks;
- Legal/regulatory/governance risks;
- Enterprise management/human factors;
- Political/societal factors;
- Country-specific/multi-country/cross-cultural factors;
- Public opinion;
- Environmental factors and force majeure events;
- Procurement methods (public private partnership (PPP), outsourcing); and
- Process factors (for example, where multiple performing organizations are involved and their processes do not align).

.5 Risk Urgency Assessment

Risks requiring near-term responses may be considered urgent. Priority indicators can include time to effect a risk response, symptoms and warning signs, and the risk rating.

.6   Impact Assessments of Interdependencies

Risks are analyzed to determine the impact of interdependencies between risks at the program level, inter-component risks at the project level, as well as organizational, operational, and strategic risks.

Program risk is not the sum of component risks. Combined project and external risks can have a positive or negative correlation. They can be neutral or can give rise to new risks. In the case of positive correlation, the program risk is increased. In the case of negative correlation, the program risk is decreased.

A mechanism is needed to ensure that project level risks are evaluated, assessed for inter-dependencies, and are taken into consideration. This may require the use of analytical mathematical models and simulation as described below.

.7   Data Gathering and Representation Techniques

- Brainstorming. Described in Section 11.2.2.2.
- Delphi Technique. Described in Section 11.2.2.2.
- RBS to WBS correlation matrix; see example in Figure 11-9.
- Causal maps.

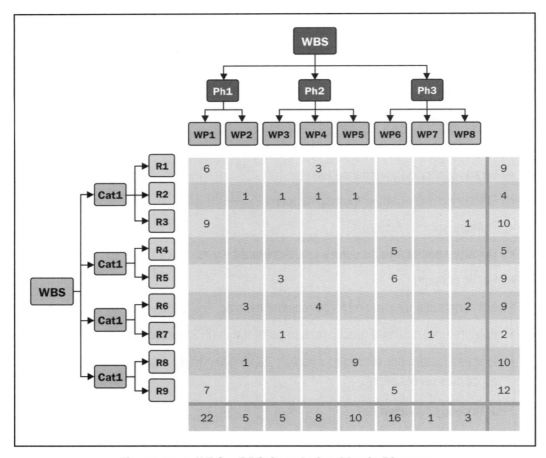

Figure 11-9. WBS—RBS Correlation Matrix Diagram

.8 Quantitative Risk Analysis and Modeling Techniques

Modeling is used to assess the effect of risk interdependencies, see Figure 11-10. Experienced modeling practitioners and specialist texts should be used for applying modeling to the program. As some inputs may have considerable uncertainty, personal judgment of the modeling results may be necessary.

Project	PjRiskID	PgRiskID	1	2	3	4	5	6	7	8	9	10	11	12	13
Project A	3	1	X												
	13	2		X											
	15	7							X						
Project B	6	2		X											
	12	3			X										
	13	6						X							
	24	5					X								
Project C	1	4				X									
	5	2		X											
	6	6						X							
	14	8								X					
	33	5					X								
Project D	2	9									X				
	3	3			X										
	6	6						X							
	33	4				X									
	34	7							X						

Figure 11-10. Program—Project Interdependencies

Particular attention should be paid to the analysis of life cycle program costs. Analysis techniques of specific use for the program environment include:

- Financial analysis methods, such as life cycle cost (LCC), return on investment (ROI), internal rate of return (IRR), net present value (NPV) expected monetary value (EMV), value engineering cost benefit analysis, and others;

- Utility theory;

- Sensitivity analysis;

- Force field analysis;

- Simulations (Monte Carlo analysis);

- Scenarios; and

- Industry-segment-specific risk analysis techniques.

.9 Independent Reviewers

Persons from outside the program and its components who have significant experience in similar programs are consulted.

11.3.3 Analyze Program Risks: Outputs

.1 Program Risk Register Updates

The program risk register is updated to include the results of the analysis. If responses have been identified, reference to them should be included. Details on how the analysis was conducted should be provided for any assumptions. For communication of the results, some organizations use RAG (Red/Amber/Green) status flags.

Cross references between risks should be updated to improve the management of risk inter-dependencies.

11.4 Plan Program Risk Responses

Plan Program Risk Responses is the process of selecting the most suitable response not only to improve opportunities and reduce the threats to the program objectives but also to plan and implement the responses (Figures 11-11 and 11-12). It involves identifying the risk owner and allocating resources (budget, schedule, and project plan) to address the response for priority risks.

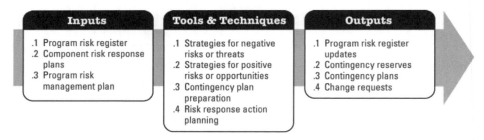

Figure 11-11. Plan Program Risk Responses: Inputs, Tools & Techniques, and Outputs

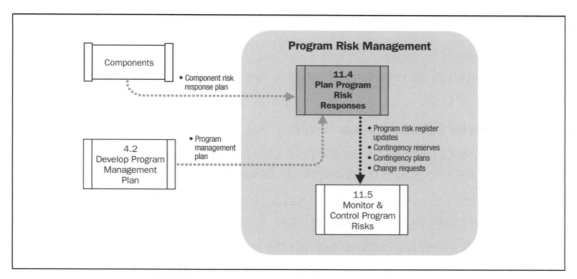

Figure 11-12. Plan Program Risk Response Data Flow Diagram

11.4.1 Plan Program Risk Responses: Inputs

.1 Program Risk Register

This includes all of the results of the Program Risk Identification and Analysis processes as well as any prior risk response planning– namely the prioritized list of risks with their characteristics, any existing responses, and estimates of overall program risk.

.2 Component Risk Response Plans

It is important to review the risk response plans of the components for proposed actions that could affect the program risk responses—for better or worse.

.3 Program Risk Management Plan

Key elements of the program risk management plan used to help identify the level of response required include roles and responsibilities, budgets, schedule activities, risk categories, the RBS, and stakeholders' risk tolerances.

11.4.2 Plan Program Risk Responses: Tools and Techniques

There are tools available to measure alternative risk responses for their benefit to the program. It may be necessary to develop multiple responses and fallback solutions for important risks and plan for contingency in terms of budget, time, and effort.

.1 Strategies for Negative Risks or Threats

- **Avoid.** Risk avoidance may be the most cost-effective strategy. It is most effectively developed during the early phases of the program or its components.

- **Transfer.** At the program level, risk interdependencies make the transfer of risk problematic. Careful evaluation for intentional exclusion of risk, or unintentional inclusion, is necessary.

- **Mitigate.** Taking early actions to reduce the probability and impact of the risk on the program.

- **Accept.** Some risks cannot be eliminated or addressed through a viable strategy. These risks may require acceptance by not acting and dealing with the threats as they occur.

.2 Strategies for Positive Risks or Opportunities

- **Exploit.** Positive impacts to the program are possible, provided the necessary resources to realize the benefits exist.

- **Share.** Outsourcing and making better use of external partnerships may be required in order to capture the opportunity.

- **Enhance.** Affecting key drivers to increase the expected value of the opportunity.

- **Accept.** This strategy indicates that the program team has decided not to change program plans and will deal with the opportunities as they occur.

.3 Contingency Plan Preparation

Despite planning efforts, a risk event may still occur. The most common active acceptance strategy is to establish a contingency reserve, including amounts of time, money, or resources needed to handle known—or even sometimes potential, unknown—threats or opportunities.

.4 Risk Response Action Planning

The selected strategies must be translated into practical actions and integrated into the program plan for execution. Actions that are available at the program level for executing specific strategies include redefining the program scope and changing priorities of constituent components.

11.4.3 Plan Program Risk Responses: Outputs

.1 Program Risk Register Updates

Components of the program risk register that may be updated at this point include:

- Risk owners and assigned responsibilities;
- Agreed-upon response strategies;
- Specific actions to implement the chosen response strategy;
- Symptoms and warning signs of risk occurrence;
- Budget and schedule activities required to implement the chosen responses;
- Contingency reserves of time and cost designed to provide for stakeholder risk tolerances;
- Contingency plans and trigger conditions that call for their execution;
- Fallback plans for use as a response to a risk that has occurred, and the primary response proves to be inadequate;
- Residual risks that are expected to remain after planned responses have been taken, as well as those that have been deliberately accepted; and
- Secondary risks that arise as a direct outcome of implementing a risk response.

.2 Contingency Reserves

A contingency reserve should be established to provide for risk responses. It may be necessary to seek approval for additional reserves when these are almost depleted.

.3 Contingency Plans

For each risk in the register that requires a contingency plan, it should include information about its trigger conditions, cost effect, impact on the schedule, resources needed, and plan status (planned, ready, activated, obsoleted).

.4 Change Requests

A planned risk response may impact the schedule, cost, resources, or quality of deliverables. A change to the program management plan or any of the project management plans may be required.

11.5 Monitor and Control Program Risks

Planned risk responses should be continuously monitored for new and changing risks. Monitor and Control Program Risks is the process of identifying, analyzing, and planning for new risks, tracking identified risks and those on the watch list, as well as reanalyzing existing risks. It includes monitoring trigger conditions, contingency plans, residual risks, and evaluating the effectiveness of risk responses. Monitoring reduces the impact of risk by identifying, analyzing, reporting, and managing risks on a continuous basis. Risk Monitoring and Control is an ongoing process for the life of the program (Figures 11-13 and 11-14).

Other purposes are to determine if:

- Program assumptions are still valid;

- Assessed risk has changed from its prior state, with analysis of trends;

- Proper risk management policies and procedures are being followed; and

- Cost or schedule contingency reserves should be modified in line with the risks of the program.

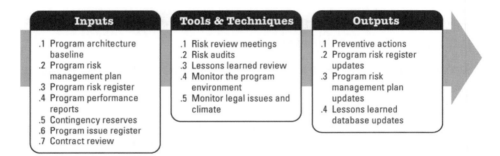

Figure 11-13. Monitor and Control Program Risks: Inputs, Tools & Techniques, and Outputs

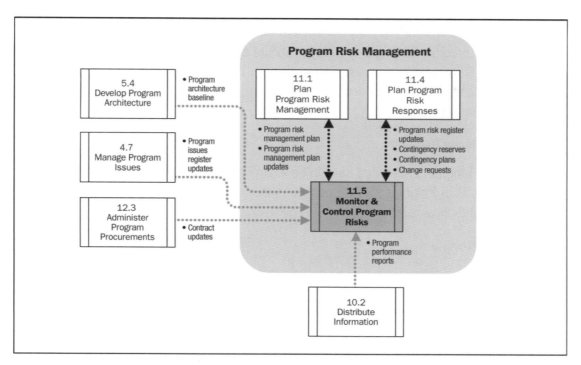

Figure 11-14. Monitor and Control Program Risks Data Flow Diagram

11.5.1 Monitor and Control Program Risks: Inputs

.1 Program Architecture Baseline

The detailed program roadmap is useful when examining current risks and determining if new risks exist.

.2 Program Risk Management Plan

This plan contains key inputs that include the assignment of people, including the risk owners and those selected to analyze risk. The plan also specifies schedules and other resources necessary for the Monitoring and Control process.

.3 Program Risk Register

The program risk register has key inputs that include identified risks, risk owners, agreed-upon risk responses, specific implementation actions, symptoms and warning signs of risks, residual and secondary risks, a watch list of low priority risks and contingency reserves (time and cost).

.4 Program Performance Reports

Program performance information including cost, time, scope, outcomes delivered, benefits realized, capabilities enabled, and validity of the business case are important inputs to risk monitoring and control.

.5 Contingency Reserves

The use of program contingency reserves should be reviewed along with an assessment of their effectiveness. This will aid program management in determining if risks to the program are being effectively managed. It also provides feedback to program management on any project that needs to be recovered or terminated.

.6 Program Issue Register

The list of program issues that need to be examined in order to evaluate whether the responses defined in the Plan Program Risk Responses process were suitable when the corresponding risks materialized and became issues.

.7 Contract Review

Contracts being entered into by the program should be reviewed to ensure that risks are managed. It is important to include the proper company resources in the process, such as legal and/or contract department. If some of the projects are service oriented, are the proper safeguards being agreed upon concerning liability? Is contract wording clear? Are the proper waivers and disclaimers included? Even if an organization has a formal process for contract negotiation and approval, the risks associated with the contract should be evaluated, not just at contract negotiation but also as an additional source of new risks for the program.

11.5.2 Monitor and Control Program Risks: Tools and Techniques

.1 Risk Review Meetings

Risk review meetings should be held on a recurring basis to evaluate the existing risks and to identify if any new risks have arisen. Any new assessment and evaluation efforts are also identified at these meetings. The items to be reviewed include the following:

- Program risk register,
- Changes in the probability-impact assessments,
- Assumptions analysis, and
- Performance of risk response actions.

Trends in performance data and the status of reserves are valuable indicators of the health of the overall program. Other methods of program variance and trend analysis may be used for monitoring overall program performance. Outcomes from these analyses may forecast potential deviation of the program at completion from cost and schedule targets. Deviation from the program roadmap may indicate the potential impact of threats or opportunities.

.2 Risk Audits

This would normally be part of a program quality review that occurs at various points in the program life cycle. The results of those audits should be reported to, and reviewed by, the program management team.

.3 Lessons Learned Review

Review lessons learned to determine if there are actions, tools, or techniques that can be applied to improve the management of program risks.

.4 Monitor the Program Environment

The program environment must be monitored for changes that could affect the program's direction or scope. Environment changes can be sudden and severe resulting in significant changes to the program. Monitoring should be visible to all program participants and regarded as an important part of the Program Risk Management Knowledge Area.

.5 Monitor Legal Issues and Climate

Legal issues can affect programs. For example, insurance programs (especially those that are technology oriented) can be susceptible to class action lawsuits. The result is often an edict from the government to determine and payout unexpected sums of money. This often results in changes in program priorities and scope. Monitoring this type of risk can give the program manager some additional time to plan for this risk.

11.5.3 Monitor and Control Program Risks: Outputs

.1 Preventive Actions

Recommendations to management on the use of program contingency reserves, program change control requests, and directives to the project standards should result from the program risk assessment and analysis performed in Section 11.5.2.1.

.2 Program Risk Register Updates

The program risk register is updated on a recurring basis. Updates include changes to existing risks and any newly identified risks. For new risks, it is important to include their assessment, analysis of results, and response plans. The risk monitoring program tracks progress of each program risk, including meeting minutes, actions implemented, and information on the results. The managers of the subsidiary projects supply all this information about their projects to the program.

.3 Program Risk Management Plan Updates

Any changes to the program management risk plan should be documented, discussed, and agreed upon by program management. These could include, but are not limited to, program administration, changes in the process used to report risk, and the metrics needed to properly evaluate risk.

.4 Lessons Learned Database Updates

Lessons learned from the risk monitoring process are documented and compiled not only for use by the existing program and future programs but also for input to the final end of program report during the program closeout.

CHAPTER 12

PROGRAM PROCUREMENT MANAGEMENT

Chapter 12 describes the processes, inputs, tools, and outputs associated with performing procurement for a program. The procurement process is critical in ensuring the success of a program. It is during this process through careful analysis and planning, that economies of scale can be obtained in procurement for the components of the program. Additionally, careful planning and analysis ensures overall quality and integration of components and activities throughout the program. For these reasons, well-documented and designed procurement processes are required. Procurement departments within the parent organization should be involved in the very initial stages of the procurement process. For international procurements, often the organization's legal department is involved to ensure legally compliant wording is incorporated into the procurement documents and contracts.

The Program Procurement Management processes are:

12.1 Plan Program Procurements—Plan Program Procurements is the process of (a) determining what to procure and when and (b) developing procurement strategies. This process precedes all other procurement efforts.

12.2 Conduct Program Procurements—This is the process that details how to conduct the procurement activities of a program. It includes strategies, tools, methods, metrics gathering, reviews and update mechanisms, standard assessment parameters, and reporting requirements to be used by each component of the program in conducting the procurement activities for the program.

12.3 Administer Program Procurements—Administer Program Procurements is the process involved in managing the contracts during the program to ensure that the deliverables meet requirements, deadlines, cost, and quality established in the contract.

12.4 Close Program Procurements—Close Program Procurements are those processes that formally close out each contract on the program after ensuring that all deliverables have been satisfactorily completed, that all payments have been made, and that there are no outstanding contractual issues.

Figure 12-1 shows the sequencing and the inputs, tools and techniques and outputs of the various subprocesses associated with performing program procurement. Procurement requires input from the various components in the program. This is particularly true regarding input of financial and resource information. Careful consideration must be given to ensure that each of the components meet the required minimal quality and utility specifications required by all other parts of the program. This is especially true when the output from a component is used as an input into a downstream component in the program. Figure 12-2 shows the process flow for Program Procurement Management and highlights the interdependencies.

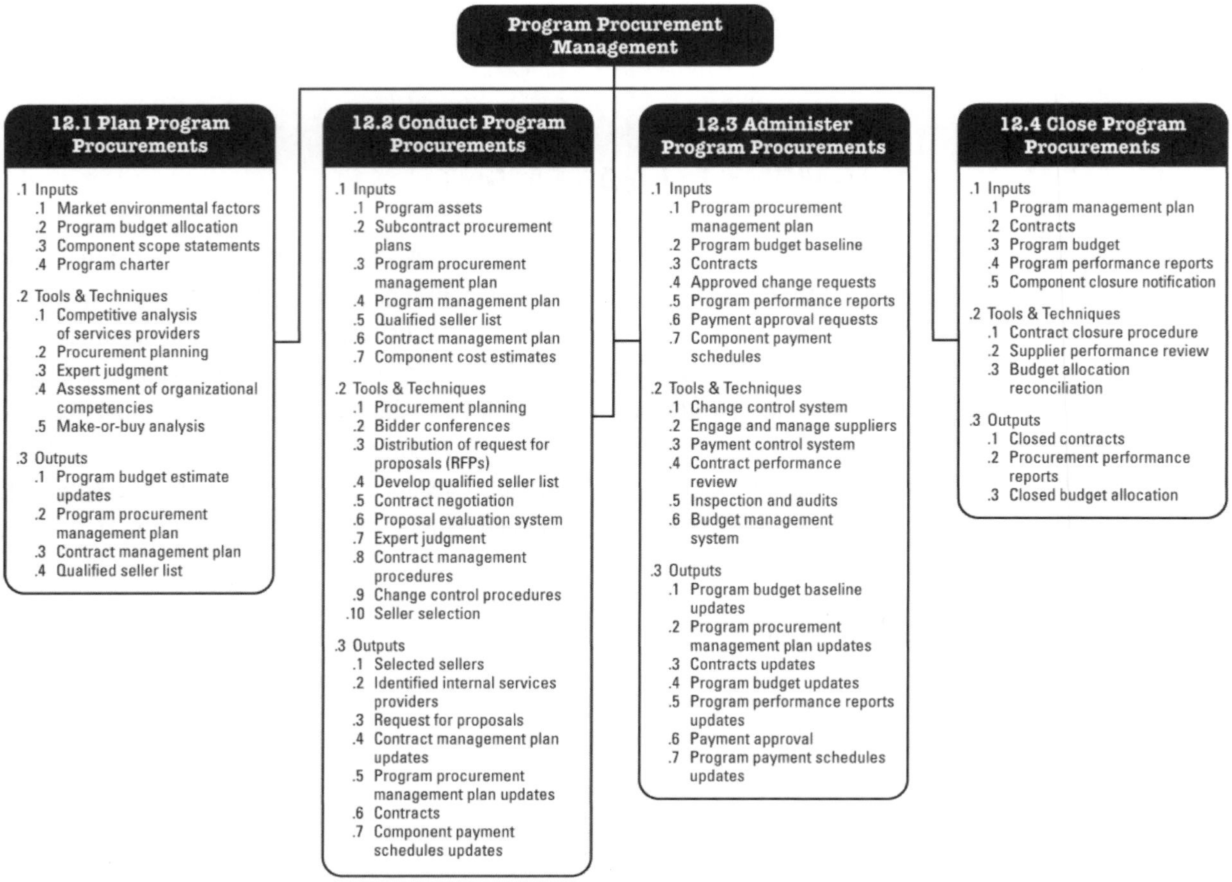

```
                    ┌─────────────────────────┐
                    │  Program Procurement    │
                    │      Management         │
                    └─────────────────────────┘
```

12.1 Plan Program Procurements

.1 Inputs
 .1 Market environmental factors
 .2 Program budget allocation
 .3 Component scope statements
 .4 Program charter

.2 Tools & Techniques
 .1 Competitive analysis of services providers
 .2 Procurement planning
 .3 Expert judgment
 .4 Assessment of organizational competencies
 .5 Make-or-buy analysis

.3 Outputs
 .1 Program budget estimate updates
 .2 Program procurement management plan
 .3 Contract management plan
 .4 Qualified seller list

12.2 Conduct Program Procurements

.1 Inputs
 .1 Program assets
 .2 Subcontract procurement plans
 .3 Program procurement management plan
 .4 Program management plan
 .5 Qualified seller list
 .6 Contract management plan
 .7 Component cost estimates

.2 Tools & Techniques
 .1 Procurement planning
 .2 Bidder conferences
 .3 Distribution of request for proposals (RFPs)
 .4 Develop qualified seller list
 .5 Contract negotiation
 .6 Proposal evaluation system
 .7 Expert judgment
 .8 Contract management procedures
 .9 Change control procedures
 .10 Seller selection

.3 Outputs
 .1 Selected sellers
 .2 Identified internal services providers
 .3 Request for proposals
 .4 Contract management plan updates
 .5 Program procurement management plan updates
 .6 Contracts
 .7 Component payment schedules updates

12.3 Administer Program Procurements

.1 Inputs
 .1 Program procurement management plan
 .2 Program budget baseline
 .3 Contracts
 .4 Approved change requests
 .5 Program performance reports
 .6 Payment approval requests
 .7 Component payment schedules

.2 Tools & Techniques
 .1 Change control system
 .2 Engage and manage suppliers
 .3 Payment control system
 .4 Contract performance review
 .5 Inspection and audits
 .6 Budget management system

.3 Outputs
 .1 Program budget baseline updates
 .2 Program procurement management plan updates
 .3 Contracts updates
 .4 Program budget updates
 .5 Program performance reports updates
 .6 Payment approval
 .7 Program payment schedules updates

12.4 Close Program Procurements

.1 Inputs
 .1 Program management plan
 .2 Contracts
 .3 Program budget
 .4 Program performance reports
 .5 Component closure notification

.2 Tools & Techniques
 .1 Contract closure procedure
 .2 Supplier performance review
 .3 Budget allocation reconciliation

.3 Outputs
 .1 Closed contracts
 .2 Procurement performance reports
 .3 Closed budget allocation

Figure 12-1. Program Procurement Management Overview

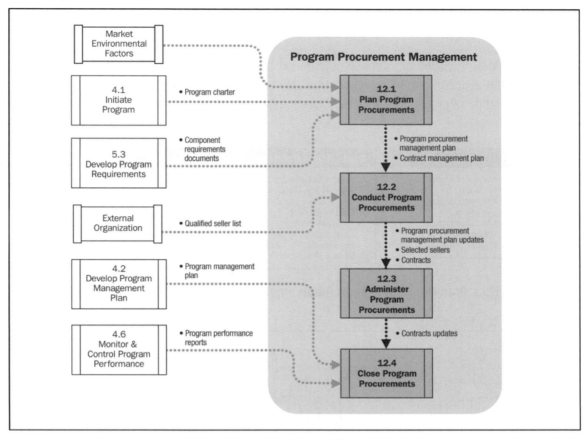

Figure 12-2. Program Procurement Management Data Flow Diagram

12.1 Plan Program Procurements

Planning program purchases and acquisitions must be performed in a manner where funds are utilized in the most appropriate fashion for all program components. Planning purchases may require creating and altering contracts throughout the individual life cycles of each component.

The program procurement planning process includes strategies, tools, methods, metrics gathering, reviews and update mechanisms, standard assessment parameters and reporting requirements to be used by each component in the procurement planning activities of the program (Figures 12-3 and 12-4).

A primary tool for this process is to analyze the program scope statement, any product descriptions, and the program WBS. Make-or-buy decision techniques are applied to the results of the analyses to determine which program WBS elements will be produced using internal resources available to the program and which ones will be obtained from outside suppliers. Once these determinations are made and approved, this information is passed to the contracts planning process, where potential sources are identified and formal contracting documents are created.

Proper risk management planning must be performed. If a vendor from one component is no longer an available resource, concurrent or subsequent components may experience delays or cancellation.

Contracts should be revisited at intervals determined by the program management team. Not only does revisiting ensure the supplier is meeting its contractual responsibility but also determines if product pricing has significantly changed. For example, a 20% increase in gasoline prices in 1 year or construction rebar rising 25% in 1 year.

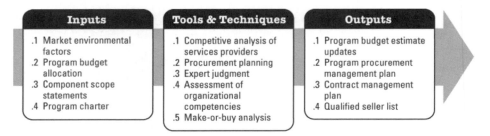

Figure 12-3. Plan Program Procurements: Inputs, Tools & Techniques, and Outputs

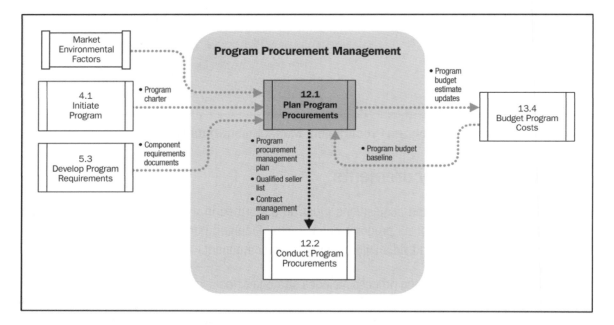

Figure 12-4. Plan Program Procurements Data Flow Diagram

12.1.1 Plan Program Procurements: Inputs

.1 Market Environmental Factors

Market environmental factors include local laws, acts and regulations (national, state, municipal) relating to contracts, tendering, procurement agencies, and other factors influencing business activities and good governance. This is further complicated when programs or components extend beyond national borders. Failure to pay sufficient attention to these factors could result in the program or one of its components unintentionally engaging in illegal activities.

.2 Program Budget Allocation

The program budget must take into account all individual component budgets. Where possible, costs can be shared across components for labor and material. The program manager determines the best use of monetary funds when performing budget allocation.

.3 Component Scope Statements

A clear understanding of the specific components needed to accomplish the program becomes evident as the architecture of the solution is developed. When sufficient detail is obtained, scope statements for the individual components can be created. These will drive the component-level contract statements of work.

.4 Program Charter

Described in Section 4.1.3.2.

12.1.2 Plan Program Procurements: Tools and Techniques

.1 Competitive Analysis of Services Providers

Identify potential suppliers to provide the specific products and services required for each component.

.2 Procurement Planning

Planning develops the procurement and contracting approach and generates the program procurement management plan. Participants in this process may include the program manager, appropriate program stakeholders, as well as the individual(s) in the organization responsible for managing procurement, contracts, or other legal aspects.

.3 Expert Judgment

Expert judgment is expertise based on knowledge and experience in an area. Such expertise may be provided by any group or person with specialized education, knowledge, skills, or experience applicable to the area under analysis.

In the procurement process, expert judgment will be required for knowledge about the law and contracts, as well as with regard to specific items that will be procured (e.g., services and/ or products). For international procurements, specific knowledge will be required about the contracts laws in the various countries in which the procurement is being pursued.

.4 Assessment of Organizational Competencies

The program's parent organization is assessed to determine whether its internal resources can provide any of the program components or the skills required in any portion of the program.

.5 Make-or-Buy Analysis

The make-or-buy analysis is a technique that is performed at the beginning of the Plan Program Procurement process. The analysis determines whether a particular product or service can be produced internal to the program or must be contracted to an outside vendor. If the decision is made to buy, the remainder of the procurement process is followed. This analysis is performed on each potential component.

12.1.3 Plan Program Procurements: Outputs

.1 Program Budget Estimate Updates

In the Plan Program Procurements process, the overall program budget is decomposed into more detailed component-level budgets. The budgets are used in the contracting process to evaluate the vendor responses.

.2 Program Procurement Management Plan

The program procurement management plan includes descriptions of all activities and deliverables necessary to define, integrate, and coordinate procurement. The program procurement management plan's content and complexity varies depending upon the application area and complexity of the desired results. It is updated and revised through the Monitor and Control Program Changes process (Section 15.7).

The program procurement management plan describes how suppliers are identified; the organization's capabilities for evaluating, procuring, and managing the procured services and products; how contract management will be conducted; the types of contracts entered into; payment for services and products delivered; and the finalization and termination of contracts.

Included in the program procurement management plan are (at a minimum):

- **Component statements of work updates**. The project statement of work compiles all the constituent component statements of work and the work specific to a component. The project statement of work guides the procurement process for a given component. It identifies how work will be managed by different components, whether work should be done internally or

---

externally, whether the external efforts should be managed by way of umbrella or individual contracts, and so on.

- **Contract type.** A variety of different contract types is possible. The needs of a particular component should define the appropriate contract. In some cases a simple time and materials contract is appropriate. In other cases, a cost-plus contract is appropriate. The specific types of contracts that may be utilized on the program should be defined and documented.

- **Identification of required and available resources**. Part of the procurement decision process involves determining the resources required for the program (part of the program planning processes) and seeing if they are available within the organization. If not, they must be obtained from outside sellers.

- **Sourcing decisions**. This decision determines whether a company will make the product in question or will purchase from an outside vendor. For example, a word processing program would be much easier to purchase off the shelf rather than create.

- **Identification of required procurements**. The required procurements identification will be used for the entire program. Cost savings can be realized through using procured items in the various components of a program. Improper planning of shared resources or not purchasing the proper material for each component may incur additional costs.

- **Proposals**. The processes, procedures, and evaluation criteria are required for objectively evaluating proposals received from vendors. In some cases, an external agency may be hired to evaluate vendor proposals to eliminate any possibility of bias on the part of the program organization.

- **Qualified seller lists**. Qualified seller lists can be developed from the organizational assets, if available, or can be developed by the program management team. General information is widely available through the Internet, library directories, relevant local associations, trade catalogs, and similar sources. Detailed information on specific sources can require more extensive effort, such as site visits or contact with previous customers.

.3 Contract Management Plan

For significant purchases or acquisitions, a plan to administer the contract is prepared based upon the specific buyer-specified items within the contract. This includes documentation, delivery, and performance requirements that the buyer and seller must meet. The plan covers the contract administration activities throughout the life of the contract.

.4 Qualified Seller List

The output of the competitive analysis of sellers is a list showing which vendors are qualified to bid on the program's components.

12.2 Conduct Program Procurements

Conduct Program Procurements processes are performed in order to acquire the desired services, resources, or materials that the program requires to meet its objectives (Figures 12-5 and 12-6).

The outputs from this process include the program contract management plan, updated budget estimates, and an updated program procurement management plan that lists potential internal service providers or selected suppliers, requests for proposals, agreed contracts, and the eventual supplier engagement.

Relevant to the procurement process are contractual agreements for insurance or services to protect the program. The relevant parties' responsibilities with regard to potential risks should be documented and incorporated into the program files.

Supplier selection involves evaluating the best options for the selection and appointment of a service provider or supplier of goods. The inputs, tools and techniques, and outputs associated with the process are shown in Figure 12-5.

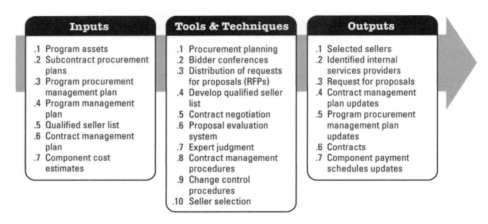

Figure 12-5. Conduct Program Procurements: Inputs, Tools & Techniques, and Outputs

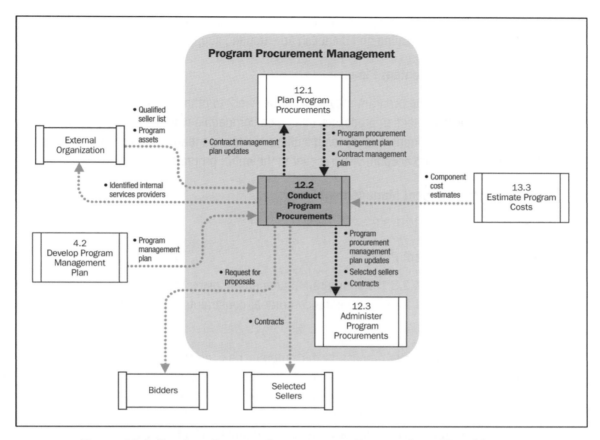

Figure 12-6. Conduct Program Procurements Process Data Flow Diagram

12.2.1 Conduct Program Procurements: Inputs

.1 Program Assets

Program assets are identified and assessed to determine how they contribute to performing source and supplier selection. The organization may have formal policies and procedures in place that must be adhered to during the procurement source selection process.

The parent organization may not have the capacity, resources, or skills required to perform source selection. It may be necessary to develop those processes and resources or to consider the services of an external party who has the necessary capacity, skills, and resources.

An organization may provide formal and informal procurement-related templates, policies, procedures, guidelines, organizational structures (e.g., legal and procurement departments), and management systems to assist in developing the procurement management plan and selecting the appropriate type of contract. Organizational policies may constrain procurement decisions. These policy constraints can include limiting the use of simple purchase orders, requiring all purchases above a certain value to use a specific contract, limiting the ability to make specific make-or-buy decisions, and requiring specific types or sizes of sellers. Organizations in some application areas also have an established multi-tier supplier system of selected and pre-qualified sellers to reduce the number of direct sellers to the organization and establish an extended supply chain.

.2 Subcontract Procurement Plans

Components within the program may subcontract work to other organizations. Their procurement processes and source-selection processes should be compatible with those of the parent program. In the event where a component must develop a unique or non-standard approach, the effect and impact of this must be taken into account with respect to the entire program.

.3 Program Procurement Management Plan

Described in Section 12.1.3.2.

.4 Program Management Plan

Described in Section 4.2.3.1. The program management plan should be reviewed for known risks, prerequisites, conditional factors, acceptance criteria, constraints, and assumptions that will affect procurement.

Especially relevant to this process is the program risk register. The program risk register is a compilation of risks identified by the respective projects in the program that may impact the scope, time, and cost of the program. The risks that relate to longer than anticipated lead times or unsatisfactory delivery of goods are considered and may require modifications to the program management plan. Risk identification may assist with the selection of another suitable seller. As part of the mitigation plan, other sellers are identified or the management plan modified to accommodate the risk.

.5 Qualified Seller List

Described in Section 12.1.3.4.

.6 Contract Management Plan

Described in Section 12.1.3.3.

.7 Component Cost Estimates

Described in Section 13.3.3.2.

12.2.2 Conduct Program Procurements: Tools and Techniques

.1 Procurement Planning

Described in Section 12.1.2.2.

.2 Bidder Conferences

Bidder conferences (also known as contractor conferences, vendor conferences, and pre-bid conferences) are meetings with prospective sellers prior to preparation of a bid or proposal. The objective is to ensure that all prospective sellers have a clear and common understanding of the procurement (e.g., technical requirements and contract requirements). Prospective sellers are able to ask to questions. Responses to questions can be incorporated into the procurement documents as amendments. All potential sellers are given equal standing during this initial buyer and seller interaction to produce the best bid.

.3 Distribution of Request for Proposals (RFPs)

In addition to bidder conferences, potential sellers are notified of the procurement process through industry newspapers, procurement web sites, or mailing out copies of the documents. These documents may be RFPs, requests for information (RFIs), request for quote (RFQ), invitations to bid, or other forms.

A suitable system for this process needs to be in place. It must be able to manage and track the flow of information to and from suppliers, and address the contractual elements, comments, queries, and feedback.

.4 Develop Qualified Seller List

Qualified sellers are those who are asked to present proposals and/or quotations in response to the procurement needs. This list is developed from the organizational assets, if such lists or information are readily available, or may be developed by the program management team. General information is widely available through the Internet, library directories, relevant local associations, trade catalogs, and similar sources. Detailed information on specific sources can require more extensive effort, such as site visits or contact with previous customers. Procurement documents can also be sent to determine if some or all of the prospective sellers have an interest in becoming a qualified potential seller.

.5 Contract Negotiation

Contract negotiation clarifies the structure and requirements of the contract so that mutual agreement can be reached prior to signing the contract. Final contract language reflects all agreements reached. Subjects covered include responsibilities and authorities, applicable terms and laws, technical and business management approaches, proprietary rights, contract financing, technical solution, overall schedule, payments, and cost. Contract negotiations conclude with a document that is signed by both buyer and seller. The final contract can be a revised offer by the seller or a counter offer by the buyer.

.6 Proposal Evaluation System

Many different techniques can be used to rate and score proposals, but all use expert judgment and evaluation criteria. The evaluation criteria can involve both objective and subjective components. Formalized proposal evaluations use predefined weightings. Inputs received from multiple reviewers during the Select Sellers process are compiled and any significant differences in scoring are resolved. An overall assessment and comparison of all proposals can be developed using a weighting system that determines the total weighted score for each proposal. A screening system that uses data from a seller rating system may also be used.

- **Weighting system.** A weighting system quantifies qualitative data to minimize personal prejudice on seller selection. Most systems assign a numerical weight to each of the evaluation criteria, rate the prospective sellers on each criterion, multiply the weight by the rating, and total the resultant products to compute an overall score.

- **Screening system.** A screening system involves establishing minimum requirements of performance for one or more of the evaluation criteria, and can employ a weighting system and independent estimates. For example, a prospective seller might be required to propose a project manager who has specific qualifications before the remainder of the proposal would be considered. The screening systems provide a weighted ranking from best to worst for all sellers who submitted a proposal.

- **Seller rating system.** Seller rating systems use information such as the seller's past performance, quality ratings, delivery performance, and contractual compliance. The seller performance evaluation documentation generated during the Administer Program Procurement process for previous sellers is one source of relevant information. The rating system is used in conjunction with the proposal evaluation's screening system.

.7 Expert Judgment

Expert judgment is used in evaluating seller proposals. The evaluation of proposals is accomplished by a multi-discipline review team with expertise in each of the areas covered by the procurement documents and proposed contract. This can include expertise from functional disciplines, such as contracts, legal, finance, accounting, engineering, design, research, development, sales, and manufacturing.

.8 Contract Management Procedures

A successful relationship also depends on non-technical factors like the establishment and maintenance of trust, and good working relationships. This can sometimes be more effectively maintained at the program level since most of the disputes will typically arise at the component level. Contract management ensures that the contract terms are being followed: both the customer and supplier are fulfilling their obligations. The customer enables the performing organization to complete the deliverable; pays the agreed price; and accepts the deliverable upon completion. The supplier provides the deliverable as specified in the statement of work and project scope statement as applicable. If the administration is performed at the component level, then the role at the program level will be monitoring and control.

.9 Change Control Procedures

A contract change control system defines the process by which the contract can be modified. It includes the paperwork, tracking systems, dispute resolution procedures, and approval levels necessary for authorizing changes. The contract change control system is integrated with the Monitor and Control Program Changes process.

.10 Seller Selection

During the Conduct Program Procurement process, the qualified sellers are narrowed down to a final few that meet the technical and managerial requirements and whose costs are within the expected cost goals. Negotiations are performed in order to select the final seller to which the contract will be given.

12.2.3 Conduct Program Procurements: Outputs

.1 Selected Sellers

The sellers selected are those sellers who have been judged to be in a competitive range based upon the outcome of the proposal or bid evaluation.

.2 Identified Internal Services Providers

Internal services within the performing organization which are able to deliver the required services or goods.

.3 Request for Proposals

Appropriate request for proposals for work at the program level are sent to the list of identified qualified sellers so they can respond.

.4 Contract Management Plan Updates

A plan to administer the contract is prepared based upon buyer-specified items within the contract such as documentation, delivery, and performance requirements that the buyer and seller must meet. The plan covers the contract administration activities throughout the life of the contract.

.5 Program Procurement Management Plan Updates

The program procurement plan is updated to reflect approved changes and corrections.

.6 Contracts

Finalized contractual agreements from which procurement work performance is measured.

.7 Component Payment Schedules Updates

Described in Section 13.2.3.3. Once contracts have been approved and signed by both parties, the payment schedules for the contracts are fed into the financial system so that contract payments can be made in accordance with the contract requirements.

12.3 Administer Program Procurements

In effect, every agreement between a supplier and a customer is a contract. The agreement describes the customer need and how the supplier will satisfy that need. It further describes how the relationship will be conducted and the recourse should a party not conform to the agreement.

Such agreements may bring together unrelated parties (separately owned or controlled companies and other organizations) or different units within the same organization. From the perspective of the customer (purchaser or buyer) and supplier (seller or performing organization), there should be no distinction in the commitment whether it is external or internal. The performing organization may be internal or external.

Agreements and contracts need to take into account the laws of the countries involved and any applicable local statutes and regulations (e.g., municipal regulations). In most countries, any agreement is, by its nature, a contract and would be regarded as such by law. Many agreements require legal analysis.

The Administer Program Procurements process ensures that the conditions and requirements of the agreement are understood and adhered to, and that the formal relations between the customer and supplier are not terminated before all requirements have been met (Figures 12-7 and 12-8).

The agreement typically describes actions to be taken if conditions are not met or if a breakdown occurs between the parties (usually referred to as a "breach").

In some cases, service level agreements (SLAs) are used in place of formal contracts. SLAs are intended for delivery of ongoing services as a part of normal organization operations. They are not suited to controlling program components, despite the fact that components are sometimes regarded as services. Since agreements describe relationships, and their purpose may be to provide products or services to one or more constituent components in a program, it is wise to coordinate these at the program level.

Administer Program Procurements requires an understanding of the agreement terms. The program and project management plans must have sufficient control mechanisms in place for monitoring and control. This includes identifying when agreement conditions are violated, inadvertently or by design, that deliverables are delivered as specified, that the relationship is terminated as stipulated, and that any post-program commitments are fulfilled as agreed. It also ensures that any changes and corrective actions affecting the agreement(s) are properly approved and managed.

For large programs, such as major civil engineering programs, aerospace and defense systems, or major construction programs, the contracting process engages primary contractors, who in turn subcontract part of the work to other contractors. The selection process criteria for these subcontracts must be defined at the program level to ensure consistency in meeting program goals. For contracts and subcontracts that occur across international boundaries, special care must be taken to ensure that local customs do not take precedence over program efforts, but that local laws are taken into account when writing the contracts. The country of origin of the contract is typically defined as the country whose laws will be followed in the contract.

Good governance requires that all contractual instruments are properly controlled, changed only according to a formal change control process, and available for scrutiny at any time by authorized parties.

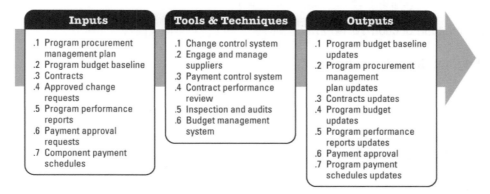

Figure 12-7. Administer Program Procurements: Inputs, Tools & Techniques, and Outputs

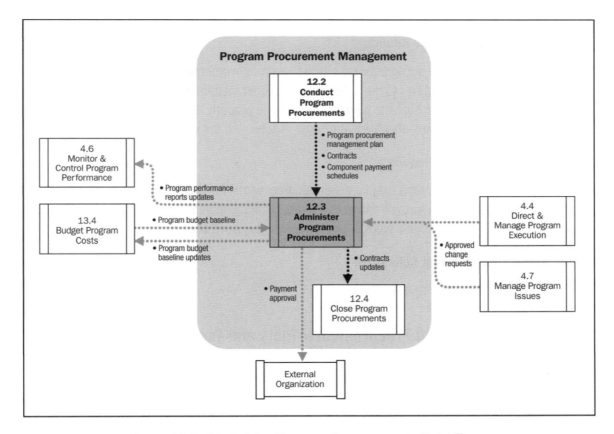

Figure 12-8. Administer Program Procurements Data Flows

12.3.1 Administer Program Procurements: Inputs

.1 Program Procurement Management Plan

Described in Section 12.1.3.2.

.2 Program Budget Baseline

Described in Section 13.4.3.1.

.3 Contracts

Described in Section 13.4.1.4.

.4 Approved Change Requests

Changes to an agreement must follow a formal process, as outlined in the program change control procedure.

.5 Program Performance Reports

Regular seller performance status reports are required in order to effectively manage the contracts. The status reports, in addition to the schedule and budget metrics, should include the approval status of seller deliverables to ensure the work has been done properly. Status reports provide management with information about how effectively the seller is achieving the contractual objectives.

.6 Payment Approval Requests

Payment approval requests may be generated from within the program, a component, or performing organization. Payment approval requests should be accompanied by evidence that all conditions associated with the applicable work packet or deliverable have been met.

.7 Component Payment Schedules

Described in Section 13.4.3.3.

12.3.2 Administer Program Procurements: Tools and Techniques

.1 Change Control System

There are many benefits to coordinating agreements across components at the program level. It ensures consistency, synergy, effectiveness, and efficiency. With purely administrative matters being dealt with at the program level, components are able to focus on delivery. An effective procurement management system is necessary.

The procurement management information system should include a records management system that defines how, what and where procurement–related documentation and records are stored for easy retrieval and referencing. The system is part of the organization and program's assets. Some

---

organization's programs may have their own records management systems, which require interfacing with/into the organization's system(s). Alternatively, the program may use the organization's systems.

.2 Engage and Manage Suppliers

Engage and manage suppliers consists of all components required for engaging suppliers and service providers in order to achieve the procurement objectives for the program and its components.

In order to effectively manage a variety of suppliers, some of whom might be international and subject to different laws and regulations, a wide variety of information is needed. At a minimum, the following items must be considered:

- **Contracts.** A contract is a mutually binding agreement that obligates the seller to provide the specified products, services, or results, and obligates the buyer to provide monetary or other valuable consideration. A contract is a legal relationship subject to remedy in the courts. The agreement can be simple or complex depending on the complexity of the deliverables. A contract includes terms and conditions, and may include the seller's proposal or marketing literature, and any other documentation that the buyer is relying upon to establish what the seller is to perform or provide. The program management team must tailor the contract to the specific needs of the program component that is being contracted. Depending upon the application area, contracts can also be called an agreement, subcontract, or purchase order. Most organizations have documented policies and procedures specifically indicating who can sign and administer such agreements on behalf of the organization.

- The type of contract must be appropriate for the type of purchase. The contract type and its terms and conditions set the degree of risk being assumed by both the buyer and seller. When the work is international or when a contractor is not in the same country as the program, the contract must clearly state which country's laws will be followed as well as the arbitration procedures and remedies for non-conformance.

- **Contract Management Plan.** Described in Section 12.1.3.3.

- **Program Procurement Management Plan.** Described in Section 12.1.3.2.

- **Performance Reports.** Performance reports provide information on the component's performance with regard to scope, schedule, cost, resources, quality, and risk. They can also be used to provide management with information about how effectively the seller is achieving the contractual objectives. Contract performance reporting is integrated into performance reporting.

- **Change Management.** Approved change requests can include modifications to the terms and conditions of the contract, including the contract statement of work, pricing, and description of the products, services, or results to be provided. All changes are formally documented in writing and approved before being implemented.

.3 Payment Control System

An effective payment control system should be in place at the program level. This ensures that any problems in the payment process can be resolved in a timely manner.

Procurement contracts may exist that are accessible to one or more program components, while others are specific to a single component. Establishing effective mechanisms ensures that the contract terms are adhered to and duplicate payments are not made.

The payment control system, which may be a manual or automated process, should include mechanisms and controls to ensure that required approvals are obtained and evidence is presented that all conditions have been met, before a payment request is authorized and executed.

.4 Contract Performance Review

Regular performance reviews verify that the customer and the performing organization(s) are adhering to the agreement(s). Any lapses and variations should be identified. Offending parties should be informed as quickly as possible so that corrections may be made to bring performance in line with requirements. This ensures minimum disruption to the program and components. Initial communications may be verbal and informal, with subsequent communications becoming more formal. As a last resort, the legal remedies specified in the contract may be needed to rectify problems. These are almost always harmful to the program objectives.

Change requests, or recommended corrective action requests, should be raised where the performance problems are a result of deficiencies in the contract(s).

.5 Inspection and Audits

A procurement audit confirms whether the seller delivered on its contractual obligations and that the statement of work and its components was achieved. It also addresses whether the contract terms, conditions, and warranties were met from an administrative and legal perspective. Procurement audits involve reviewing and verifying all procurement-related documentation, such as purchase orders, delivery notes, payments, after-sales warranties and guarantees, provisions for ongoing (post- project / program) service from seller etc. Based on the findings, it may be necessary to request changes or to recommend corrective actions.

Inspections and audits should take note of adherence to contracts, as applicable, noting whether procurement was done during contract term (after start and before end dates) and according to the contract stipulations.

.6 Budget Management System

The program budget management should be integrated with the organization's budget management system and be able to manage the overall program procurement budget. The overall budget should be monitored and managed at the program level, including contracts that are program component-specific (e.g. a project). This ensures that economies of scale and savings can be optimized as well as prevents duplications.

It is crucial that the budget management system be able to provide warnings of potential over-expenditure as well as highlight where infractions have already occurred. This is important since

---

external suppliers may refuse to complete deliverables until payment is assured, which impacts the objectives of other program components.

12.3.3 Administer Program Procurements: Outputs

.1 Program Budget Baseline Updates

Program budget allocations are updated based on contractually agreed amounts. These budget changes may affect many different components of the program management plan. They are managed by the program's financial organization.

.2 Program Procurement Management Plan Updates

The program procurement plan is updated to reflect approved changes and corrections.

.3 Contracts Updates

Changes and corrective actions may result in changes to contracts. Contracts typically state that such changes may only be made subject to certain conditions being met (e.g., that they are reduced to writing, and be agreed to by all parties).

.4 Program Budget Updates

Once amounts have been contractually agreed upon, they must be adhered to. If the amounts are out of line with what has been determined in the program budget, the program budget must be changed.

.5 Program Performance Reports Updates

Described in Section 12.3.3.5.

.6 Payment Approval

Requests for payment that have been verified to be valid are approved and forwarded to the organization's finance section for payment.

.7 Program Payment Schedules Updates

Described in Section 13.4.3.2.

12.4 Close Program Procurements

Program procurement may be closed when all procurement activities on a program are concluded. This involves notifying program and component stakeholders, including suppliers and project management teams, and the organization's finance department. In addition to reviewing contract termination clauses, residual stipulations and clauses need to be noted and the appropriate parties informed (Figures 12-9 and 12-10).

Contracts are reviewed to determine if all conditions are met, will be met after the closure of procurement activities (for example, during the realization of benefits), and whether warranties are applicable.

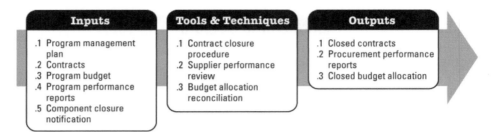

Inputs	Tools & Techniques	Outputs
.1 Program management plan .2 Contracts .3 Program budget .4 Program performance reports .5 Component closure notification	.1 Contract closure procedure .2 Supplier performance review .3 Budget allocation reconciliation	.1 Closed contracts .2 Procurement performance reports .3 Closed budget allocation

Figure 12-9. Close Program Procurements: Inputs, Tools & Techniques, and Outputs

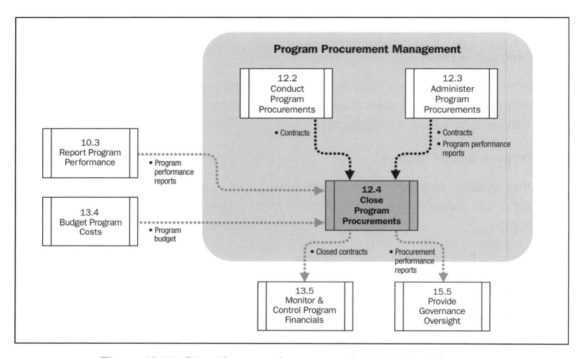

Figure 12-10. Close Program Procurements Data Flow Diagram

12.4.1 Close Program Procurements: Inputs

.1 Program Management Plan

The program management plan is reviewed to identify any special actions to be taken when closing program procurements.

.2 Contracts

All contract documentation is scrutinized to ensure that contract closure stipulations are adhered to and any residual stipulations are dealt with appropriately.

.3 Program Budget

The program budget is reviewed to assess whether there is sufficient budget available to conclude and close the contract.

.4 Program Performance Reports

Program performance reports, including component performance reports, are scrutinized to establish whether all issues raised were addressed satisfactorily.

.5 Component Closure Notification

The closure of a component indicates that there will not be any additional procurement requests, and that procurement closure activities may be required.

12.4.2 Close Program Procurements: Tools and Techniques

.1 Contract Closure Procedure

Contract closure is the process of closing out a contract executed during the program and on behalf of the program, in accordance with the contract's terms and conditions. This process also applies to cases of premature contract termination.

The performing organization's policies, processes, and procedures that outline the requirements for formally and legally closing and/or terminating contractual agreements are reviewed and addressed. This includes predefined verification criteria intended to protect the organization (and other parties) from breach of contract. In the case of premature termination, contract closure involves documenting actual work performed as well as work not performed, the circumstances of termination, and the updating of contract records.

Contracts are scrutinized to verify that all conditions have been met. Evidence is reviewed that the deliverables of the contract have been successfully delivered. Any unaccounted variations and deviations are noted for follow-up action.

Follow-up on activities and other residual aspects of contracts, such as warranties and remedies, are noted and addressed as a part of component closure.

.2 Supplier Performance Review

The program management team needs to be aware that this will possibly be the last opportunity for recourse to address performance deficiencies with suppliers.

.3 Budget Allocation Reconciliation

It is typical for there to be variations in categorization, allocation, and summarization between program and program component plans, contracts, and organizational charts of account, making it difficult to relate expenditure between different program and organization components.

Where necessary, differences should be cross-referenced and explained with notes to show how they relate. This is especially important as the organizational financial reporting and auditing cycles are often not synchronized with contract closure events. While this process affects contracts, it is performed by the program's financial organization.

12.4.3 Close Program Procurements: Outputs

.1 Closed Contracts

All contract documentation is transferred to a secure archive. Many countries have legislation that stipulates how long contract documentation must be kept. In any event, documentation should be available for as long as the contract itself stipulates (for example, in residual clauses).

All appropriate suppliers, program components, and stakeholders must be informed that a contract is no longer in force to ensure that no new procurements are made against the contract.

.2 Procurement Performance Reports

The results of contract performance reviews are documented and distributed to appropriate stakeholders. Items that require follow up are recorded in the program issues register.

Updates to the organization's program assets are noted (e.g., evaluation criteria, qualified seller lists, templates, contractual terms and conditions etc.) to benefit and/or improve the program procurement process for future use. In other words, these updates are the lessons learned specific to program procurement management.

.3 Closed Budget Allocation

Budget allocations to closed contracts are finalized and closed when all approved payment requests have been processed. Any remaining budget allocations may be returned to the overall program budget, in accordance with the program cost management plan.

CHAPTER 13

PROGRAM FINANCIAL MANAGEMENT

Program Financial Management includes all of the processes involved in identifying the program's financial sources and resources, integrating the budgets of the individual program components, developing the overall budget for the program, and controlling costs throughout the life cycle of both the component and program. Figure 13-1 shows the processes involved in the effort and Figure 13-2 shows the primary data flow through the processes.

The processes are:

13.1 Establish Program Financial Framework—Identifying the overall financial environment for the program and pinpointing the funds that are available according to identified milestones.

13.2 Develop Program Financial Plan—Creating the processes for developing and managing the program budget and the payment schedules to the components.

13.3 Estimate Program Costs—Developing the initial program cost estimates that will be presented to the decision makers for approval and further funding.

13.4 Budget Program Costs—Developing the detailed budgets for the program and for the components based on the estimates provided by the components.

13.5 Monitor and Control Program Financials—Influencing the factors that create cost variances, controlling those variances at the program level, and closing out the program and component finances.

These processes interact with each other, with processes in other Knowledge Areas, and with processes at the component level, which are described in *A Guide to the Project Management Body of Knowledge (PMBOK® Guide) – Fourth Edition*.

Since programs are typically very high in cost compared to projects, program financial management is concerned with the overall financial management of the program rather than managing individual component costs.

Since programs by definition are comprised of multiple components, program budgets must include the costs for each individual component as well as monies to pay for the resources and facilities to manage the program itself. Program costs can run into many millions or billions of dollars, euros, or other currencies. A different financial structure and oversight is often imposed on programs because of their inherently higher costs. Unlike components, where the project manager is generally not assigned until after the component has been approved, program managers are often involved in the program from the initial pre-approval stages all the way through to program completion.

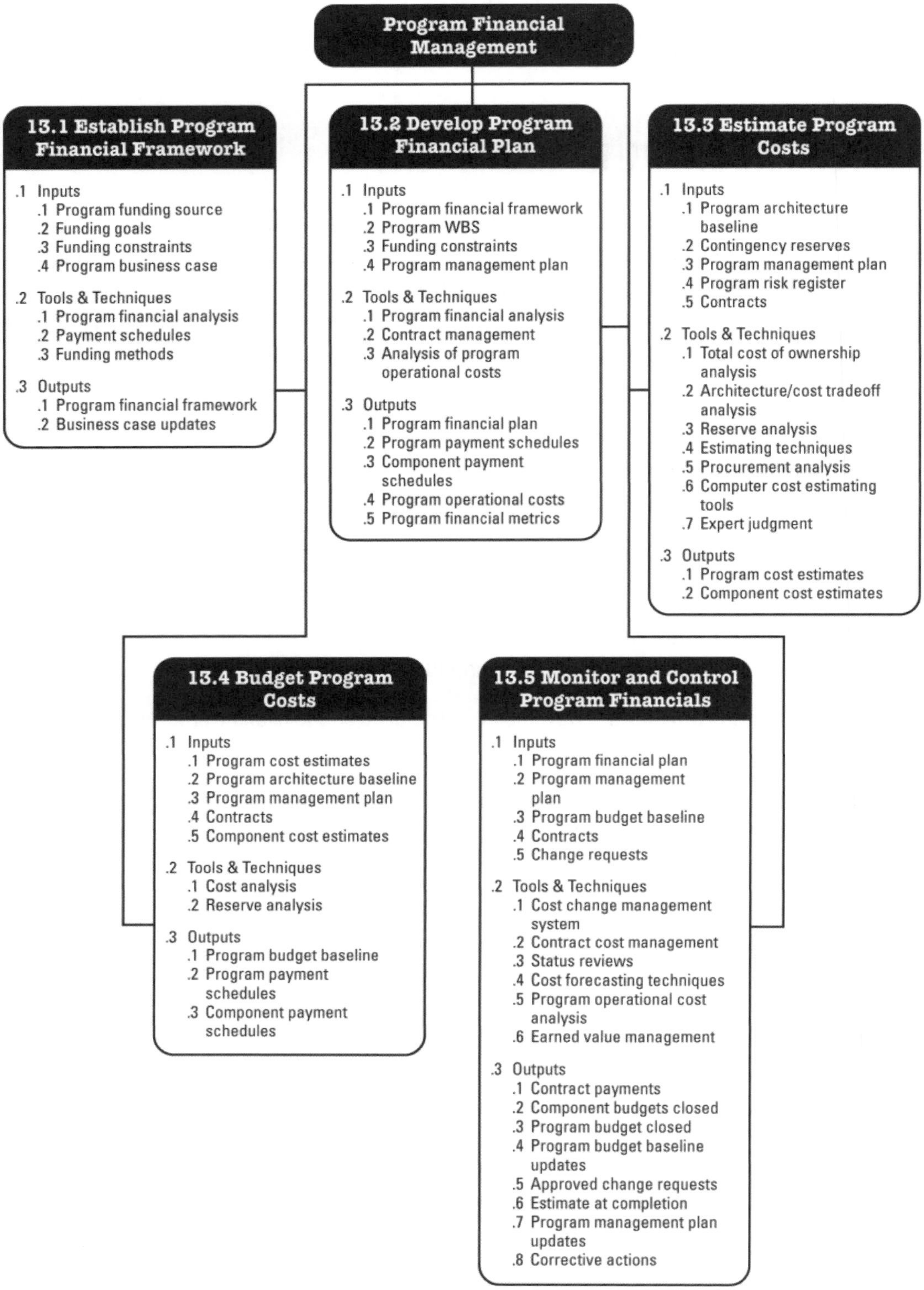

Program Financial Management

13.1 Establish Program Financial Framework

.1 Inputs
  .1 Program funding source
  .2 Funding goals
  .3 Funding constraints
  .4 Program business case

.2 Tools & Techniques
  .1 Program financial analysis
  .2 Payment schedules
  .3 Funding methods

.3 Outputs
  .1 Program financial framework
  .2 Business case updates

13.2 Develop Program Financial Plan

.1 Inputs
  .1 Program financial framework
  .2 Program WBS
  .3 Funding constraints
  .4 Program management plan

.2 Tools & Techniques
  .1 Program financial analysis
  .2 Contract management
  .3 Analysis of program operational costs

.3 Outputs
  .1 Program financial plan
  .2 Program payment schedules
  .3 Component payment schedules
  .4 Program operational costs
  .5 Program financial metrics

13.3 Estimate Program Costs

.1 Inputs
  .1 Program architecture baseline
  .2 Contingency reserves
  .3 Program management plan
  .4 Program risk register
  .5 Contracts

.2 Tools & Techniques
  .1 Total cost of ownership analysis
  .2 Architecture/cost tradeoff analysis
  .3 Reserve analysis
  .4 Estimating techniques
  .5 Procurement analysis
  .6 Computer cost estimating tools
  .7 Expert judgment

.3 Outputs
  .1 Program cost estimates
  .2 Component cost estimates

13.4 Budget Program Costs

.1 Inputs
  .1 Program cost estimates
  .2 Program architecture baseline
  .3 Program management plan
  .4 Contracts
  .5 Component cost estimates

.2 Tools & Techniques
  .1 Cost analysis
  .2 Reserve analysis

.3 Outputs
  .1 Program budget baseline
  .2 Program payment schedules
  .3 Component payment schedules

13.5 Monitor and Control Program Financials

.1 Inputs
  .1 Program financial plan
  .2 Program management plan
  .3 Program budget baseline
  .4 Contracts
  .5 Change requests

.2 Tools & Techniques
  .1 Cost change management system
  .2 Contract cost management
  .3 Status reviews
  .4 Cost forecasting techniques
  .5 Program operational cost analysis
  .6 Earned value management

.3 Outputs
  .1 Contract payments
  .2 Component budgets closed
  .3 Program budget closed
  .4 Program budget baseline updates
  .5 Approved change requests
  .6 Estimate at completion
  .7 Program management plan updates
  .8 Corrective actions

Figure 13-1. Program Financial Management Overview

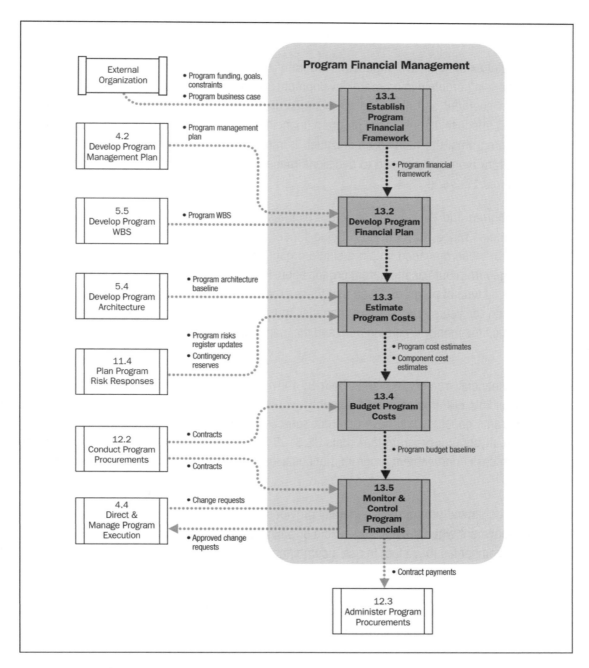

Figure 13-2. Program Financial Management Data Flow Diagram

13.1 Establish Program Financial Framework

To a much greater extent than in components, program costs occur earlier, often years earlier, than benefits. The core of the financing problem in program development is to obtain funds to bridge the gap between paying out monies for development and obtaining the benefits of the programs. Covering this large negative cash balance in the most effective manner is the program financing problem. Because of the large amount of money involved in most programs, the funding organization is rarely a passive partner but instead has significant inputs to the program management and to decisions made by both the technical leads and by the program manager. See Figures 13-3 and 13-4.

The type of program and the funding structure dictates the financial environment to which the program exists. Funding models range from (a) those being funded entirely within a single organization (as is usual for IT programs), (b) those managed within a single organization but funded separately, or (c) those entirely funded and managed from outside the parent organization. Public works programs such as highways, bridges, or dams are a special type of program. Given that these programs use public money, are often extremely large in cost, and can run for years, the program manager must have a thorough understanding of the financial environment in which the money is coming from and the mandatory financial audits that are part of government contracting.

The program financial framework varies both by the type of program, for example large construction, aerospace, shipbuilding, ERP implementations, public works, etc., but also by the size of the program. Larger, longer-scale programs generally will have different sources of funding than smaller, shorter-term programs. An eight year long skyscraper program that costs US $100 million will require a different financial framework than an internal process improvement program that costs less than US $2 million and will be completed within one year.

Funding for large capital programs is generally provided by external sources, such as bank loans against the promise of repayment when the building is sold or payment out of future income from leases. For smaller capital programs, companies may elect to use a combination of retained earnings, find equity partners in the financing, issue bonds, or sell stocks to the financial markets in order to generate sufficient funds. Common sources of funding in the United States for large construction components include real estate investment trusts (REITs), pension funds, and insurance companies. For similar-size components in other countries, government-backed funding may be made available, making the government an investor and/or a part owner of the end result.

Figure 13-3. Establish Program Financial Framework Inputs, Tools & Techniques, and Outputs

---

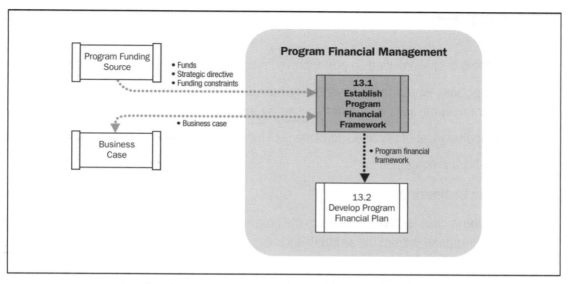

Figure 13-4. Establish Program Financial Framework Data Flow Diagram

13.1.1 Establish Program Financial Framework: Inputs

The program financial framework is established at the beginning of the program and is performed in conjunction with the financing organization. Inputs to the process include identification of the major funding source (or sources), funding goals, constraints, and the business case for the program.

.1 Program Funding Source

Programs have a variety of potential funding sources depending on the program's type, size and complexity; whether it is international or local; and whether it is entirely internally funded or requires outside funding sources.

.2 Funding Goals

The funding organization can have different goals than the program manager. The funding organization may wish to maintain a steady outflow of funds on a consistent basis; it may wish to obtain revenue from the program as quickly as possible; it may wish to delay payments as long as possible; or have other specific financial goals. The program manager must identify and be cognizant of the funding organization's goals so that they can be accommodated by the program's financial structure.

.3 Funding Constraints

Funding constraints may include:

- Payment accepted only in the local currency,

- Percentage of the contract is held as retainage (typically 5% in the construction industry),

- Funding is only available on an annual or semiannual basis as investments are redeemed,

- Funding cannot proceed until the government bonds paying for the program have been created and sold,

- Funding is only provided on pre-approved milestones after going through an approval process,

- Compulsory employment for some specified percentage of semi-skilled and unskilled local labor under the sons-of-the-soil policies by the local government,

- Compulsory use of specified percentage of indigenously produced products in the program, and

- Buy-back arrangements.

.4 Program Business Case

The business case is developed before the program is approved. It is obtained from the client, the funding organization, or from the program sponsor.

13.1.2 Establish Program Financial Framework: Tools and Techniques

.1 Program Financial Analysis

Program financial analysis involves identifying sources and schedules of funding, the program's financial environmental factors, trends in labor and materials costs and availability, and contract costs. It also involves performing design/cost tradeoffs and other finance-related analysis as required. For international development programs this analysis can be complex.

The analysis should provide sufficient information, which is necessary for approving the program and making decisions on design trade-offs. These analyses might include benefit-cost analysis (BCA), return on investment (ROI), net present value (NPV), trend analysis, and other financial tools as required.

.2 Payment Schedules

These identify the schedules and milestone points at which payments are made to contractors. A financial framework is essential for expending program funds efficiently. This is because program funds are spent well in advance of any revenue or benefits realization.

.3 Funding Methods

Programs may be funded by a variety of methods, depending on the factors identified earlier. The program manager considers the method of funding when managing program costs and expenditures. Some funding methods include:

- Being funded entirely internally through retained earnings or by the issuance of debt or the sale of stock,

- Being funded by government entities through tax monies collected or by the sale of government bonds,

- Being funded by external funding organizations such as a consortium of banks, financial institutions, or even venture capital funds,

- Obtaining mortgages for smaller construction programs, or

- Receiving loans to bridge temporary shortfalls in funding.

13.1.3 Establish Program Financial Framework: Outputs

.1 Program Financial Framework

The program's financial framework is the plan for coordinating what funding is available, under what constraints it is available, and how the money is paid out. The financial framework defines and describes the program funding flows in such a way that the money is spent as efficiently and with the least waste possible.

.2 Business Case Updates

During the analysis of the overall financial framework, changes may be identified that impact the original business case justifying the program. Based on these changes, the business case is modified with full involvement of the decision-makers.

13.2 Develop Program Financial Plan

Developing the program financial plan is a difficult part of initiating a program. A program may have multiple sources of funding, is typically of long duration, may have multiple contractors (each with its own payment schedule), and can be international in development work. The program financial plan must take into account items such as risk reserves, potential cash flow problems, international exchange rate fluctuations, future interest rate increases or decreases, local laws regarding finances, trends in material costs, contract incentive and penalty clauses, and extent of retainage of contractor payments, etc. (Figure 13-5).

For programs that are funded internally, either out of retained earnings, through bank loans or the sale of bonds, the program manager must consider scheduled contract payments, inflation, the factors listed above, and other environmental factors.

Inputs	Tools & Techniques	Outputs
.1 Program financial framework .2 Program WBS .3 Funding constraints .4 Program management plan	.1 Program financial analysis .2 Contract management .3 Analysis of program operational costs	.1 Program financial plan .2 Program payment schedules .3 Component payment schedules .4 Program operational costs .5 Program financial metrics

Figure 13-5. Develop Program Financial Plan: Inputs, Tools & Techniques, and Outputs

There are so many environmental factors outside of the program manager's control that may lead to significant financial changes that are outside of the original business case. This can include items such as unforeseen reversals of international currencies or unexpected increases in material costs. While some items can be predicted, at least in trend, unexpected changes can have deleterious impacts on a program's finances.

For example, in the construction industry, from 2006 to 2007, the cost of both concrete and steel rebar jumped an unexpected 25% due to higher-than-expected demand from Asian countries. Program managers who had not mitigated their cost risk by buying futures in these items or purchasing insurance found themselves having to deal with higher costs than their planned funding could provide. In order to deal with unexpected financial crises like these, part of the financial plan must include processes for requesting additional funding as needed.

Contractors and subcontractors have limited financing options. This is especially true in the construction industry where subcontractors are usually smaller than the prime contractor and have limited access to capital during the construction phase. The program manager must take this into consideration when developing the payment schedule. In the drive to lower costs, even the retainage held back on construction contracts may place a poorly financed subcontractor under financial pressure and may impact the construction schedule.

In many programs, regardless of industry type, the cash flow for contractors resembles the graph in Figure 13-6 showing the time lag between money expended by the contractor and reimbursement from the program.

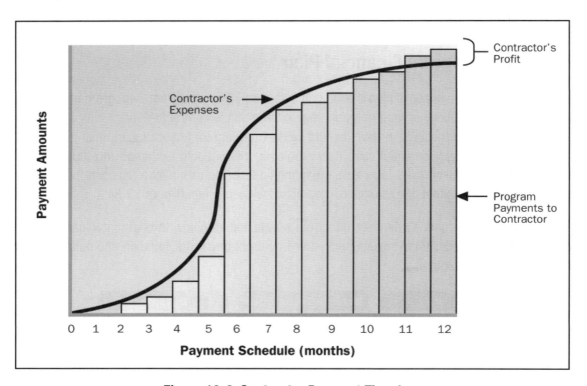

Figure 13-6. Contractor Payment Time Lag

This is of particular importance with international components. Subcontractors may have limited access to funds and credit in their part of the world than their prime contractor counterparts.

For programs that are funded through government agencies, the financial plan must take into account the fact that funding may be provided on an annual basis rather than funded entirely at the beginning of the program. A funding schedule must be considered when developing the overall financial plan. Figure 13-7 shows the data flow diagram for this process.

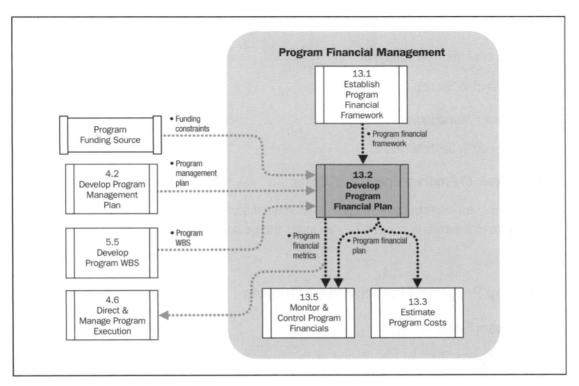

Figure 13-7. Develop Program Financial Plan Data Flow Diagram

13.2.1 Develop Program Financial Plan: Inputs

.1 Program Financial Framework

Described in Section 13.1.3.1.

.2 Program WBS

Described in Section 5.5.3.1.

.3 Funding Constraints

Programs can be long-term and costly. Obtaining 100% of the funding upfront is rare. In most cases, funding is released at program milestones or on a time basis such as annually. The program's financial plan must identify the milestones and the payment schedules tied to them.

.4 Program Management Plan

Described in Section 4.2.3.1.

13.2.2 Develop Program Financial Plan: Tools and Techniques

.1　Program Financial Analysis

Described in Section 13.1.2.1.

.2　Contract Management

Described in Section 12.3.2.

.3　Analysis of Program Operational Costs

The program infrastructure required to manage the program should be identified and incorporated into the overall baseline budget. This includes the personnel, resources, and program management office.

13.2.3 Develop Program Financial Plan: Outputs

.1　Program Financial Plan

The program financial plan is part of the program management plan and documents all of the program's financial aspects: funding schedules and milestones, baseline budget, contract payments and schedules, financial reporting processes and mechanisms, and the financial metrics.

.2　Program Payment Schedules

The program payment schedules identify the schedules and milestone points where funding is received by the funding organization.

.3　Component Payment Schedules

Described in Section 13.1.2.2.

.4　Program Operational Costs

These identify the operational and infrastructure costs associated with managing the program.

.5　Program Financial Metrics

These are the detailed metrics by which the program's benefits are measured. As changes to cost and scope occur during the life of the program, these metrics are measured against the initial metrics used to approve the program. Decisions to continue the program, to cancel it, or to modify it are based on the results.

13.3 Estimate Program Costs

Program costing is done in multiple stages with approval gates between each stage. These gates are necessary to allow full control and governance over the large program budgets. The most accurate estimates can be developed for short-term programs in which labor is the most significant cost driver. The least accurate estimates will be those for long term programs in which the primary cost drivers are materials and equipment. See Figures 13-8 and 13-9.

A typical example is the development of a skyscraper. An organization develops the initial idea for a new high-rise building, has some preliminary architectural design done and a model created. Using the model and detailed financial analysis of future cash flows and returns, the building is proposed to a funding organization which approves the concept and funds it. The funding is provided in stages for purchasing land and performing regulatory-defined studies, detailed architectural design, engineering design, construction, and transition.

Another example is estimating the cost of a new highway bridge across a bay in the early program phases. An initial architecture/cost analysis is performed for alternative designs, such as a truss bridge versus a suspension bridge. Once the initial architecture is determined, a preliminary estimate is made based on the conceptual design. When the design is completed and the engineering details are defined, a more detailed estimate is developed. Once the specifications are complete, the baseline engineering estimates are created and the detailed material costs are determined.

Programs can be so complex that estimating cannot be done without the involvement of contractors who have the knowledge required to design and build the end product. When the program is a new chemical processing plant, a new commercial airplane, or a new automobile model, contractors may be involved in the estimating early in the analysis cycle to provide detailed knowledge that the end user or the prime contractor may not possess.

Typically, an initial order-of-magnitude estimate is performed to allow the financial decision-makers to decide if the program should be funded. If the initial estimates are within the financial boundaries, a more detailed estimate is performed, often after doing a requirements collection and assessment. The requirements effort may involve an internal assessment or it may involve multiple contractors. The goal is to develop the architecture to a level sufficient to determine if the program is feasible within the cost expectations of the funding organization.

Once the second level of assessment has been performed and the program is approved for the next stage, detailed estimates are obtained from each of the contractors or groups involved in the program. These processes are often heavily involved with the procurement and contracting processes. At this point, the technical details are often sufficiently developed to allow reasonable cost estimates to be made by each group or contractor. For risky, advanced technology programs, a significant amount of reserve should be set aside so that areas of technical risk can be provided with additional funding as issues arise.

A critical determination prior to any estimating being done is to define the cost goal. Will the estimates minimize the cost of developing the end product, or will the estimates minimize the total cost of ownership (TCO)? The solution may be different for these two goals. Part of the TCO analysis includes future known upgrades, replacements, or refurbishments. For example, for a chemical processing plant, the cost of future refurbishments is a factor in both the initial design as well as the TCO analysis. For a new highway construction program, the cost of regular maintenance of the road and eventual replacement after its design life is exceeded are factors in the TCO analysis.

Section 13.2 on Develop Program Financial Plan, stated that many program environmental factors are outside of the program manager's control, such as currency fluctuations and materials costs. Although the program may have material costs specified in contracts, when there are extreme changes in the costs there is no guarantee that the vendor can satisfy the contract without going out of business. For programs that require significant materials purchases, the possibility of future changes in material prices should be taken into account when estimating overall costs. Preparations for mitigating underestimates should be part of the overall estimation process.

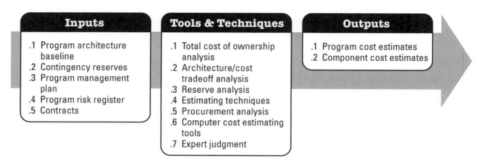

Figure 13-8. Estimate Program Costs Inputs, Tools & Techniques, and Outputs

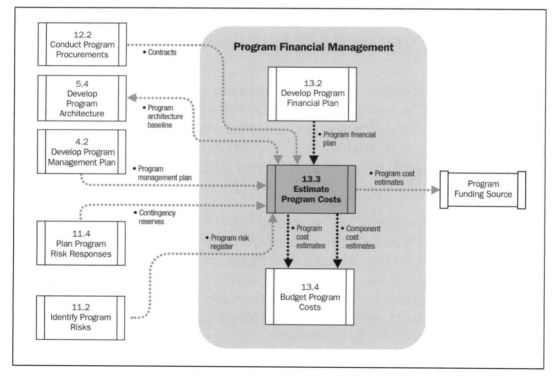

Figure 13-9. Estimate Program Costs Data Flow Diagram

13.3.1 Estimate Program Costs: Inputs

.1 Program Architecture Baseline

Described in Section 5.4.3.1.

.2 Contingency Reserves

Contingency reserves are monies set aside to pay for unexpected changes to the requirements or program environmental factors and to pay for anticipated risks.

.3 Program Management Plan

Described in Section 4.2.3.1.

.4 Program Risk Register

Described in Section 11.2.3.1.

.5 Contracts

The specific types of contracts as well as their amount and payment schedules are an input to estimating the program costs.

13.3.2 Estimate Program Costs: Tools and Techniques

.1 Total Cost of Ownership Analysis

Analysis of the total cost of ownership allows the most cost-effective design to be created for the life of the final product. This includes not only the development and implementation costs, but the on-going costs of maintenance and eventual decommissioning. Methods may include value engineering (VE), value analysis (VA), or other approaches.

.2 Architecture/Cost Tradeoff Analysis

Different architectures can have significantly different cost implications. When different solutions exist, tradeoff analysis is performed to compare different architectural solutions and their cost implications.

.3 Reserve Analysis

It is important to conduct an analysis of the reserve amount needed to respond to unexpected changes in the program scope or environmental factors as well as to recover from risks that occur.

.4 Estimating Techniques

Estimating techniques for each component within the program should follow the techniques outlined in the *A Guide to the Project Management Body of Knowledge* – Fourth Edition. Estimating techniques for the program components outside of the individual components can include historical estimating techniques from previous similar programs, updated appropriately, or analysis of the resource needs to manage the program.

.5 Procurement Analysis

Procurement analysis evaluates the cost of each individual component within the program, based on the type of contract, payment schedule, material purchases, and other cost factors as well as the costs of the procurement process itself.

.6 Computer Cost Estimating Tools

Computer tools can be highly useful in determining the program's current cost of materials and labor. Where programs involve multiple components and contractors, it is important that the major contractors utilize the same, or compatible, tools. Compatibility eliminates errors created by multiple reporting formats and the tools use of data of different vintages. Incompatibility of software tools can create significant problems during the development phase.

.7 Expert Judgment

Software tools can accurately sum up a bill of materials based on a design and create the cost of the materials. However, software tools are generally not sufficient to accurately estimate the total cost of the complex large scale program. According to the American Association of Cost Engineers (AACE), cost engineering is defined as that area of engineering practice, where engineering judgment and experience are utilized in the application of scientific principles and techniques to the problem of cost estimation, cost control, and profitability.

13.3.3 Estimate Program Costs: Outputs

.1 Program Cost Estimates

The overall cost estimates for the program is the primary output of the Estimate Program Costs process. The cost estimate occurs in stages based on the level of detail available at the time of the estimate. At the point where detailed engineering specifications are completed, the program costs can be baselined and the program manager should manage to that baseline.

.2 Component Cost Estimates

Another output of this process is the cost estimates for the individual components within the program. Component costs are baselined and become the budget for that particular component. If the component is being performed by a contractor, this cost is written into the contract.

13.4 Budget Program Costs

Developing the program's budget involves compiling all available financial information and listing all income and payment schedules in sufficient detail so that the program's costs can be tracked. For most programs, the details of every expense are not known in the early planning phases of the program. As the program develops, the budget becomes increasingly detailed and refined (Figures 13-10 and 13-11).

The majority of the program's costs is traceable to the individual components within the program and is not due to the overhead in managing the program. When contractors are involved, the details of the budget come from the contracts. The program overhead is added to the initial budget figure before a baseline budget can be prepared.

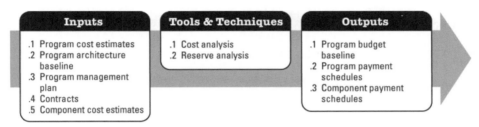

Figure 13-10. Budget Program Costs Inputs, Tools & Techniques, and Outputs

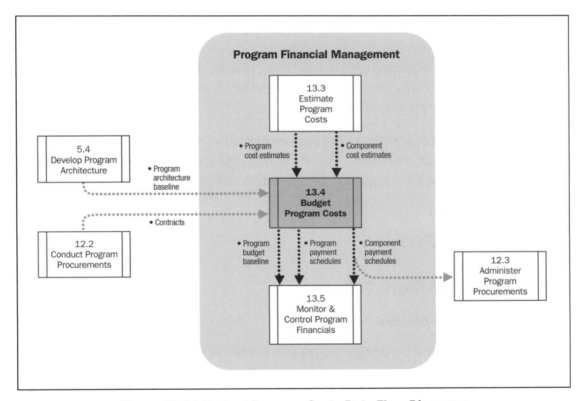

Figure 13-11. Budget Program Costs Data Flow Diagrams

13.4.1 Budget Program Costs: Inputs

.1 Program Cost Estimates

Described in Section 13.3.3.1.

.2 Program Architecture Baseline

Described in Section 5.4.3.1.

.3 Program Management Plan

Described in Section 4.3.1.1.

.4 Contracts

For those programs which utilize contractors, this input is described in Section 12.2.3.6.

.5 Component Cost Estimates

Described in Section 13.3.3.2.

13.4.2 Budget Program Costs: Tools and Techniques

.1 Cost Analysis

A primary tool for developing the program budget is an analysis of each program component's cost structure: funding amounts, schedules, and constraints; contract amounts, payment schedules, and constraints; and program-associated overhead.

The result of the cost analysis is a thorough understanding of the money flow through the program: how and when the funds are received from the funding organization and where and how payments are made to the contractors and to support the program management infrastructure.

.2 Reserve Analysis

Described in Section 13.3.2.3.

13.4.3 Budget Program Costs: Outputs

.1 Program Budget Baseline

The primary output of the budgeting process is the overall program budget highlighting the flow of monies into and out of the program. Once baselined, the budget becomes the primary financial target that the program is measured against.

.2 Program Payment Schedules

Described in Section 13.2.3.2.

.3 Component Payment Schedules

The component payment schedules show how and when contractors will be paid in accordance with the contract provisions.

13.5 Monitor and Control Program Financials

Once the program has received initial funding and has started paying expenses, the financial effort moves into tracking, monitoring, and controlling the program's funds and expenditures (Figures 13-12 and 13-13). This is managed by the program manager with oversight by the governance group and by the auditors.

Monitoring the program's finances and controlling expenditures within budget are critical aspects of ensuring the program meets the goals of the funding agency or of the higher organization. A program whose costs exceed the planned budget may no longer satisfy the business case used to justify it and may be subject to cancellation. Even minor over-runs are subject to audit, governance oversight, and must be justified.

There are extensive examples in the literature of programs whose costs ran far out of control. The frequency and financial consequences are such that strong governance and oversight are established.

There are a number of causes for program cost overruns. Organizations mature in program management are more adept at keeping costs under control than those with little project management experience. In the area of public works, a primary cause of cost overruns is the impact of stakeholders who wish to stop or significantly change the program after it has started due to its perceived negative impact. These actions may tie up the program development, sometimes for years, in litigation to cancel the program. Finally, industries developing highly risky advanced technology products face cost over-runs due to the inherent technical risks.

Monitoring and controlling includes:

- Identifying factors that create changes to the financial baseline,
- Monitoring the environmental factors for potential impacts,
- Managing changes when they occur,
- Monitoring contract expenditures to ensure funds are disbursed in accordance with the contracts,
- Identifying impacts to the program components from overruns or underruns,
- Communicating changes to the financial baseline to the governance groups and to the auditors, and
- Managing the expenditure of the program infrastructure to ensure costs are within expected parameters.

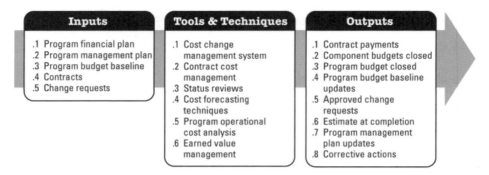

Figure 13-12. Monitor and Control Program Financials Inputs, Tools & Techniques, and Outputs

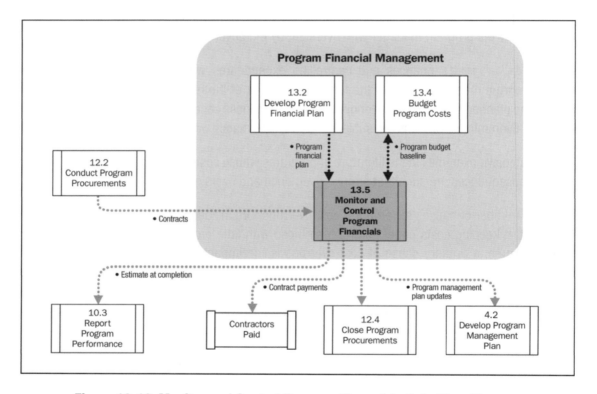

Figure 13-13. Monitor and Control Program Financials Data Flow Diagram

13.5.1 Monitor and Control Program Financials: Inputs

.1 Program Financial Plan

Described in Section 13.2.3.1.

.2 Program Management Plan

Described in Section 4.2.3.1.

.3 Program Budget Baseline

Described in Section 13.4.3.1.

.4 Contracts

Described in Section 12.2.3.6.

.5 Change Requests

Requested changes can come from any component within the program or from outside the program by the funding organization or other groups. All changes are assessed for financial impact to the components and to the overall program.

13.5.2 Monitor and Control Program Financials: Tools and Techniques

.1 Cost Change Management System

The cost change management system defines the procedures by which the financial baseline will be analyzed and changed in response to approved changes. It analyzes the impacts to individual components of the program and to the overall program.

.2 Contract Cost Management

Described in Section 12.3.2.

.3 Status Reviews

Component financial expenditures are reviewed on a regular basis to ensure compliance with contracts and with the baseline in both cost and schedule.

.4 Cost Forecasting Techniques

Forecasting techniques such as estimates to complete (ETC) and estimate at completion (EAC) are performed on a regular basis to predict future cost performance against the baseline and to predict the final program costs.

.5 Program Operational Cost Analysis

In addition to the costs associated with each component within the program, there are costs associated with the program management and infrastructure. These are also monitored and controlled.

.6 Earned Value Management

Earned value management (EVM) is a basic approach to monitoring program progress. It is used for each component in the program and for the overall program. The EVM tools and techniques should be compatible between the program and the individual components so that component progress can be readily measured by the program.

13.5.3 Monitor and Control Program Financials: Outputs

.1 Contract Payments

Contract payments are made in accordance with the contracts, with the financial infrastructure of the program, and with the status of the contract deliverables.

.2 Component Budgets Closed

As each individual component completes its work, the budget for that component is closed within the overall program budget.

.3 Program Budget Closed

As the program completes, the program budget is closed and the final financial reports are communicated in accordance with the stakeholder management plan. Any unspent monies are returned to the funding organization.

.4 Program Budget Baseline Updates

As changes are approved that have significant cost impacts, the program's budget baseline is updated accordingly and the budget is re-baselined.

.5 Approved Change Requests

Approved changes to either the program or to an individual component are incorporated into the appropriate budget.

.6 Estimate at Completion

New financial forecasts for the program are prepared on a regular basis and communicated in accordance with the stakeholder management plan.

.7 Program Management Plan Updates

Updates to the program management plan from the financial monitoring and control are made aappropriate.

.8 Corrective Actions

Corrective actions are taken as required in response to unanticipated changes or in response to problems that have arisen.

CHAPTER 14

PROGRAM STAKEHOLDER MANAGEMENT

The Program Stakeholder Management Knowledge Area defines program stakeholders as individuals and organizations whose interests may be affected by the program outcomes, either positively or negatively. These stakeholders play a critical role in the success of any program. Stakeholders of a program can be internal or external to the organization. Internal stakeholders cover all levels of the organization's hierarchy. Many stakeholders provide valuable inputs and also have the ability to influence programs — they can either help or hinder depending on the perceived benefits or threats. The program manager must understand the stakeholders and the way they may exert their influence, and their source of power.

Program stakeholder management identifies how the program will affect stakeholders (e.g., the organization's culture, the local population, current major issues, resistance or barriers to change) and then develops a communication strategy to engage the affected stakeholders, manage their expectations, and manage acceptance of the objectives of the program.

Program stakeholder management extends beyond project stakeholder management and considers additional levels of stakeholders resulting from broader interdependencies among projects, the larger scope, and impacts beyond the executing organization. A stakeholder management plan, combined with the communication plan, should ensure an active exchange of accurate, consistent, and timely information that reaches all relevant stakeholders. Communication planning focuses on the proactive and targeted development and exchange of key messages, and engages key stakeholders at the right time and in the right manner. Refer to Plan Communication process under the Program Communication Management Knowledge Area (Section 10.1).

Stakeholder management is an important factor in implementing successful organizational change. In this context, program plans should clearly show an understanding of and integration with generally accepted methods of organizational change management. This includes identifying the key individuals who have an interest in or will be affected by the changes and ensuring they are aware of, supportive of, and part of the change process. To facilitate the change process, the program manager must communicate to stakeholders a clear vision of the need for change, as well as the initiative's specific objectives and the resources required. The program manager must utilize strong leadership skills to set clear goals, assess readiness for change, plan for the change, provide resources/support, monitor the change, obtain and evaluate feedback from those affected by the change, and manage issues with people who are not fully embracing the change.

Figure 14-1 provides an overview of the Program Stakeholder Management processes as follows:

> **14.1 Plan Program Stakeholder Management**—Plan Stakeholder Management covers planning how stakeholders will be identified, analyzed, engaged, and managed throughout the life of the program.

14.2 Identify Program Stakeholders—Identify Program Stakeholders addresses the systematic identification and analysis of program stakeholders and creates the stakeholder register.

14.3 Engage Program Stakeholders—The process of engaging Program Stakeholders is where the program management team ensures that stakeholders are involved in the program.

14.4 Manage Program Stakeholder Expectations—Manage Program Stakeholder Expectations is the process of managing communications to satisfy the requirements of, and resolve issues with, program stakeholders.

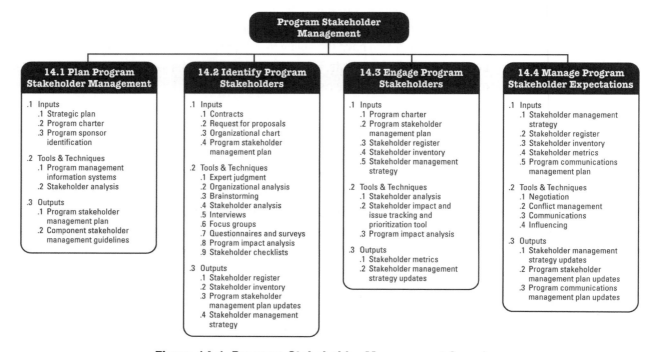

Figure 14-1. Program Stakeholder Management Overview

14.1 Plan Program Stakeholder Management

Plan Program Stakeholder Management process covers planning how stakeholders will be identified, analyzed, engaged, and managed throughout the life of the program. It outlines how the activities, tools and techniques, and resources are to be used. In this process the primary stakeholders are program sponsor, Governance Board, and the key stakeholders. Program stakeholder management revolves around these primary stakeholders.

This process brings out the program stakeholder management plan which contains detailed plans on how effective stakeholder management is realized. This process also comes out with component stakeholder management guidelines, which provides insights on how the stakeholders of various components of a program are managed.

Figure 14-2 refers to the input, tools and techniques, and outputs required to produce the necessary output in this process. These are described in detail in the following sections. Figure 14-3 shows the data flow through the processes.

Figure 14-2. Plan Program Stakeholder Management: Inputs, Tools & Techniques, and Outputs

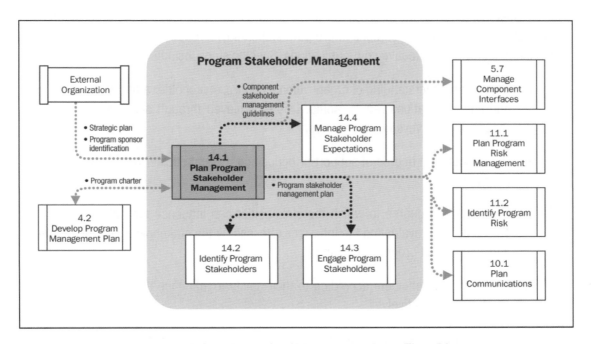

Figure 14-3. Plan Stakeholder Management Data Flow Diagram

14.1.1 Plan Program Stakeholder Management: Inputs

.1 Strategic Plan

The strategic plan provides insight into the larger organizational or political environment and assists in identifying the scope of stakeholder management.

.2 Program Charter

Described in Section 4.1.2.

.3 Program Sponsor Identification

The program sponsor is one of the primary stakeholders whose interests should be considered in planning stakeholder management.

14.1.2 Plan Program Stakeholder Management: Tools and Techniques

.1 Program Management Information Systems

Described in Section 4.2.2.1.

.2 Stakeholder Analysis

In stakeholder analysis, the program team gains an understanding of the organization culture as well as the needs and expectations of program stakeholders. A detailed plan is developed to engage stakeholders through effective communications. Specific steps include:

1. Gaining an understanding of organizational culture, stakeholder attitudes toward the program, and communications requirements. This is achieved through stakeholder interviews, focus groups, and surveys/questionnaires.

2. Determining the degree of support or opposition the stakeholder has for the objectives of the program.

3. Evaluating the degree to which the stakeholder can influence the outcome of the program. This is done by evaluating the interest expressed by the stakeholder and the degree to which they can impact program outcomes.

4. Prioritizing stakeholders according to their ability to influence the program outcomes, either positively or negatively.

5. Developing a stakeholder communications strategy to define the methods and frequency of communication with stakeholders.

6. Developing the stakeholder register to include a summary of stakeholder analysis results including the degree of stakeholder influence, the likely disposition towards the program and the impact of the program on the stakeholder.

7. Updating the program stakeholder management plan, as required, to refine the strategies for managing stakeholders and program communications.

8. Determining how receptive the stakeholder is to communications from the program.

14.1.3 Plan Program Stakeholder Management: Outputs

.1 Program Stakeholder Management Plan

The program stakeholder management plan documents how stakeholders will be identified, analyzed, engaged, and managed throughout the life of the program. It contains the activities, tools and techniques, and resources to be used.

.2 Component Stakeholder Management Guidelines

The guidelines for project-level stakeholder management should be provided to the individual projects or groups of projects under the program.

14.2 Identify Program Stakeholders

Identify Program Stakeholders addresses the systematic identification and analysis of the program stakeholders and creates the stakeholder register which lists the various internal and external stakeholders who may be impacted by the program directly or indirectly. This register serves as the primary input for the distribution of program reports and other communications.

This process also identifies the impacts, either positive or negative, on the stakeholders and determines approaches for managing these relationships. At the end of this process, the program stakeholder management plan is updated with the changes or additional outputs that come as a result of this process.

This process uses a technique which analyzes the stakeholders and maps them into various categories. Stakeholders vary in their interest in a program. Some simply require information for planning purposes, while others want to directly influence the objectives and execution of the program. Mapping is useful in determining:

- Type of stakeholder against an area of interest,
- Type of interaction required based on the stakeholder's influence versus the level of importance of the stakeholder,
- Ability of a stakeholder to influence versus the impact that the program will have on the stakeholder, and
- Type of stakeholder who defines the command, control loops, and communication mechanisms.

Figure 14-4 refers to the inputs, tools and techniques, and outputs required to produce the necessary output in this process. These are described in details in the following sections. Figure 14-5 shows the data flow through the processes.

Figure 14-4. Identify Program Stakeholders: Inputs, Tools & Techniques, and Outputs

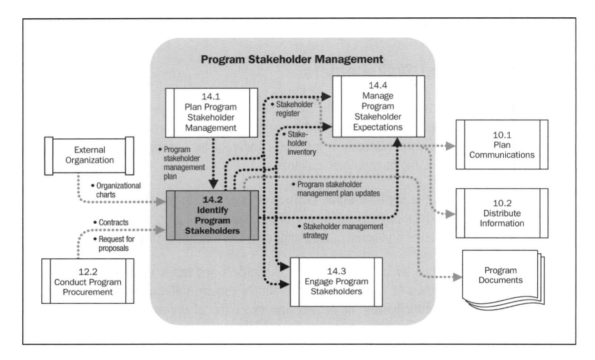

Figure 14-5. Identify Program Stakeholders Data Flow Diagram

14.2.1 Identify Program Stakeholders: Inputs

.1 Contracts

Contracts are agreements between two or more persons (individuals, businesses, organizations, or government agencies). It includes the contract of award for the program itself as well as various project-related contracts, being part of the program and any other third party contracts under which parts of the programs and or projects were subcontracted to other vendors. Refer to Section 12.2.3.6 for more details.

.2 Request for Proposals

The request for proposal will typically include the identification of contracted program sponsor(s) and may mandate individuals or organizations that must be treated as stakeholders. Refer to Section 12.2.3.3 for more details.

.3 Organizational Chart

It includes all the organizational charts of various different organizations impacted directly or indirectly as a result of the program like suppliers, government agencies, NGOs, subcontractors, and marketing agencies, etc.

.4 Program Stakeholder Management Plan

The program stakeholder management plan documents how stakeholders will be identified, analyzed, engaged, and managed throughout the life of the program. It also outlines the processes, tools and techniques, and resources to be used.

14.2.2 Identify Program Stakeholders: Tools and Techniques

.1 Expert Judgment

Individuals with experience working with the organizations and personalities involved in the program aid in the identification and characterization of stakeholders.

.2 Organizational Analysis

Analysis of the organizational players involved in the program and their formal and informal roles can be a valuable technique for revealing stakeholders with a significant but perhaps not obvious role to play in the program. As part of this analysis, external organizations that might have a strong interest in the program are also analyzed.

.3 Brainstorming

A brainstorming session among the initial program team members and stakeholders is useful in identifying potential stakeholders, their roles, their significance to the program, and their likely interests.

.4 Stakeholder Analysis

Described in Section 14.1.2.2.

.5 Interviews

Stakeholder interviews are structured discussions with some program stakeholders used to better understand the organizational culture, concerns related to the program, and the impact of the program. Interviews work particularly well in programs involving organizational process changes. During the interview, the program team uses a series of open-ended questions to solicit stakeholder feedback. Sample questions might include:

- How do you perform your job today?
- What information do you rely on to perform your job?
- What tools do you use to perform your job?

- How will you be impacted by the program outcomes?

- How will your workgroup react to the changes introduced by the program?

- What would help your team adjust to the changes resulting from the program?

- What type of communications would you like to see from the program team?

.6 Focus Groups

Focus groups may be used to solicit feedback from groups of stakeholders regarding their attitude towards the program and appropriate approaches for communications and impact mitigation. This approach presents open-ended questions, similar to those used in interviews, but allows groups of participants to interact with each other. This results in a deeper understanding of the program impacts than can be achieved through individual interviews or questionnaires/surveys.

.7 Questionnaires and Surveys

Questionnaires and surveys may be used to solicit feedback from stakeholders. Stakeholders are provided with a series of standard questions to evaluate their attitudes towards the program and determine appropriate approaches for communications and impact mitigation. This approach allows the program team to solicit feedback from a greater number of stakeholders than is possible with interviews or focus groups.

.8 Program Impact Analysis

Using the stakeholder analysis as input, the program team develops a comprehensive summary of how each stakeholder and stakeholder group will be impacted by the program. Negative impacts are identified and mitigation plans are developed to minimize their effect.

.9 Stakeholder Checklists

A simple checklist or matrix listing typical roles and interests found in programs or projects of similar scope can also be used to identify stakeholders and their respective roles.

14.2.3 Identify Program Stakeholders: Outputs

.1 Stakeholder Register

The stakeholder register is the primary output of this process. It should be established and maintained in such a way that members of the program team can access it easily for use in reporting, distributing program deliverables, and formal and informal communications. Key program stakeholders include:

- **Program Director.** The individual with executive ownership of the program or programs.

- **Program Manager.** The individual responsible for managing the program.

- **Project Managers.** The individuals responsible for managing the individual projects within the program.

- **Program Sponsor.** The individual or group who champions the program initiative, is responsible for providing project resources and often ultimately for delivering the benefits.

- **Customer.** The individual or organization that will use the new capabilities/results of the program and derive the anticipated benefits. The customer is a core stakeholder in the program's final result and will determine whether the program is judged to be ultimately successful or not.

- **Performing Organization.** The group that is performing the work of the program through projects.

- **Program Team Members.** The individuals performing program activities.

- **Project Team Members.** The individuals performing constituent project activities.

- **Funding Organization.** The part of the organization or the external agency that is providing funding for the program is a significant stakeholder.

- **Program Management Office (PMO).** The organization responsible for defining and managing the program-related governance processes, procedures, templates, etc. Also to provide support to individual program management teams or project managers by handling administrative functions centrally, even though this is done differently by different organizations, and where the name "program management office" may be used interchangeably with the PMO.

- **Program Governance Board/Steering Committee.** The group responsible for ensuring that program goals are achieved and providing support for addressing program risks and issues.

Additional stakeholders may exist within the organization or external to it. Some examples of external stakeholders include:

- Suppliers affected by changing policies and procedures,

- Governmental regulatory agencies imposing new policies or providing permits,

- Competitors and potential customers with an interest in the program, and

- Groups representing consumer, environmental or other interests (including political interests).

Stakeholders may also include individuals and groups who are not directly affected by the results of the program but maintain an interest in the initiative. Groups or individuals who are competing for limited resources or pursuing goals which conflict with those of the program should also be considered as stakeholders, since they can affect the program results.

.2 Stakeholder Inventory

The stakeholder inventory provides a comprehensive summary of how each stakeholder and stakeholder group will be impacted by the program, an assessment of the likely stakeholder responses, identified stakeholder issues and planned mitigation approaches.

.3 Program Stakeholder Management Plan Updates

The process of developing the stakeholder register may result in the need to update the program stakeholder management plan to reflect the more comprehensive set of stakeholders.

.4 Stakeholder Management Strategy

Stakeholder management strategy captures mitigation approaches coming out of the Identify Program Stakeholders process, which outlines specific steps to be taken to manage the impacts of the program on stakeholders. These may include:

- Comprehensive training to allow stakeholders to understand and adjust to the changes resulting from the program;

- Development of job aids, such as process documentation, manuals or quick references, to support stakeholders working with new processes and/or systems; and

- Intensive communication and involvement in the program.

14.3 Engage Program Stakeholders

The Engage Program Stakeholders process occurs when the program management team ensures that stakeholders are involved in the program. Effective stakeholder engagement requires thorough knowledge of the stakeholders' needs and potential impacts and issues. It also requires interacting effectively with stakeholders to communicate strategic objectives and status, influence stakeholder expectations, and resolve conflicts.

Stakeholder knowledge and experience can be used to contribute to the program outcomes. Figure 14-6 refers to the inputs and tools and techniques required to produce the necessary outputs in this process. These are described in detail in the following sections. Figure 14-7 shows the data flow through the processes.

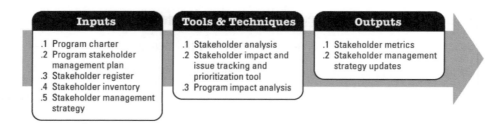

Inputs
.1 Program charter
.2 Program stakeholder management plan
.3 Stakeholder register
.4 Stakeholder inventory
.5 Stakeholder management strategy

Tools & Techniques
.1 Stakeholder analysis
.2 Stakeholder impact and issue tracking and prioritization tool
.3 Program impact analysis

Outputs
.1 Stakeholder metrics
.2 Stakeholder management strategy updates

Figure 14-6. Engage Program Stakeholders: Inputs, Tools & Techniques, and Outputs

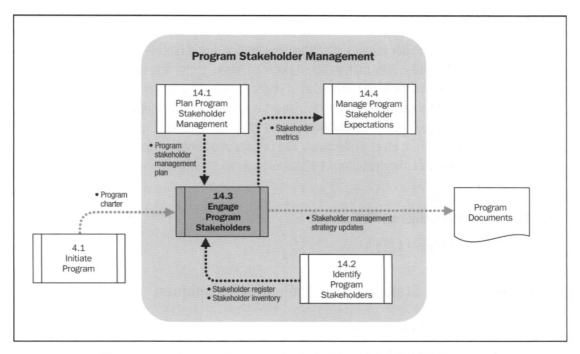

Figure 14-7. Engage Program Stakeholders Data Flow Diagram

14.3.1 Engage Program Stakeholders: Inputs

.1 Program Charter

See Section 4.1.3.2 for more details. The program charter establishes high-level expectations for the delivery of program benefits. It also defines program risks and dependencies at a high level. Knowledge of the program benefits, risks, and dependencies provides a basis for engaging successfully with stakeholders.

.2 Program Stakeholder Management Plan

The stakeholder management plan and guidelines define how the program and project teams will interact with stakeholders, including defining the tools and techniques to be used to effectively engage stakeholders. It will also define the metrics that will be used to measure performance of stakeholder engagement activities, such as stakeholder meeting attendance and communication plan delivery.

.3 Stakeholder Register

The program manager uses the stakeholder register to ensure that no stakeholders are overlooked. Although engagement with some stakeholders will be a higher priority than with others, the program manager has the responsibility to ensure that all stakeholders have had an opportunity to participate in the process and have their issues addressed. The stakeholder register is updated during this process to reflect new/revised stakeholders discovered after the program is under way.

.4 Stakeholder Inventory

Although the stakeholder register identifies stakeholders and high-level roles and responsibilities, it does not contain detailed information about potential stakeholder impact, issues, and concerns. The stakeholder inventory contains a current log of impacts identified during stakeholder analysis, issues raised by stakeholders during engagement, and tracking of impact mitigation and issue resolution status. Each component project will have stakeholder management guidelines that must also be considered at the program level. Collectively, the project stakeholders are also program stakeholders, since dissatisfaction by individual project stakeholders can negatively impact stakeholder acceptance of the overall program.

.5 Stakeholder Management Strategy

Described in Section 14.2.3.4.

14.3.2 Engage Program Stakeholders: Tools and Techniques

.1 Stakeholder Analysis

Described in Section 14.1.2.2.

.2 Stakeholder Impact and Issue Tracking and Prioritization Tool

As the program team works with stakeholders, they will learn about stakeholder issues and concerns that must be tracked to closure. Use of a tool to document, prioritize, and track issues and stakeholder impacts will ensure that stakeholder's concerns are appropriately addressed. When the list of stakeholders is small, a simple spreadsheet may be an adequate tracking tool. For programs with complex risks and issues affecting large numbers of stakeholders, a more sophisticated tracking and prioritization system may be required.

.3 Program Impact Analysis

Stakeholder issues and concerns are likely to affect program costs, schedules, and priorities. Impact analysis tools and techniques can help the project manager understand the urgency and probability of stakeholder-related program risks.

14.3.3 Engage Program Stakeholders: Outputs

.1 Stakeholder Metrics

Stakeholder metrics, defined in the stakeholder management plan, are tracked and reviewed regularly to identify potential risks caused by non-participation by stakeholders. Participation trends should be analyzed, and root cause analysis performed to identify and address causes of non-participation.

.2 Stakeholder Management Strategy Updates

Stakeholder meetings will typically serve two purposes: (1) to communicate program status; and (2) to hear issues and concerns raised by stakeholders. Issues and concerns should be captured in the stakeholder issue inventory, and conflict resolution techniques performed to reach negotiated compromises.

These negotiated compromises which come out of Engage Program Stakeholders are captured in the stakeholder management strategy as updates, an output of the Identify Program Stakeholder process.

14.4 Manage Program Stakeholder Expectations

Manage Program Stakeholder Expectations is the process of managing communications to satisfy the requirements of, and resolve issues with, program stakeholders.

Effective negotiation techniques are used to satisfy stakeholders who may have conflicting requirements. Use of conflict management skills helps in case the situation escalates into a conflict within the team or other stakeholders.

Participation of the stakeholders is also monitored and ensures that their expectations are met, which is vital for the success of the program.

Figure 14-8 refers to the inputs, tools and techniques, and outputs required to produce the necessary output in this process. These are described in details in the following sections. Figure 14-9 shows the data flow through the processes.

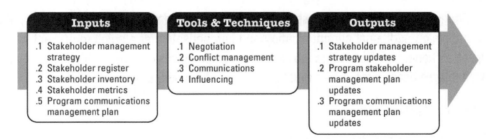

Figure 14-8. Manage Program Stakeholder Expectations: Inputs, Tools & Techniques, and Outputs

---

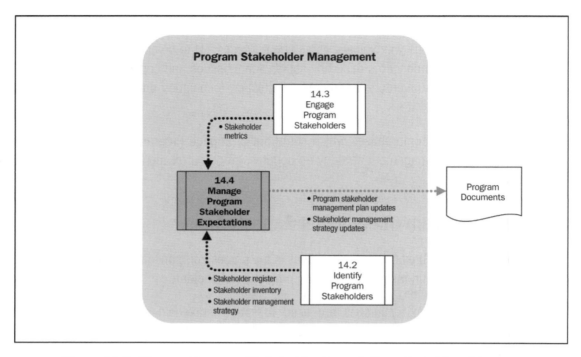

Figure 14-9. Manage Program Stakeholder Expectations Data Flow Diagram

14.4.1 Manage Program Stakeholder Expectations: Inputs

.1 Stakeholder Management Strategy

When a project or program negatively affects a stakeholder, the team must develop strategies for minimizing the impact to keep stakeholders engaged. The first step is to ensure that the stakeholders' expectations of the program are based on current, accurate information. Subsequently, the team may need to develop additional communication and compensation strategies to prevent a stakeholder or group of stakeholders from affecting other less-affected stakeholders. When negative impacts are unavoidable, mitigation strategies must be provided fairly and in a timely manner.

.2 Stakeholder Register

The stakeholder register includes a high-level summary of stakeholder needs, and can be used to determine if a specific stakeholder group's expectations are becoming unrealistic.

.3 Stakeholder Inventory

By continually tracking stakeholder issues and concerns in the stakeholder inventory, the team gains an understanding of stakeholder expectations and proactively communicates with those stakeholders to manage their expectations.

.4 Stakeholder Metrics

The history of stakeholder participation provides important background that could influence stakeholder expectations. For example, if a stakeholder group has not been actively participating, it is likely that they may have inaccurate expectations as a result.

.5 Program Communications Management Plan

Described in Section 10.1.3.1.

14.4.2 Manage Program Stakeholder Expectations: Tools and Techniques

.1 Negotiation

Effective negotiation skills and techniques can help the team work with stakeholders to resolve issues and conflicts that arise during the program. Large programs with diverse stakeholder groups may also need to facilitate negotiation sessions between stakeholders when their needs conflict.

.2 Conflict Management

The program manager's conflict management approach defines how conflicts among program stakeholders will be managed and defines escalation paths.

.3 Communications

Communications is the primary tool for managing stakeholders.

.4 Influencing

The ability to affect the beliefs, actions, and attitudes of other people.

14.4.3 Manage Program Stakeholder Expectations: Outputs

.1 Stakeholder Management Strategy Updates

The stakeholder management strategy is updated with any changes in the mitigation approaches and/or negotiated compromises identified during the Manage Program Stakeholder Expectations process.

.2 Program Stakeholder Management Plan Updates

The program stakeholder management plan should be updated regularly to ensure that all stakeholders are actively involved and that their expectations are appropriate and realistic.

.3 Program Communications Management Plan Updates

Updates to the program communications management plan are done regularly as stakeholders change and as their communications needs change.

CHAPTER 15

PROGRAM GOVERNANCE

Chapter 1 described the purpose of Program Governance and how it fits within the program management framework. Program Governance ensures decision-making and delivery management activities are focused on achieving program goals in a consistent manner, addressing appropriate risks, and fulfilling stakeholder requirements. Governance for programs is different than governance for most projects, because the scope and impact of a program is typically complex. Examples of factors contributing to this complexity are multi-year timelines, competition between projects for scarce resources, diverse stakeholder requirements, as well as inter-project and enterprise-level risks and issues.

The Program Governance processes include:

15.1 Plan and Establish Program Governance Structure. The process of identifying governance goals and defining the governance structure, roles, and responsibilities.

15.2 Plan for Audits —The process for ensuring the program is prepared for both external and internal audits of program finances, processes, and documents, and demonstrates compliance with approved organizational program management processes.

15.3 Plan Program Quality—The process of identifying quality standards applicable to the program, the processes, and the standards to be applied, and ensuring compliance to these standards.

15.4 Approve Component Initiation—The process of defining the decision-making structures and processes, enabling initiating and changing the program and/or components within the program.

15.5 Provide Governance Oversight—The process for providing governance and auditability throughout the course of the program.

15.6 Manage Program Benefits—The process for ensuring governance of expected program benefits is delivered consistently throughout the program life cycle.

15.7 Monitor and Control Program Changes—The process for ensuring the appropriate level of governance is applied to decision making of proposed changes to the program plan.

15.8 Approve Component Transition—The process for ensuring transition of knowledge, responsibilities, and benefit realization from the program to ongoing operations.

Program Governance activities are conducted through all phases of the program life cycle and require organizations to establish and enforce policies that address the following:

- Common procedures for all components within the program;
- Appropriate controls to ensure consistent application of procedures;

- Approach for developing and documenting program assumptions and decisions;

- Approach for managing program change;

- Quantifiable measures for evaluating the success of individual projects and the program;

- Common practices for capturing risks, issues, benefit measurements, and lessons learned. Figure 15-1 shows an overview of the processes involved in the effort.

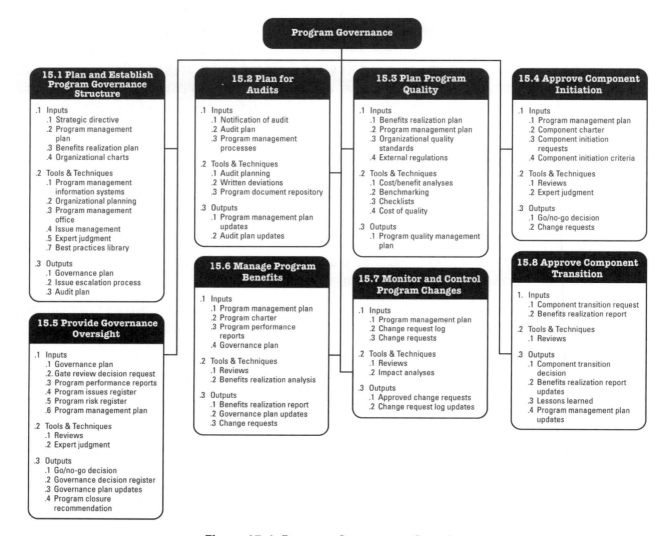

Figure 15-1. Program Governance Overview

15.1 Plan and Establish Program Governance Structure

Effective Program Governance relies on a governance framework that can be used across the program. Just like quality cannot be inspected into a product, governance must be proactive and not performed afterwards.

The program management team, in conjunction with major stakeholders, establishes the key governance principles and ensures that the correct structure is in place to encourage effective and appropriate governance. The program management team verifies that the governance approaches are being followed.

Factors that affect governance can differ depending upon the sector or industry that the organization serves, for example, national or local government, banking and financial advisory services, personal and hospitality services, food and health, security, etc. Governance principles need to consider environmental factors as well, since most countries have extensive regulations and laws that cover activities in these areas.

The governance structure ensures the program's goals and objectives are aligned with the strategic goals and objectives of the enterprise(s) for which the program is being developed. Programs, by their nature, may overlap a number of enterprises, with one or more being customers, performing organizations, suppliers, or stakeholders. The governance framework ensures that important interfaces are managed carefully to minimize program and inter-component conflicts.

Effective governance ensures that this strategic alignment and the value that has been promised is realized and benefits delivered; that all stakeholders are appropriately communicated with and kept aware of progress and issues; that appropriate tools and processes are used in the program; that decisions are being made rationally and with justification; and that the responsibilities and accountabilities are clearly defined and applied. All of this is done within the policies and standards of the partner organizations and is measured to ensure compliance.

Although Program Governance structure is specific for each organization and situation, it is fulfilled through the following common roles (see Figures 15-2 and 15-3):

- **Executive Sponsor.** The individual or group who is responsible for providing project resources and ensuring program success. Program sponsors represent the senior managers who are responsible for defining the direction of the organization and for the investment decisions.

- **Program Board (Steering Committee).** Empowered to make decisions regarding program scope, budget, and schedules and to resolve escalated issues and risks.

- **Program Manager.** Responsible for setting up and managing the program, ensuring that it is performing according to plan and that the program goals and objectives remain aligned to the overall strategic objectives of the organization.

- **Project Managers.** Responsible for effective planning, execution, tracking, and delivery of their component projects, in line with the corresponding program objectives.

- **Program Management Office.** Provides support to program and project management teams by handling administrative functions centrally. Responsible for defining and managing the program-related governance processes, procedures, and templates, etc., and controlling the collection of information and the generation of performance reports on behalf of program or project managers.

- **Project Teams and Team Members.** Responsible for performing planned activities to ensure the project continues to successful completion.

Figure 15-2. Plan and Establish Program Governance Structure: Inputs, Tools & Techniques, and Outputs

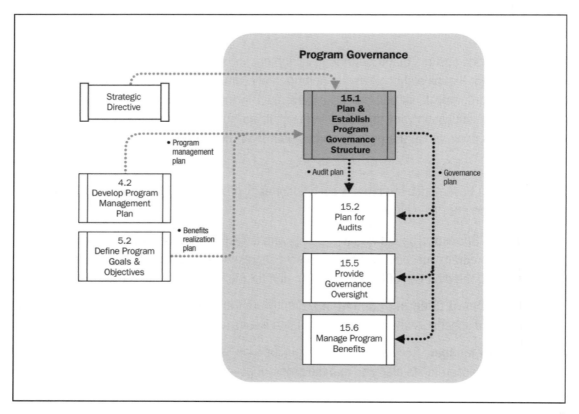

Figure 15-3. Plan and Establish Program Governance Structure: Data Flow Diagram

15.1.1 Plan and Establish Program Governance Structure: Inputs

.1 Strategic Directive

Decisions made as a result of the governance process may affect strategic alignment and program benefit delivery, so an understanding of the overall strategic directive for the program is essential.

.2 Program Management Plan

The program management plan and its constituent subplans set the format and establish the criteria for developing and controlling different aspects of the program. The governance structure ensures that the program is being managed effectively, including decisions that affect overall delivery of program benefits.

The following subplans of the overall program management plan are essential inputs to the Program Governance process:

- **Program Charter.** The program charter provides authorization to the program management team to use organizational resources to execute the program and it links the program to the business case or to the organization's strategic priorities. Key elements of the program charter that support Program Governance are reporting requirements, approval processes, and levels.

- **Program Business Case.** The primary objective of a business case is to highlight the value of the program and how it should be delivered to the organization for resources expended. Program Governance processes enable business case oversight related to the justification of resource expenditure and alignment with the benefits to be delivered.

- **Sponsor and Stakeholder Requirements.** Sponsor and stakeholder requirements specify the minimum acceptable criteria for a successful program. Unless these are clearly understood, resources may be applied to activities and components that do not deliver maximum benefits. These requirements support governance activities by making it easier for the program management team to obtain feedback and authorization from sponsors and stakeholders when required.

.3 Benefits Realization Plan

Projects and programs both deliver benefit. Value is delivered when these benefits are utilized by the organization, community, or other program or project beneficiaries. The benefits realization plan identifies when and how these benefits are expected to be realized and may specify mechanisms that should be in place to ensure that the benefits are fully realized over time. Benefits are sometimes not realized until long after the end of active work on a program.

Examples of benefits realization measures are whether or not benefits exceed their input costs and whether they are delivered timely. This analysis requires linking benefits to expenditures (not just financial), measurement criteria, and measurement and review points. The benefits realization plan will also be used in the Manage Program Benefits process (Section 15.6) to verify that benefits are being realized, and provide feedback to program management and governance plans as needed to ensure successful benefit delivery.

.4 Organizational Charts

Organizational charts indicate authority levels within the organization and scope of control. It is important that feedback and authorization is received as quickly and clearly as possible so as to not impede program progress. These charts are the initial foundation for the governance plan structure and organization.

15.1.2 Plan and Establish Program Governance Structure: Tools and Techniques

.1 Program Management Information Systems

An effective program management information system includes tools and mechanisms to store information about programs and aid in the quick recovery of such information. The program management information system usually consists of a mix of manual and automated tools, techniques, processes and procedures to assist the program management team provide effective oversight of the program.

To benefit Program Governance, the program management information system should include mechanisms to search external local and international databases for regulatory information when appropriate.

.2 Organizational Planning

Programs use a wide variety of different organizational structures. Very large programs may utilize multiple organizational structures within different parts of the overall program structure.

For example, one set of program components may be a weak matrix (where change management activities are involved), another set may be organized according to a strong matrix (where multiple suppliers are engaged in delivering a capability to perform a service), and another set of components may be strictly projectized (for example, where a new computer system is being developed).

.3 Program Management Office

A program management office (PMO) can provide an effective way of sharing and optimizing scarce or common resources. Program Governance ensures that these services, at the required quantity and quality, are available in a timely manner. The PMO can also assist with communications according to sponsor and stakeholder requirements. Where a PMO is used, the PMO structure, responsibilities, and implementation approach can vary widely depending upon organizational needs.

.4 Issue Management

Issue escalation is an activity that occurs within the governance process. Skillful tracking, managing, and resolution of program-level and inter-component issues enable effective governance. See Section 4.7 for further information on Manage Program Issues.

.5 Expert Judgment

Described in Section 4.1.2.1.

.6 Best Practices Library

Described in Section 4.2.1.3.

15.1.3 Plan and Establish Program Governance Structure: Outputs

.1 Governance Plan

The program governance plan describes the governance goals, structure, roles and responsibilities, and logistics for executing the governance process. The program governance plan is referenced throughout the Program Governance process. Governance subprocesses provide feedback for refining the program governance plan to ensure it is operating effectively.

The plan should include the following sections:

- **Program Governance Goals.** The governance goals for the program and its constituent components, documented and communicated with component teams and stakeholders. Component charter documents and project management plans need to show the priority of these goals and provide advice on how they need to be met.

- **Program Governance Structure and Composition.** The governance structure and composition describes how Program Governance will be implemented, describes roles and responsibilities, processes, stage gate requirements, and execution.

- **Program Governance Role and Responsibility Definitions.** By answering the following questions, the overall roles and responsibilities for a program can be identified and described:

  - What is the composition of the program board? What is the frequency of meetings? How are issues escalated to the board? How does the board communicate its decisions?

  - What is the role and responsibility of the program executive sponsor and constituent sponsors?

  - What are the roles and responsibilities of the program director and constituent component owners?

  - What is the role of the program management office?

  - Who will be accountable for delivery?

  - Who will ensure that benefits are realized and the value is delivered?

  - Who will ensure that architectural principles are not violated?

  - Who will provide administrative, guidance, consulting, and oversight service to the program and constituent components?

  - Who will ensure appropriate, effective, efficient, and timely communication with all stakeholder groups and specific stakeholders?

- **High Level Governance Plan and Meeting Schedules.** The structure of the governance plan is devised and becomes a part of the program management plan. It includes the output of all governance planning activities, including schedules of governance activities and meetings such as health checks, gate reviews, and audits.

- **Gate Review Requirements.** One of the most important aspects of Program Governance is ensuring the program components are being managed effectively. The program management team must ensure that program components have an ongoing mandate or closed if they will not achieve their stated objectives.

  Matters to be considered include strategic alignment, investment appraisal, monitoring and control of opportunities and threats, benefit assessment, and the monitoring of program outcomes. Phase gate reviews, shown in Figure 2-2, are a recommended approach to aiding program control and program management, as well as facilitating Program Governance. Phase-gate reviews are carried out at key decision points in the program life cycle and provide an objective check against the exit criteria of a completed phase to determine readiness to proceed to the next phase in the program life cycle. Phase-gate reviews also provide an opportunity to assess the program with respect to a number of strategic and quality-related criteria including:

  o Program and its constituent components are still aligned with the organization's strategy;

  o Expected benefits are in line with the original business plan;

  o Level of risk remains acceptable to the organization; and

  o Identified generally accepted good practices are being followed.

  Phase-gate reviews are often based upon the core investment decisions within the life cycle. The focus of each is specific to the phase just completed by the program. Each of these reviews functions as a "go" or "no-go" decision point on the program as a whole. Program Governance may also include recurring program reviews that do not correspond with the end of a phase. Requirements for gate reviews should address the following:

  o What is to be gated?

  o How is it gated (the process)?

  o Who is responsible?

  o What are the measurement criteria?

  In practice, phase gate reviews are sometimes called stage gate reviews or go/no-go decision points.

- **Component Initiation Criteria.** The initial gate review for a component is at component initiation. It is particularly important to have very clear criteria for this gate to ensure that the right components are initiated at the right time. Further detail can be found in Section 2.2.1. These criteria are inputs to the Approve Component Initiation process (Section 15.4).

- **Periodic Health Checks.** Phase-gate reviews are not a substitute for periodic program performance reviews. These reviews assess performance against expected outcomes and against the need to realize and sustain program benefits into the long term. Program health checks are one way to ensure that the program is reviewed and checked on a regular basis. Health checks tend to be more informal than phase gates or audits and are considered less threatening by component teams. Their objective is to:

  o Approach intermittent and inevitable failures in a positive and constructive manner. This will ensure that the lessons learned will prevent future similar failures and improve the overall processes.

  o Focus on areas, rather than specific points, to ensure the overall program is successful.

  o Uncover alternatives when problems are identified. While there may be no single solution to a problem, there are always ways of managing it.

  o Start with a high level overview and drill down more deeply where this is indicated.

  o Evaluate whether processes and procedures are able to achieve the objectives for which they were designed.

.2 Issue Escalation Process

An effective issue escalation and resolution process ensures important issues are escalated appropriately, and resolved in a timely manner.

The escalation process typically operates at two levels: within the program between component teams and the program management team; and between the program management team and organizational executive management or other stakeholders.

.3 Audit Plan

External and internal audits should be conducted at regular and predefined intervals, for example, at phase end reviews, or at major milestones. The audit plan describes the objectives and timing of audits.

15.2 Plan for Audits

Programs are being increasingly audited. All programs in the government sector are subject to audit to ensure the taxpayer's money is being spent in a reasonable fashion and to ensure that what is being delivered is what was contracted for. Programs in the construction sector are subject to audits by the financial funding organization. Even programs that are entirely internal to an organization may be audited by the organization's audit office. The program manager should be prepared for audits, either from external agencies or from the internal audit organization. See Figures 15-4 and 15-5.

Audits can have several goals. From the standpoint of the program manager, the preplanned and random audits have essentially the same objectives—either to examine the program finances to ensure the money is being spent as planned, or to review the program management processes to ensure that the program is being managed in accordance with the organization's approved processes. In order to prepare for these types of audits, the program manager should simply follow the organization's approved program management processes in managing the program. If the program manager feels that a process is not appropriate or not necessary for a particular program, then a deviation from the processes should be requested and approval of that deviation documented. In general, an auditor will be looking for unapproved deviations from the management processes.

Another possible goal of an audit is to specifically look for evidence of fraud or extreme mismanagement. This is undertaken rarely and only in cases where there is evidence or strong suspicion of such issues.

Figure 15-4. Plan for Audits: Inputs, Tools & Techniques, and Outputs

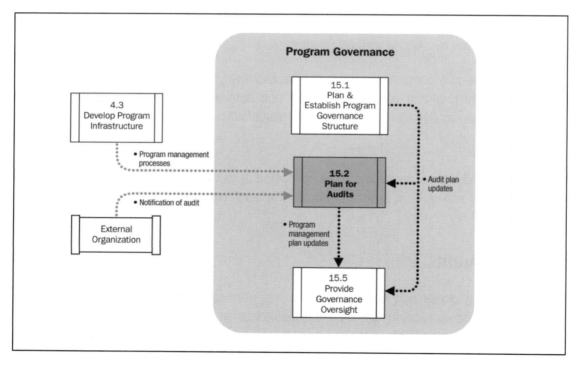

Figure 15-5. Plan for Audits: Data Flow Diagram

Audits may be done either during the program execution or after the program is complete. In either case the program manager's best preparation for these audits is:

- Follow all the organization's documented and approved processes for program management;

- Obtain written approval for any deviation from the documented processes; and

- Document all decisions, plans, status and performance reports, financial reports, action items, risks and issues, change requests, meeting minutes, contracts, and all other items that show how the program is being managed.

Audits take time, both time by the auditors and time by the program staff to be interviewed by the auditors. If an audit is pre-planned the program schedule should be examined to ensure that there is sufficient time for staff to sit through audit meetings and interviews without impact to the schedule.

15.2.1 Plan for Audits: Inputs

.1 Notification of Audit

Most audits are pre-planned and the program manager will be notified of them in advance in order to prepare for the audit and to prevent the audit from interfering with the program schedule. The program manager should be aware that the program may be randomly audited with no warning.

.2 Audit Plan

If the program has developed an internal audit plan, as part of overall program management plan, this would be an additional input to the process. An example would be a scheduled series of self-assessment audits to ensure compliance with program management processes and standards.

.3 Program Management Processes

The documented project or program management processes must be used to plan out the auditing effort and forms the auditor's guidelines for how the program and its components should be managed.

15.2.2 Plan for Audits: Tools and Techniques

.1 Audit Planning

The program manager must ensure that all documented program management processes are followed. The project managers for the components must ensure that all documented project management processes are followed.

.2 Written Deviations

When it does not make sense for a particular program to follow documented processes, a written deviation must be submitted and approved before the process deviation can occur.

.3 Program Document Repository

For all program management processes, maintain documentation that validates the processes are being followed.

15.2.3 Plan for Audits: Outputs

.1 Program Management Plan Updates

The most effective way to prepare for audits is to maintain the program management documentation and ensure it is readily available to the auditors. By proactively preparing for audits, the program management team can be respond quickly and accurately to both planned and unplanned audit events.

.2 Audit Plan Updates

Upon completion of each audit, audit results should be recorded in the audit plan with feedback to the governance planning function if changes to any of the program management, governance, or audit plans are needed to address audit outcomes.

15.3 Plan Program Quality

The majority of quality planning will occur at the component level (including quality assurance and quality control). There will also be significant quality requirements identified as part of the procurement and other individual processes. See Figures 15-6 and 15-7.

Each of the components is responsible for establishing appropriate mechanisms for assuring the quality of their progress and outputs. It may be useful for the program to be involved in component-level reviews of items critical to the successful delivery of the program benefits.

Plan Program Quality is concerned with identifying and communicating those elements where the program needs to specify quality standards or oversights that help enable the program to achieve its benefits and to ensure a consistent cross-component application of specific quality requirements.

The program quality management plan should include quality requirements that are cross-component or minimal requirements for individual components. It will be used as an input to individual component planning.

Example 1: A program has several components where IT infrastructure is being developed and installed. The program establishes a uniform standard for testing fiberoptic cables and for measuring data transmission rates.

Example 2: A program is building a campus for a company to consolidate operations. The program quality management plan establishes a minimal set of testing and standards to be used for all buildings or establishes a component to perform all quality inspections for all concrete pours for all buildings.

©2008 Project Management Institute. *The Standard for Program Management* — Second Edition

There is a close coupling between this section and procurement planning, as both can benefit from standardization of products, standards, and tests, and in establishing economies of scale for acquiring these items.

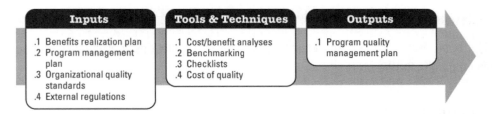

Figure 15-6. Plan Program Quality: Inputs, Tools & Techniques, and Outputs

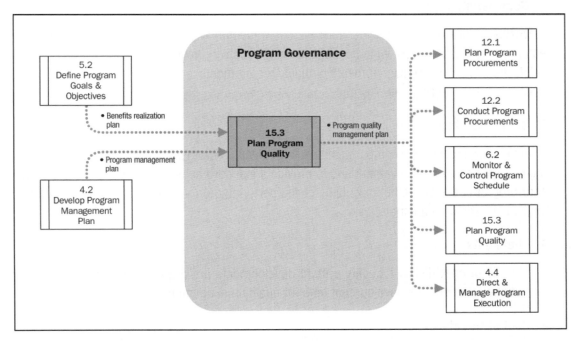

Figure 15-7. Plan Program Quality: Inputs, Tools & Techniques, and Outputs

15.3.1 Plan Program Quality: Inputs

.1 Benefits Realization Plan

Program quality will primarily be defined by successful benefits realization. A complete understanding of the scope and nature of the benefits enable the program manager to define appropriate quality standards and measures.

.2 Program Management Plan

All elements of the program management plan are useful inputs for planning program quality, especially the elements from Program Scope Management (Section 5).

.3 Organizational Quality Standards

Each organization may have established minimal quality standards that must be used by all organization programs and projects.

.4 External Regulations

The team must evaluate and identify any external regulations that need to be considered when planning quality for the program.

15.3.2 Plan Program Quality: Tools and Techniques

.1 Cost/Benefit Analyses

Quality planning must consider cost/benefit tradeoffs. The primary benefit of meeting quality requirements is less rework which means higher productivity, lower costs, and increased stakeholder satisfaction. The primary cost of meeting quality requirements is the expense associated with quality management activities.

.2 Benchmarking

Benchmarking involves comparing actual or planned program practices to those of other programs to generate ideas for improvement and to provide a standard by which to measure performance. The other programs can be within or outside of the performing organization, or can be within the same application area or in another.

.3 Checklists

The use of checklists for quality system developments are a great aid to ensure items are not missed and to reduce the development time for quality management plans.

.4 Cost of Quality

Cost of quality refers to the total cost of all efforts to achieve product or service quality and includes all work to ensure conformance to requirements, as well as all work resulting from nonconformance to requirements. There are three types of costs that are incurred: prevention costs, appraisal costs, and failure costs, where the latter is broken down into internal and external costs.

15.3.3 Plan Program Quality: Outputs

.1 Program Quality Management Plan

The quality management plan should include:

- Minimal quality standards for components;
- Minimal testing requirements for components;

- Minimal requirements for quality planning, quality control, and quality assurance for components;

- Any program level quality assurance or quality control activities required; and

- Roles and responsibilities for program level quality assurance and quality control activities required.

15.4 Approve Component Initiation

Approve Component Initiation is the process of performing the program management activities to initiate a component within the program. This process can occur during any program phase except closing. The timing to initiate a component is normally controlled by the program management plan. Program needs change over time, and the program team may need to update the program management plan for newly identified components. See Figures 15-8 and 15-9.

The Approve Component Initiation process at the program level includes:

- Developing a business case that will secure funding for, and allocate budget to, the component;

- Ensuring ongoing operations that are part of the program are properly funded and aligned with the needs of the program;

- Ensuring a project manager is assigned to components defined as projects;

- Ensuring an operations manager familiar with the program is assigned to ongoing operations;

- Communicating the component-related information to stakeholders;

- Communicating the ongoing operations to stakeholders, as needed;

- Initiating a governance structure that will monitor and track benefit delivery and progress of the component at the program level; and

- Assigning a sponsor for each component.

Approve Component Initiation may trigger the redeployment of human and other resources from one component to another. This is managed at the program level and may require other program process activity if the managers of the releasing component are unable or unwilling to release the resources required.

Finally, all program-level documentation and records dealing with the component must be updated to reflect the changes to the components affected.

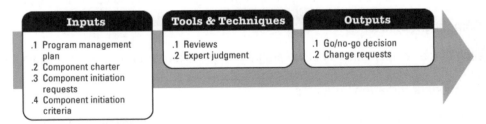

Figure 15-8. Approve Component Initiation: Inputs, Tools & Techniques, and Outputs

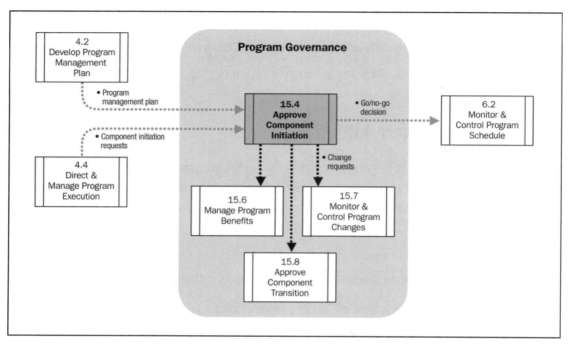

Figure 15-9. Approve Component Initiation: Data Flow Diagram

15.4.1 Approve Component Initiation: Inputs

.1 Program Management Plan

The program management plan provides overall guidance for initiating components within the program. The elements of the plan that are most useful for this process are:

- **Program Charter.** The program charter, including the program scope statement, guide individual component charters and may provide the following information for all components:

  o Define the various daily operational components and identify when they become part of the program.

  o Ensure the component has been properly identified as part of the program.

- **Program Strategic Plan.** The company's strategic plan should be the defining document for the program and should be reflected in the program charter. The program team should be familiar with the strategic plan and ensure that the program and its components support the plan.

.2 Component Charter

Each of the components within the program requires a charter before it can begin its work.

.3 Component Initiation Requests

A component initiation request evaluates the component against the organization's approved selection criteria. A decision is made on whether the component should be initiated.

The program team may redefine priorities of program components. Component initiation may be delayed or accelerated as defined by the program team and its needs.

.4 Component Initiation Criteria

The evaluation criteria and decision process may be formal or informal. These criteria should have been defined during the initial planning program process defined in Section 15.1, and included in the program governance plan.

15.4.2 Approve Component Initiation: Tools and Techniques

.1 Reviews

Approve Component Initiation is typically the first gate review in a program. Gate reviews are described in Section 15.1 Plan and Establish Program Governance Structure.

.2 Expert Judgment

Described in Section 4.1.2.1.

15.4.3 Approve Component Initiation: Outputs

.1 Go/No-Go Decision

The criteria for approval of component initiation must be clearly defined in the governance plan.

.2 Change Requests

Component changes that could affect the overall program's benefit delivery should be reviewed and approved by the governance board. Change requests are handled in Monitor and Control Program Changes.

15.5 Provide Governance Oversight

Governance is defined as the process of developing, communicating, implementing, monitoring, and assuring the policies, procedures, organizational structures, and practices associated with a given program. Governance is oversight and control. The following are examples of governance oversight functions:

- Monitoring program outcomes and ensuring accepted good practices are being followed; and

- Monitoring measures that focus on strategic alignment; investment appraisal; monitoring and controlling risk opportunities and threats acceptable to the organization; and ensuring expected benefits are in line with the original business plan.

Governance activities are usually carried out by means of a program governance board (or program steering committee), as prescribed in the organization structure part of the program governance plan created in Section 15.1. When a governance board is used, it is recommended that governance meetings be planned on a regular, scheduled basis, and not just performed in an ad-hoc manner. Regular, planned meetings ensure that the governance board is providing adequate oversight, and reduce the risk of it becoming low priority for board members.

Program governance oversight involves execution of the governance plan through the supporting governance goals, structure and framework. It ensures that governance is in place and feedback is received to improve the components and the program. Governance oversight should also be an internal-looking practice, where continuous improvement of the governance process and framework should be employed. See Figures 15-10 and 15-11.

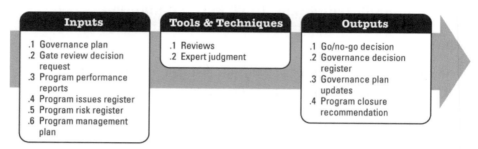

Figure 15-10. Provide Governance Oversight: Inputs, Tools & Techniques, and Outputs

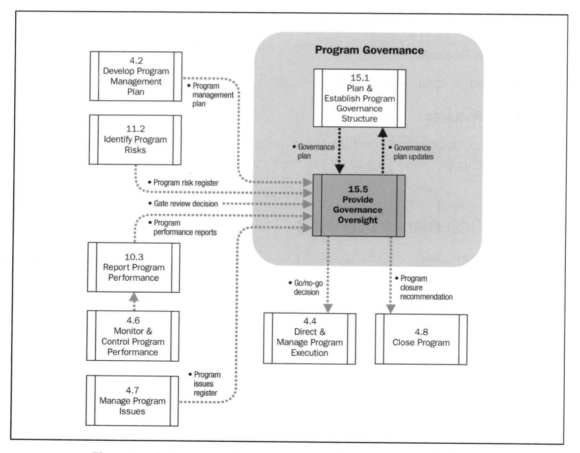

Figure 15-11. Provide Governance Oversight: Data Flow Diagram

15.5.1 Provide Governance Oversight: Inputs

.1 Governance Plan

The program governance plan provides guidance for the governance oversight process. All sections of the plan described in Section 15.1 are important for this process.

The gate requirements are especially crucial. Gates can be checkpoints where an assessment is beneficial, such as when a component transitions from one phase to another. Gates identify defects or risks early in the process, where the cost to eliminate is lower in the beginning phases of the program. The input gate requirements are key criteria that form the basis for governance board decisions.

.2 Gate Review Decision Request

Most governance board decision requests will be made for component gate reviews, as described in Section 15.1. Other decision requests could be made to resolve an issue, review a proposal, or address a risk. The request is usually formal in nature and contains supporting documentation to facilitate board decisions. Program and component changes will typically follow the Monitor and Control Program Changes process described in Section 15.7 before approaching the governance board for a final decision. Changes that do not affect the overall program's performance will usually be handled in accordance with Section 15.7 and not require governance board review.

.3 Program Performance Reports

The status report, financial report, and resource deviation report are examples of reports submitted to the governance board to support its role of oversight and control. Other reports reviewed by the governance board may include analysis results, recommendations, proposals, or alternatives made by team members and/or from subject matter experts that are internal or external to the component. Audit reports from planned and unplanned audits are an example of external viewpoints that can be used as a 'check and balance' opinion for the governance board's decision process.

.4 Program Issues Register

Described in Section 4.4.3.4.

.5 Program Risk Register

Described in Section 11.2.3.1.

.6 Program Management Plan

Described in Section 4.2.3.1. The program management plan is an essential input for effective program governance, since it contains all of the subsidiary plans that define the framework and program management processes to be followed for the current program.

15.5.2 Provide Governance Oversight: Tools and Techniques

.1 Reviews

Governance board or steering committee meetings are the most common method used to perform governance oversight activities. Regularly scheduled review meetings, with well-planned agendas and documented decision records, enhance the effectiveness of the governance process.

.2 Expert Judgment

Described in Section 4.1.2.1.

15.5.3 Provide Governance Oversight: Outputs

.1 Go/No-Go Decision

The decision record and meeting minutes from the gate review will also highlight any risks as the component/program completes one phase and moves to the next phase. These risks are often categorized into high risk, medium risk, and manageable risk. Depending upon the criteria set by the governance framework, phase transition may proceed even though a number of high risks may be identified.

.2 Governance Decision Register

Decisions are documented formally using meeting minutes, action item logs, or other forms of decision records. Governance board decisions are used as feedback to improve the result of the components/program. Decisions that require program changes are handled in the Monitor and Control Program Changes process (see Section 15.7).

.3 Governance Plan Updates

This is the feedback loop for the governance framework, where continuous improvement is built into the process by assessing the effectiveness of the governance framework to the improved result of the components/program.

This is also the feedback loop for the governance process, where continuous improvement is built into the process by assessing the effectiveness of the governance process to achieve an improved result for the components/program.

.4 Program Closure Recommendation

When the last component within a program has been closed, the governance board or steering committee for the program will review the overall program delivery and benefits realization, and decide on whether to recommend that the program be closed. This program closure recommendation would typically be proposed to the program's sponsor(s) for the final closure decision. After program closure, there may still be ongoing activities to ensure continued benefits realization. Tracking and management of those long-term benefits may either be by transition to ongoing operations, or become a part of other new or existing program(s).

15.6 Manage Program Benefits

Actively managing program benefits is an indication that governance is being followed and the organization's strategic plan goals are met by the program. The Manage Program Benefits process ensures there is a defined set of reports or metrics reported to the program management office, program stakeholders, governance committee, and/or sponsors. By consistently monitoring and reporting benefits metrics, stakeholders can assess the overall health of the program, and take action as required to ensure successful benefit delivery. See Figures 15-12 and 15.13.

Inputs	Tools & Techniques	Outputs
.1 Program management plan .2 Program charter .3 Program performance reports .4 Governance plan	.1 Reviews .2 Benefits realization analysis	.1 Benefits realization report .2 Governance plan updates .3 Change requests

Figure 15-12. Manage Program Benefits: Inputs, Tools & Techniques, and Outputs

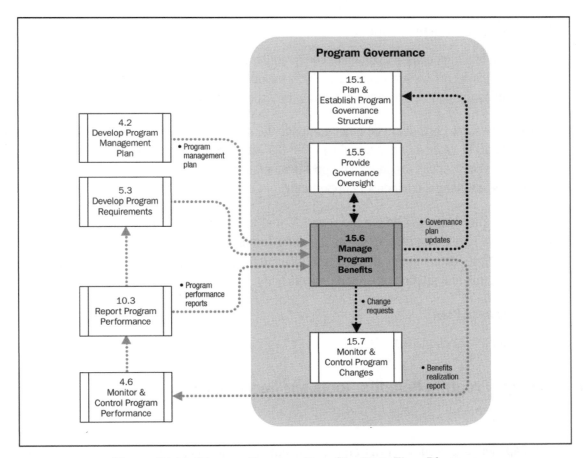

Figure 15-13. Manage Program Benefits: Data Flow Diagram

15.6.1 Manage Program Benefits: Inputs

.1 Program Management Plan

The program management plan and its constituent subplans establish the criteria for developing and controlling the program. The plan is reviewed, noting when benefit realization events are scheduled, and ensuring that they are included in phase-gate reviews and the decisions emanating from these reviews.

The program team frequently reviews the program management plans to ensure they reflect the current state of the program. As updates are noted, the change process may be launched. The program team ensures that the changes are communicated to the components for implementation and action.

.2 Program Charter

Described in Section 4.1.3.2. Program components need to review the program charter to derive planned benefits. This should be done with oversight from the program management office. The program management office will have final approval of the benefits required by the components.

.3 Program Performance Reports

Program health checks are conducted on a regular basis. The findings may be useful for proposing program adjustments, where necessary. These include schedule variations (speeding up or delaying the start of components), allocation of work to be done between components, and so on.

A key aspect to consider is whether components, or even the program as a whole, are still viable. This would occur when it becomes evident that the value proposition has changed, for example, if the overall life cycle cost will exceed the proposed benefits, or if the benefits will be delivered too late (for example, when there is a window of opportunity).

The program team will define the report format and due date (e.g., phase ends) to each of the components. The report may result in the early termination of some components and initiate the process to close the component. It may also result in the program team reallocating resources among the components and starting other components early.

.4 Governance Plan

Described in Section 15.1.3.3.

15.6.2 Manage Program Benefits: Tools and Techniques

.1 Reviews

Component and program plans, and the management and control of these plans, must be reviewed to verify that the delivery of benefits has not been compromised by decisions made during the execution of the program and its components. To facilitate effective review, benefits should be described in an effective manner, explaining how they add value. If benefits are not presented in a coherent fashion,

---

then the value may not be understood. One objective of the benefits review is to reassure stakeholders that all is going well in the program components. This could also be verified by conducting periodic audits, and reviewing the audit results with key stakeholders.

.2 Benefits Realization Analysis

The benefits review requires analysis of the planned versus actual benefits across a wide range of factors. In particular, some of the aspects that should be analyzed and assessed as part of the benefits management process include:

- **Strategic alignment.** Focuses on ensuring the linkage of enterprise and program plans; on defining, maintaining and validating the program value proposition; and on aligning program management with enterprise operations management. How will the realization of benefits affect the flow of operations of the organization as the benefit realization is introduced, and how negative effects may be minimized? How will the disruptiveness inherent in components be managed by the organization?

- **Value delivery.** Focuses on ensuring that the program delivers the promised benefits and that these benefits translate into value. A benefit, translates into value when it is used to benefit the enterprise in some manner. This may involve service level agreements or specific results that are achieved. Sometimes there is a window of opportunity for a benefit to be turned into value. One should determine whether the window was compromised by actual events in the program or constituent components (for example, a delay, a cost overrun, or feature reduction)? Investments may also have time value, where shifts in component schedules can have additional financial impact.

- **Resource management.** Focuses on ensuring that the appropriate resources are made available to components at the appropriate time for optimal utilization. That is, resources (applications, information, infrastructure, people, money, etc.) are identified and made available to the components at the right time and returned to the enterprise when their purpose has been served. Resource management also ensures there are appropriate resources to ensure benefit realization when these are ready to start.

- **Risk management.** Focuses on risk awareness by senior enterprise officers; understanding of enterprise risk tolerance; managing inter-component and enterprise-level risks; and monitoring and supporting effective risk management within components. It has to do more with the manner in which risk to benefit realization is managed in the enterprise than management of specific risks.

- **Performance measurement.** Focuses on tracking and monitoring strategy implementation, component completion, resource usage, process performance, and component delivery. Since programs long outlive components, it may be necessary to establish service level agreements, or influence operational service level agreements so that the program value proposition is maintained. The performance of components, especially their impact on other components (in the program and outside of it), is monitored to ensure that the ability to deliver benefits is not compromised.

15.6.3 Manage Program Benefits: Outputs

.1 Benefits Realization Report

Metrics and reporting outline the deviation of the planned program benefits versus the actual ongoing program results and are produced as defined in the program governance plan.

- **Benefits Realization Plan Versus Actual.** The benefits realization plan identifies how and when benefits are delivered to the organization. For a benefit to have value, it must be realized to a sufficient degree and in a timely manner. The plan must be monitored regularly to determine that actual events and changes in plans at both the component and overall program level have not precluded the possibility of benefit realization as planned. The benefits realization plan is evaluated against the actual benefit of the component. This analysis is done by the program team. The actual benefits are reported in the benefit report.

- **Benefits Report.** Benefits may be realized before the formal work of the program has ended and will likely continue long after the formal work has completed. The program management team ensures that all benefits have been delivered and accepted prior to the closure of the program (see Section 2.2.4). Benefits are quantified so that their realization may be measured. This includes the dimensions of the benefit (e.g., the date when realization must start) and a quantification of the benefit (e.g., hours saved, profit increased, market share increased, competitor strength reduced, etc.). Governance must evaluate that this is taking place within the required parameters so that changes to the components or the program as a whole can be proposed. The benefit report measures the component against the benefits realization plan. The report, which is analyzed by the program team and reported to the enterprise executives, may cause the component to be realigned, terminated, or started early.

.2 Governance Plan Updates

An outcome of benefits realization analysis could be recommended changes to the governance processes, plan, roles and responsibilities and/or structure. As changes are identified, other related plans may also need to be updated.

- **Updated Governance Process.** The governance process is reviewed and modified to capture changes made to the governance process. These changes are captured in the lessons learned, as appropriate.

- **Updated Governance Plan.** The governance plan is updated to account for any lessons learned and changes brought about by changes to the constituent component plans and the overall program plan.

- **Updated Governance Roles and Responsibilities.** Governance roles and responsibilities are changed as lessons are learned, and changes to the constituent component plans and the overall program plan are made. These changes aim to restore the timeliness and magnitude of benefit realization.

- **Updated Governance Structure.** The governance structure is modified as lessons are learned, and changes to the constituent component plans and the overall program plan are made. These changes would aim to restore the timeliness and magnitude of benefit realization.

.3 Change Requests

Change requests are generated where reviews identify that benefits realization will be compromised. These changes would aim to restore the timeliness and magnitude of benefit realization. Change requests can be targeted at constituent components or to the program as a whole.

15.7 Monitor and Control Program Changes

The Monitor and Control Program Changes process is the process that ensures the appropriate level of governance is applied to decision making regarding proposed changes to the program plan. Proposed changes may be accepted, rejected or modified in this process. See Figures 15-14 and 15-15.

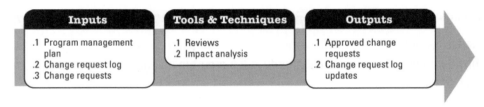

Figure 15-14. Monitor and Control Program Changes: Inputs, Tools & Techniques, and Outputs

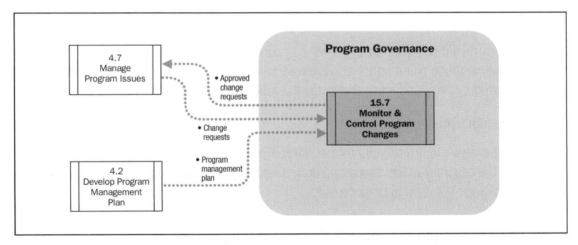

Figure 15-15. Monitor and Control Program Changes: Data Flow Diagram

15.7.1 Monitor and Control Program Changes: Inputs

.1 Program Management Plan

The program management plan and its constituent subplans provide the starting point for consideration of changes that develop and influence the program. The plan also identifies benefits that may be affected by proposed changes.

The program change control team will review the current program management plan to ensure that proposed changes are consistent with the current direction of the program. As changes are approved, the program team ensures that the changes are reflected in the program management plan.

.2 Change Request Log

This is the document used to record and describe or denote change request details in this process.

.3 Change Requests

Change requests are raised for consideration through the integrated change control process. They are considered by the appropriate authority in the program management team and approved, rejected, or modified for further consideration.

15.7.2 Monitor and Control Program Changes: Tools and Techniques

.1 Reviews

Changes provided for or arising from components and programs plans, and the management and control of these plans, must be reviewed to verify that the delivery of benefits has not been compromised by decisions made during the execution of the program and its components.

.2 Impact Analysis

Impact analysis is a technique that explores the effect of the proposed changes on the program, including the accuracy of any assumptions, and identifies risks and benefits to the component arising from the change if it were to be accepted.

15.7.3 Monitor and Control Program Changes: Outputs

.1 Approved Change Requests

Decisions on acceptance, rejection, or modification of change requests are made by the people with designated authority to do so. Change decisions are made with an understanding of the documented program benefits and would be expected to be consistent with the current program benefits. As changes are approved, the program team ensures that the changes are communicated to the components for implementation and action.

.2 Change Request Log Updates

As changes are approved, the program team ensures that details of the changes are accurately recorded in the program change request log. Details are recorded for changes that are approved, rejected, or modified.

15.8 Approve Component Transition

Approve Component Transition is the process of performing program management activities to formally transition a program component into ongoing operational status. For completed components, this process is the last gate review for the component, validating that component-level closure has occurred appropriately, and ensuring that the component has achieved its objectives relative to the overall program. Components must conform to program component closure requirements as well as component closure requirements as defined by the program management plan and by the governance processes. Non-project components must be approved for transition or termination, as appropriate. The resources that become available may be reallocated to other components. Communications to a larger, or different, set of stakeholders other than those at the project level may be necessary. See Figures 15-16 and 15-17.

Program components will normally close at the end of the project life cycle. Project closure may occur if a project is terminated before the completion of its life cycle. Non-project components may revert to the operational organization or be closed. Upon closure of the last program component, the overall program is evaluated for closure. The recommendation to close the program is part of the governance oversight process described in Section 15.5.

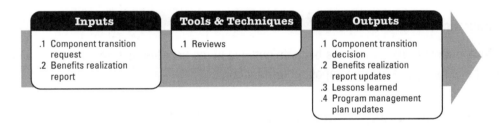

Figure 15-16. Approve Component Transition: Inputs, Tools & Techniques, and Outputs

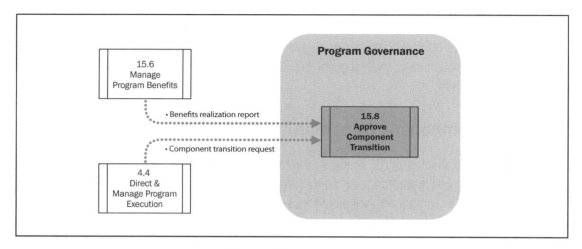

Figure 15-17. Approve Component Transition: Data Flow Diagram

15.8.1 Approve Component Transition: Inputs

.1 Component Transition Request

The governance board makes closure decisions based on component closure requests, arising either from normal project completion or from terminations. Program scope may change which may affect the various components and result in termination. The program team needs to understand how cost controls are affecting the various components. Should costs become an issue, one of the decisions may be to terminate the project early and redeploy resources.

.2 Benefits Realization Report

Components must provide the benefits outlined in the benefits realization plan. A failure to provide these benefits may result in component termination.

15.8.2 Approve Component Transition: Tools and Techniques

.1 Reviews

Component transition is typically the final gate review for a component within a program.

15.8.3 Approve Component Transition: Outputs

.1 Component Transition Decision

Decisions to transition or close components should be documented on a project transition/closure certificate and be communicated to stakeholders and component personnel, when appropriate. Decision records are stored in the program archives, and in accordance with regulations, laws, and organizational requirements.

.2 Benefits Realization Report Updates

The updated benefits realization report summarizes how successfully the component has delivered the desired benefits. It may optionally include the timeline, processes, and organization to measure future benefits.

.3 Lessons Learned

Lessons learned are captured throughout the life-cycle of the program and project.

.4 Program Management Plan Updates

Upon component closure, the program management plan and the decision log should be updated.

SECTION IV

APPENDICES

Appendix A

- Second Edition Changes

Appendix B

- Evolution of PMI's *The Standard for Program Management* – Second Edition

Appendix C

- Contributors and Reviewers of *The Standard for Program Management* – Second Edition

Appendix D

- Summary of Program Management Knowledge Areas

APPENDIX A

SECOND EDITION CHANGES

The purpose of this appendix is to give a detailed explanation of the changes included in *The Standard for Program Management* – Second Edition.

A.1 Structural Changes

There are dramatic revisions to *The Standard for Program Management* – Second Edition, with a marked difference in structure. *The Standard for Program Management* – Second Edition is structured to integrate the addition of Knowledge Areas for program management, which were previously not part of *The Standard for Program Management*, as described in Table A1, displaying a side-by-side comparison of the distinctions.

Table A1. Structural Changes

Original Standard Sections	Second Edition Sections
Section I – The Program Management Framework Chapters 1 and 2	Section I –The Program Management Framework Chapters 1 and 2
Section II – The Standard for Program Management Chapter 3 – Program Management Processes	Section II – The Standard for Program Management Chapter 3 – Program Management Processes
	Section III – The Program Management Knowledge Areas Chapters 4 through 15
Section III –Appendices Appendix D – Tools and Techniques Appendix E – Benefits Assurance and Sustainment Appendix F – Program Management Controls Appendix G – Examples of Organizational Structures of Programs Appendix H – Variance from or Extensions to Other related PMI Standards	Section IV – Appendices Appendix A – Second Edition Changes Appendix B – Evolution of PMI's *The Standard for Program Management* Appendix C – Contributors and Reviewers of *The Standard for Program Management* – Second Edition Appendix D – Summary of Program Management Knowledge Areas
Section IV - Glossary and Index	Section V –Glossary and Index

A.2 Addition of Knowledge Areas

In *The Standard for Program Management* – Second Edition, nine Knowledge Areas have been added which map to the five Process Groups.

Most of these Knowledge Areas will appear to be similar to those of the *PMBOK® Guide* – Fourth Edition Knowledge Areas, however the related inputs, outputs, tools and techniques in *The Standard for Program Management* – Second Edition are defined specifically for the management of programs. For example, while the *PMBOK® Guide* – Fourth Edition includes a Knowledge Area for Cost Management, the program management Knowledge Area is focused appropriately on Financial Management.

There are three Knowledge Areas that were deferred to the *PMBOK® Guide* – Fourth Edition, because they were felt to be adequately managed at the project level rather than at the program level. These areas were: Cost Management, Quality Management and Human Resource Management.

A.3 Elimination of Themes

The term "themes" is no longer used. Broad management themes had originally appeared in Section 1.7 of the initial *The Standard for Program Management,* referring to Benefits Management, Stakeholder Management, and Program Governance as major themes. This term has been eliminated since themes were since elaborated upon and have adequately been integrated into the program processes and Knowledge Areas.

A.4 Writing Styles

A style guide was developed and used by the project team to create and finalize the input. Attention was focused on using active voice language and content consistency throughout the document to prevent an occurrence of different writing styles.

A.5 Chapter 1 – Introduction Changes

The changes to Chapter 1 are largely to elaborate on the fundamental changes to the standard, which has been revised to reflect the standard Knowledge Areas and processes by which program management is widely practiced globally today. In Section 1.1 on the Purpose of the Standard for Program Management, the alignment of this standard with other PMI standards is highlighted, additionally referring to PMI's Code of Ethics and its importance to the practice of program management. There is also further discussion on the interactions between project, program, and portfolio management in Chapter 1, and an expansion on the program manager's role, knowledge, and skills and the organizational factors involved in program management.

The following table summarizes the changes between editions:

Table A2. Chapter 1 Summary of Changes

Initial Edition Sections	Second Edition Sections
1.1 Purpose of *The Standard for Program Management*	1.1 Purpose of *The Standard for Program Management*
1.2 What is a Program?	1.2 What is a Program?
1.3 What is Program Management?	1.3 What is Program Management?

1.4 The Relationship Between Program Management and Portfolio Management	1.4 Relationships Among Project, Program, and Portfolio
	  1.4.1 The Relationship between Program Management and Project Management
	  1.4.2 The Relationship between Program Management and Portfolio Management
	  1.4.3 The Interactions Among Portfolio, Program, and Project Management

1.5 The Relationship Between Program Management and Project Management	1.5 Program Management Office
1.6 Program Management in Organizational Planning	1.6 Role of the Program Manager 1.6.1 Program Manager Knowledge and Skills

1.7 Themes of Program Management
  1.7.1 Benefits Management
  1.7.2 Program Stakeholder Management
  1.7.3 Program Governance
	1.7 Program – External Factors
	  1.7.1 Organizational Process Assets
	  1.7.2 Enterprise Environmental Factors
	  1.7.3 Enterprise External Factors

A.6 Chapter 2 – Program Life Cycle and Benefits Management

In eliminating themes and building a stronger framework around program management, the title of Chapter 2 was changed from Program Life Cycle and Organization, to Program Life Cycle and Benefits Management. Subtle naming differences to clarify program phases were also incorporated into the revision. Chapter 2 now includes Section 2.3 on Program Benefits Management to end the chapter with a discussion of this salient aspect of program management and its importance in the program life cycle.

The following table summarizes the changes between the editions:

Table A3. Chapter 2 Summary of Changes

Initial Edition Sections	Second Edition Sections
2.1 The Program Life Cycle Overview	2.1 Program Life Cycle 　　2.1.1 Characteristics of the Program Life Cycle 　　2.1.2 Relationship to a Product's Life Cycle 　　2.1.3 Program Life Cycle and Benefits Management 　　2.1.4 Program Governance across the Life Cycle
2.2 Program Themes across the Program Life Cycle 　　2.2.1 Benefits Management and the Program Life Cycle 　　2.2.2 Stakeholder Management 　　2.2.3 Program Governance through Phase-Gate Reviews	2.2 Program Life Cycle Phases 　　2.2.1 Pre-Program Preparations 　　2.2.2 Program Initiation 　　2.2.3 Program Setup 　　2.2.4 Delivery of Program Benefits 　　2.2.5 Program Closure
2.3 Program Management Life Cycle Phases 　　2.3.1 Program Governance Across the Life Cycle 　　2.3.2 Phase One: Pre-Program Set Up 　　2.3.3 Phase Two: Program Set Up 　　2.3.4 Phase Three: Establish Program Management and Technical Infrastructure 　　2.3.5 Phase Four: Deliver the Benefits 　　2.3.6 Phase Five: Close the Program	2.3 Program Benefits Management 　　2.3.1 Delivering and Managing Benefits 　　2.3.2 Organizational Differences 　　2.3.3 Benefits Sustainment

A.7 Chapter 3 – Program Management Processes Changes

Chapter 3 has been revised to map to the Knowledge Areas being introduced in *The Standard for Program Management* – Second Edition. Chapter 3 serves as a standard for managing a program and clearly indicates the five required Program Management Process Groups and their constituent processes. Some of the processes were reshuffled to better flow as program management is practiced.

The following table summarizes the changes between the editions:

Table A4. Chapter 3 Summary of Changes

Initial Edition Sections	Second Edition Sections

3.1 Themes in the Program Management Life Cycle
   3.1.1 Benefits Management
   3.1.2 Stakeholder Management
   3.1.3 Program Governance
	3.1 Common Program Management Process Interactions
	   3.1.1 Common Inputs and Outputs

3.2 Program Management Process Groups	3.2 Program Management Process Groups

3.3 Common Program Management Process Components
   3.3.1 Inputs Common to Program Management Processes
   3.3.2 Outputs Common to Program Management Processes
	3.3 Initiating Process Group
	   3.3.1 Initiate Program
	   3.3.2 Establish Program Financial Framework

3.4 Initiating Process Group
   3.4.1 Initiate Program
   3.4.2 Authorize Projects
   3.4.3 Initiate Team
	3.4 Planning Process Group
	   3.4.1 Plan Program Scope
	   3.4.2 Define Program Goals and Objectives
	   3.4.3 Plan and Establish Program Governance Structure
	   3.4.4 Identify Program Stakeholders
	   3.4.5 Develop Program Management Plan
	   3.4.6 Develop Program Infrastructure
	   3.4.7 Develop Program Requirements
	   3.4.8 Develop Program Architecture
	   3.4.9 Develop Program WBS
	   3.4.10 Develop Program Schedule
	   3.4.11 Develop Program Financial Plan
	   3.4.12 Estimate Program Costs
	   3.4.13 Budget Program Costs
	   3.4.14 Plan Program Procurements
	   3.4.15 Plan Program Stakeholder Management
	   3.4.16 Plan Communications
	   3.4.17 Plan for Audits
	   3.4.18 Plan Program Quality
	   3.4.19 Plan Program Risk Management
	   3.4.20 Identify Program Risks
	   3.4.21 Analyze Program Risks
	   3.4.22 Plan Program Risk Responses

3.5 Planning Process Group
  3.5.1 Develop Program Management Plan
  3.5.2 Interface Planning
  3.5.3 Transition Planning
  3.5.4 Resource Planning
  3.5.5 Scope Definition
  3.5.6 Create Program WBS
  3.5.7 Schedule Development
  3.5.8 Cost Estimating and Budgeting
  3.5.9 Quality Planning
  3.5.10 Human Resource Planning
  3.5 11 Communications Planning
  3.5.12 Risk Management Planning and Analysis
  3.5.13 Plan Program Purchases and Acquisitions
  3.5.14 Plan Program Contracting

3.5 Executing Process Group
  3.5.1 Direct and Manage Program Execution
  3.5.2 Manage Program Resources
  3.5.3 Manage Program Architecture
  3.5.4 Manage Component Interfaces
  3.5.5 Engage Program Stakeholders
  3.5.6 Distribute Information
  3.5.7 Conduct Program Procurements
  3.5.8 Approve Component Initiation

3.6 Executing Process Group
  3.6.1 Direct and Manage Program Execution
  3.6.2 Perform Quality Assurance
  3.6.3 Acquire Program Team
  3.6.4 Develop Program Team
  3.6.5 Information Distribution
  3.6.6 Request Seller Responses
  3.6.7 Select Sellers

3.6 Monitoring and Controlling Process Group
  3.6.1 Monitor and Control Program Performance
  3.6.2 Monitor and Control Program Scope
  3.6.3 Monitor and Control Program Schedule
  3.6.4 Monitor and Control Program Financials
  3.6.5 Manage Program Stakeholder Expectations
  3.6.6 Monitor and Control Program Risks
  3.6.7 Administer Program Procurements
  3.6.8 Manage Program Issues
  3.6.9 Monitor and Control Program Changes
  3.6.10 Report Program Performance
  3.6 11 Provide Governance Oversight
  3.6.12 Manage Program Benefits

3.7 Monitoring and Controlling Process Group
  3.7.1 Integrated Change Control
  3.7 2 Resource Control
  3.7.3 Monitor and Control Program Work
  3.7.4 Issue Management and Control
  3.7.5 Scope Control
  3.7.6 Schedule Control
  3.7.7 Cost Control
  3.7.8 Perform Quality Control
  3.7.9 Communications Control
  3.7.10 Performance Reporting
  3.7.11 Risk Monitoring and Control
  3.7.12 Program Contract Administration

3.7 Closing Process Group
  3.7.1 Close Program
  3.7 2 Approve Component Transition
  3.7 3 Close Program Procurements

3.8 Closing Process Group
  3.8.1 Close Program
  3.8.2 Component Closure
  3.8.3 Contract Closure

3.9 Process Interactions

3.10 Program Management Process Mapping

A.8 Chapters 4 through 15 Changes

Content for Chapters 4 through 15 did not exist in the initial *The Standard for Program Management*. Knowledge Areas have been added and expanded upon, including inputs, tools and techniques, and outputs for each of these areas of program management:

Chapter 4: Program Integration Management

Chapter 5: Program Scope Management

Chapter 6: Program Time Management

Chapter 10: Program Communication Management

Chapter 11: Program Risk Management

Chapter 12: Program Procurement Management

Chapter 13: Program Financial Management

Chapter 14: Program Stakeholder Management

Chapter 15: Program Governance

The following chapters refer the reader to the *PMBOK® Guide* – Fourth Edition:

Chapter 7: Program Cost Management

Chapter 8: Program Quality Management

Chapter 9: Program Human Resource Management

It should be noted that these chapters were not included because most of the work in these Knowledge Areas is performed at the component level and not at the program level. Rather than duplicating chapters that are included in the *PMBOK® Guide* – Fourth Edition, the standard simply references the other standard.

The following table summarizes the changes between the editions:

Table A5. Chapter 4 Program Integration Management Changes

Initial Edition Sections	Second Edition Sections
	4.1 Initiate Program
	4.2 Develop Program Management Plan
	4.3 Develop Program Infrastructure
	4.4 Direct and Manage Program Execution
	4.5 Manage Program Resources
	4.6 Monitor and Control Program Performance
	4.7 Manage Program Issues
	4.8 Close Program

Table A6. Chapter 5 Program Scope Management Changes

Initial Edition Sections	Second Edition Sections
	5.1 Plan Program Scope
	5.2 Define Program Goals and Objectives
	5.3 Develop Program Requirements
	5.4 Develop Program Architecture
	5.5 Develop Program WBS
	5.6 Manage Program Architecture
	5.7 Manage Component Interfaces
	5.8 Monitor and Control Program Scope

Table A7. Chapter 6 Program Time Management Changes

Initial Edition Sections	Second Edition Sections
	6.1 Develop Program Schedule
	6.2 Monitor and Control Program Schedule

Table A8. Chapter 10 Program Communication Management Changes

Initial Edition Sections	Second Edition Sections
	10.1 Plan Communications
	10.2 Distribute Information
	10.3 Report Program Performance

Table A9. Chapter 11 Program Risk Management Changes

Initial Edition Sections	Second Edition Sections
	11.1 Plan Program Risk Management
	11.2 Identify Program Risks
	11.3 Analyze Program Risks
	11.4 Plan Program Risk Responses
	11.5 Monitor and Control Program Risks

Table A10. Chapter 12 Program Procurement Management Changes

Initial Edition Sections	Second Edition Sections
	12.1 Plan Program Procurements
	12.2 Conduct Program Procurements
	12.3 Administer Program Procurements
	12.4 Close Program Procurements

Table A11. Chapter 13 Program Financial Management Changes

Initial Edition Sections	Second Edition Sections
	13.1 Establish Program Financial Framework
	13.2 Develop Program Financial Plan
	13.3 Estimate Program Costs
	13.4 Budget Program Costs
	13.5 Monitor and Control Program Financials

Table A12. Chapter 14 Program Stakeholder Management Changes

Initial Edition Sections	Second Edition Sections
	14.1 Plan Program Stakeholder Management
	14.2 Identify Program Stakeholders
	14.3 Engage Program Stakeholders
	14.4 Manage Program Stakeholder Expectations

Table A13. Chapter 15 Program Governance Changes

Initial Edition Sections	Second Edition Sections
	15.1 Plan and Establish Program Governance Structure
	15.2 Plan for Audits
	15.3 Plan Program Quality
	15.4 Approve Component Initiation
	15.5 Provide Governance Oversight
	15.6 Manage Program Benefits
	15.7 Monitor and Control Program Changes
	15.8 Approve Component Transition

A.9 Chapters 4 – 15 Knowledge Area Summaries

Knowledge Area summaries for each of these chapters are detailed in Appendix D.

A.10 Glossary

The glossary has been expanded and updated to:

- Include those terms within *The Standard for Program Management* – Second Edition that need to be defined to support an understanding of the document's contents,

- Clarify meaning and improve the quality and accuracy of any translations, and

- Eliminate terms not used within *The Standard for Program Management* – Second Edition.

APPENDIX B

EVOLUTION OF PMI'S *THE STANDARD FOR PROGRAM MANAGEMENT*

B.1 Introduction

Since 1996, project managers and organizations have recognized the standard for managing a project: PMI's *A Guide to the Project Management Body of Knowledge* (*PMBOK® Guide*). Then in 2003, PMI introduced its first standard for organizations called the *Organizational Project Management Maturity Model* (*OPM3®*).

Early in 2003, recognizing that the project management profession encompasses a much broader field, including managing multiple projects through programs and portfolios, PMI's Standards Program Team (SPT – which includes the PMI Manager of Standards plus the Member Advisory Group) chartered the development of "a standard or standards" for program management and portfolio management processes.

Like the *PMBOK® Guide* standard for "most projects most of the time," the charter for the PPMS Program (program and portfolio management standards) was to focus on processes that are generally recognized as good practice most of the time. Moreover, the new standard or standards were to emulate the *PMBOK® Guide* – Third Edition, specifically excluding Knowledge Areas as well as tools and techniques. The new standard or standards, however, were to map content relationships to processes and Knowledge Areas aligned with the *PMBOK® Guide* – Third Edition.

B.2 Preliminary Work

In the summer of 2003, the PPMS Team formed, eventually including 416 PMI volunteers representing 36 countries under the leadership of David Ross, Project Manager, and Paul Shaltry, Deputy Project Manager.

One of the first challenges was the need to establish common agreement on the key definitions, in this case, "program," "program management," "portfolio," and "portfolio management." The PMI Standards Manager brought together all of the active standards teams to achieve consensus on these definitions. The involved team leaders agreed in time for common definitions to be included in the *PMBOK® Guide* – Third Edition and form the foundation for the program and portfolio management standards.

Next, the PPMS Team looked at whether the two subjects should be combined as one standard or treated separately. A sub-team was formed to perform a literature survey and poll the PM community to determine the differences and similarities between program and portfolio management processes. The research confirmed that while program management processes provide for the management of a group of interdependent projects, portfolio management comprises continuous, repeatable, and sustainable processes designed to map business requirements and objectives to projects and programs. As a result of this investigation, the PPMS Team concluded that the profession would be best served with two standards.

Despite the differences in these processes, the PPMS Team believed that because of the relationships between the two subjects and that these were first time standards, it would be best to manage them both under one program. The PPMS Core Team proposed this approach to the SPT, which approved the recommendation. In kind, the PPMS Team developed detailed requirements for each standard that the SPT also approved. The Core Team developed a program plan and general team orientation, which was mandatory, to help volunteers engage effectively. Development of both standards began in early 2004.

B.3 Drafting *The Standard for Program Management*

The Program Management Architecture Team (ProgMAT), jointly led by Clarese Walker and David Whelbourn, organized into four sub-teams: one for each chapter (1-3) and integration.

The team recognized early that the processes for program management closely paralleled those of project management, but were larger in scope. In addition, program management further distinguished itself by containing three broad themes that are common throughout each program: benefits management, stakeholder management, and governance.

While most of the work was done virtually, the team gathered for a meeting in Philadelphia in October 2004 to finalize the document. In the last quarter of 2004, the ProgMAT's draft standard underwent separate reviews by the PPMS Edit and Quality Teams in preparation for a broader review by, potentially, the whole PPMS Team. This broader review emulated the eventual global exposure draft review that PMI would conduct. The "mini-exposure draft" process generated over 400 comments from PPMS volunteers around the world.

The ProgMAT's work benefited from these comments and recommendations in the improvement or confirmation of content, even though a significant number of comments received were editorial. In general, this internal exposure draft process validated that the ProgMAT's draft was on target, as reviewers did not identify any major gaps.

B.4 Delivering the Initial *The Standard for Program Management*

The PPMS Core Team guided the final revisions and submitted the revised version to the general PPMS Team for a consensus vote. The overwhelming majority of those voting indicated acceptance of the proposed standard without reservation. The Core Team approved the proposed standard before turning it over to the SPT for review and approval in March 2005. The SPT engaged independent subject matter experts to augment the review process. From there, minor refinements were made and the proposed standard went on to a 90-day exposure draft process starting in June 2005.

The exposure draft period for *The Standard for Program Management* ended on August 19, 2005. PMI received 465 comments that the PPMS Adjudication Team reviewed. More than half of these comments were accepted, accepted with modification, or identified for review in the next version of the standard. The PPMS Core Team approved the actions of the Adjudication Team and directed the final edit and approval of the proposed standard. Only one adjudication action was appealed, and PMI's Adjudication Appeals Team subsequently resolved it.

In December 2005, the PPMS Core Team transferred the final draft for approval by the PMI Standards Consensus Body and subsequent publication.

B.4.1 *The Standard for Program Management* Project Core Team

The following individuals served as members, were contributors of text or concepts, and served as leaders within the Project Core Team (PCT):

David W. Ross, PMP, Project Manager

Paul E. Shaltry, PMP, Deputy Project Manager

Claude Emond, MBA, PMP

Larry Goldsmith, MBA, PMP

Nancy Hildebrand, BSc, PMP

Jerry Manas, PMP

Patricia G. Mulcair, PMP

Beth Ouellette, PMP

Tom E. Vanderheiden, PMP

Clarese Walker, PMP

David Whelbourn, MBA, PMP

Michael A. Yinger

B.4.2 Significant Contributors

In addition to the members of the Project Core Team, the following individuals provided significant input or concepts:

Fred Abrams, PMP, CPL

Greg Alexander, PhD, PE

Ronald L. Anderson, PMP, MPM

A. Kent Bettisworth

Peggy J. Brady, PMP

Nancy A. Cygan, PMP

Jeffrey J. Dworkin, PMP

Harold S. Hunt, PMP

Mary M. Kosovich, PMP, PE

Polisetty Veera Subrahmanya Kumar, PMP

Cheryl D. Logan, PMP

J. Kendall Lott, PMP

Angela Lummel, PMP

Susan MacAndrew, MBA, PMP

Russell McDowell, MEng, PMP

Laura L. Miller, PMP

Crispin (Kik) Piney, PMP

Clare J. Settle, PMP

Srikanth U.S MS, PMP

Nageswaran Vaidyanathan, PMP

Thomas Walenta, PMP

B.4.3 *The Standard for Program Management* Project Team Members

In addition to those listed previously, the following Program Management Team Members provided input to and recommendations on drafts of *The Standard for Program Management:*

Mohamed Hosney Abdelgelil

Eduardo O. Aguilo, PMP

Mounir A. Ajam, MS, PMP

Petya Alexandrova, PMP

Luis E. Alvarez Dionisi, MS, PMP

Cynthia Anderson, PMP

Jayant Aphale, PhD, MBA

V. Alberto Araujo, MBA, PMP

Alexey O. Arefiev, PMP

Julie Arnold, PMP

Darwyn S. Azzinaro, PMP

Rod Baker, MAPM, CPM

Harold Wayne Balsinger

Kate Bankston, PMP

Christina Barbosa, PMP

Randy Bennett, PMP, RCC

Susan S. Bivins, PMP

Dave M. Bond, PhD, PMP

Herbert Borchardt, PMP

Christine M. Boudreau

Lynda Bourne, DPM, PMP

Sonia Boutari, PMP

Adrienne L. Bransky, PMP

Shirley F. Buchanan, PMP

Jacques Cantin

Margareth F. Santos Carneiro, PMP, MSc

Jose M. Carvalho, PMP

Trevor Chappell, FIEE, PMP

Deepak Chauhan, PMP, APM

Keith Chiavetta

Pankaj Agrawal, PMP, CISA

Zubair Ahmed, PMP

Joyce Alexander

Shelley M. Alton, MBA, PMP

Neelu Amber

Mauricio Andrade, PMP

Michael Appleton, CMC, PMP

Jose Carlos Arce Rioboo, PMP

Mario Arlt, PMP

Canan Z. Aydemir

AC Fred Baker, PMP, MBA

Lorie A. Ballbach, PMP

Keith E. Bandt, PMP

Anil Bansal

John P. Benfield, PMP

David D. Bigness, Jr.

Jeroen Bolluijt

Stephen F. Bonk, PMP, PE

Ann Abigail Bosacker, PMP

Laurent Bour, PMP

Mark E. Bouska, PMP

David Bradford, PMP

Donna Brighton, PMP

Matthew Burrows, MIMC, PMP

James D. Carlin, PMP

Brian R. Carter, PMP

Pietro Casanova, PMP

Gordon Chastain

Eshan S. Chawla, MBA, PMP

Jaikumar R. Chinnakonda, PMP

Edmond Choi

Lisa Clark

Jose Correia Alberto, MSc, LCGI

Mark R. Cox, PMP

Damyan Georgiev Damyanov

Sushovan Datta

Stephanie E. Dawson, PMP

Nikunj Desai

Christopher DiFilippo, PMP

Vivek Dixit

Ross Domnik, PMP

Jim C. Dotson, PMP

Renee De Mond

Charles A. Dutton, PMP

Barbara S. Ebner

Michael G. Elliott

Michael P. Ervick, MBA, PMP

Linda A. Fernandez, MBA

Maviese A. Fisher, PMP, IMBA

Jacqueline Flores, PMP

Carolyn A. Francis, PMP

Kenneth Fung, PMP, MBA

Lisa Ann Giles, PMP

Sunil Kumar Goel, PMP

Andres H. Gonzalez D., ChE

Ferdousi J. Gramling

Bjoern Greiff, PMP

Naveen Grover

Claude L. Guertin, BSc, PMP

Bulent E. Guzel, PMP

Cheryl Harris-Barney

David A. Hillson, PhD, PMP

Sandy Yiu Fai Hui

Isao Indo, PMP, PE, JP

Sandra Ciccolallo

Kurt J. Clemente Sr., PMP

April M. Cox, PMP

Margery J. Cruise, MSc, PMP

Kiran M. Dasgupta, MBA, PMP

Kenneth M. Daugherty, PMP

Pallab K. Deb, B Tech, MBA

D. James Dickson, PMP

Peter Dimov, PMP, CBM

Janet Dixon, PMP, EdD

Anna Dopico, PMP

Karthik Duddala

Karen K. Dunlap, PMP, SSGB

Lowell D. Dye, PMP

Daniella Eilers

Michael T. Enea, PMP, CISSP

Clifton D. Fauntroy

Ezequiel Ferraz, PMP

Joyce M. Flavin, PMP

Robert J. Forster, MCPM, PMP

Serena E. Frank, PMP

Lorie Gibbons, PMP

John Glander

Victor Edward Gomes, BSc, PMP

Mike Goodman, PMP, MSEE

Alicia Maria Granados

Steve Gress, PMP

Yvonne D. Grymes

Papiya Gupta

Deng Hao

Holly Hickman

MD Hudon, PMP

Zeeshan Idrees, BSc

Andrea Innocenti, PMP

Suhail Iqbal, PE, PMP

Venkata Rao Jammi, MBA, PMP

Haydar Jawad, PMP

Monique Jn-Marie, PMP

Martin H. Kaerner, PhD, Ing

Kenday Samuel Kamara

Malle Kancherla, PMP

Saravanan Nanjan Kannan, PMP

Ashish Kemkar, PMP

Todd M. Kent, PMP

Sandeep Khanna, MBA, PMP

Raymond R. Klosek, PMP

Victoria Kosuda

Narayan Krish, PMP, MS

Puneet Kumar

Janet Kuster, PMP, MBA

Olaronke Arike Ladipo, MD

Robert LaRoche, PMP

Terry Laughlin, PMP

Ade Lewandowski

Jeffrey M. Lewman, PMP

Giri V. Lingamarla, PMP

Douglas Mackey, PMP

Erica Dawn Main

Ammar W. Mango, PMP, CSSBB

Hal Markowitz

Sandeep Mathur, PMP, MPD

Warren V. Mayo, PMP, CSSBB

Yves Mboda, PMP

Richard C. McClarty, Sr.

Malcolm McFarlane

Christopher F. McLoon

David McPeters, PMP

Vladimir I. Melnik, MSc, PMP

Anshoom Jain, PMP

David B. Janda

G. Lynne Jeffries, PMP

Kenneth L. Jones, Jr., PMP

Craig L. Kalsa, PMP

Michael Kamel, PEng, PMP

Soundaian Kamalakannan

Barbara Karten, PMP

Geoffrey L. Kent, PMP

Thomas C. Keuten, PMP, CMC

Karu Godwin Kirijath

Richard M. Knaster, PMP

Koushik Sudeendra, PMP

S V R Madhu Kumar, MBA, PMP

Girish Kurwalkar, PMP

Puneet Kuthiala, PMP

Guilherme Ponce de Leon S. Lago, PMP

David W. Larsen, PMP

Fernando Ledesma, PM, MBA

Corazon B. Lewis, PMP

Lynne C. Limpert, PMP

Dinah Lucre

Saji Madapat, PMP, CSSMBB

Subbaraya N. Mandya, PMP

Tony Maramara

Franck L. Marle, PhD, PMP

Dean R. Mayer

Philippe Mayrand, PMP

Amy McCarthy

Eric McCleaf, PMP

Graham McHardy

Kevin Patrick McNalley, PMP

Carl J. McPhail, PMP

Philip R. Mileham

M. Aslam Mirza, MBA, PMP

Nahid Mohammadi MS

Subrata Mondal

Balu Moothedath

Sharon D. Morgan-Redmond, PMP

Dr. Ralf Muller, PMP

Praveen Chand Mullacherry, PMP

Sreenikumar G. Nair

Carlos Roberto Naranjo P., PMP

Sean O'Neill, PMP

Rolf A. Oswald, PMP

Sukanta Kumar Padhi, PMP

Anil Peer, P.Eng., PMP

Zafeiris K. Petalas PhD Candidat

D. Michele Pitman

Todd Porter

Yves Pszenica, PMP

Peter Quinnell, MBA

Madhubala Rajagopal, MCA, PMP

Sameer S. Ramchandani, PMP

Raju N. Rao, PMP, SCPM

Carolyn S. Reid, PMP, MBA

Bill Rini, PMP

Cynthia Roberts

Allan S. Rodger, PMP

Dennis M. Rose, PMP

Julie Rundgren

Gunes Sahillioglu, MSc, MAPM

Mansi A. Sanap

Kulasekaran C. Satagopan, PMP, CQM

John Schmitt, PMP

Mark N. Scott

Sunita Sekhar, PMP

Nandan Shah, PMP

Rahul Mishra

Sandhya Mohanraj, PMP

Donald James Moore

Roy E. Morgan, PE, PMP

Saradhi Motamarri, MTech, PMP

Seetharam Mukkavilli, PhD, PMP

Kannan Sami Nadar, PMP

Vinod B. Nair, B Tech, MBA

Nigel Oliveira, PMP, BBA

Bradford Orcutt, PMP

Louis R. Pack, PMP

Lennox A. Parkins, MBA, PMP

Sameer K. Penakalapati, PMP

Susan Philipose

Charles M. Poplos, EdD, PMP

Ranganath Prabhu, PMP

Sridhar Pydah, PMP

Sueli S. Rabaca, PMP

Mahalingam Ramamoorthi, PMP

Prem G. Ranganath, PMP, CSQE

Tony Raymond, PMP

Geoff Reiss, FAPM, M.Phil

Steven F. Ritter, PMP

Andrew C. Robison, PMP

Randy T. Rohovit

Jackson Rovina, PMP

Diana Russo, PMP

Banmeet Kaur Saluja, PMP

Nandakumar Sankaran

Gary Scherling, PMP, ITIL

Neils (Chris) Schmitt

Stephen F. Seay, PMP

David Seto, PMP

Shoukat M. Sheikh

Donna- Mae Shyduik	Derry Simmel, PMP, MBA
Arun Singh, PMP, CSQA	Deepak Singh, PMP
Anand Sinha	Ron Sklaver, PMP, CISA
Michael I. Slansky, PMP	Nancy A. Slater, MBA, PMP
Christopher Sloan	Dennis M. Smith
Noel Smyth	Jamie B. Solak, MAEd
Keith J. Spacek	Gomathy Srinivasan, PMP
Srinivasan Govindarajulu, PMP	Joyce Statz, PhD, PMP
Marie Sterling, PMP	Martin B. Stivers, PMP
Curtis A. Stock, PMP	Michael E. Stockwell
LeConte F. Stover, MBA, PMP	Anthony P. Strande
Juergen Sturany, PMP	Kalayani Subramanyan, PMP
Mohammed Suheel, BE, MCP	Patricia Sullivan-Taylor, MPA, PMP
Vijay Suryanarayana, PMP	Dawn C. Sutherland, PMP
Alexander M. Tait	Martin D. Talbott, PMP
Ali Taleb, MBA, PMP	David E. Taylor, PMP
Sai K. Thallam, PMP	Ignatius Thomas, PMP
James M. Toney, Jr.	Eugenio R. Tonin, PMP
Jonathan Topp	Murthy TS, PMP
Shi-Ja Sophie Tseng, PMP	Yen K. Tu
Ian Turnbull	Dr. M. Ulagaraj, PhD
Marianne Utendorf, PMP	Ernest C. Valle, MBA, PMP
Thierry Vanden Broeck, PMP	Gary van Eck, PMP
Paula Ximena Varas, PMP	Jayadeep A. Vijayan, BTech, MBA
Alberto Villa, PMP, MBA	Ludmila Volkovich
Namita Wadhwa, CAPM	Jane B. Walton, CPA
Yongjiang Wang, PMP	Michael Jeffrey Watson
Kevin R. Wegryn, PMP, MA	Richard A. Weller, PMP
Thomas Williamson, PMP	Rick Woods, MBA, PMP
Fan Wu	Cai Ding Zheng, PMP
Yuchen Zhu, PMP	Leon Zilber, MSc, PMP

B.4.4 Final Exposure Draft Reviewers and Contributors

In addition to team members, the following individuals provided recommendations for improving *The Standard for Program Management*:

Hussain Ali Al-Ansari, Eur Ing, C Eng

Mohammed Abdulla Al-Kuwari, C Eng, PMP

Mohammed Safi Batley, MIM

Colin S. Cantlie, PEng, PMP

John M. Clifford, CAPM

John E. Cormier, PMP

Gary C. Davis, PMP

Johan Delaure, PMP

Jean-Luc Frere, Ir, PMP

Stanislaw Gasik

Harsh Grover, PMP

Charles L. Hunt

Matthew D. Kraft, PMP

Craig J. Letavec, PMP

Susan Marshall

Yan Bello Mendez, PMP

Sundara Nagarajan

Kazuhiko Okubo, PE, PMP

Jerry Partridge, PMP

Kenyon D. Potter, PE, JD

Kenneth P. Schlatter

Gregory P. Schneider, PMP

Kazuo Shimizu, PMP

Larry Sieck

Jennie R. Smith, PMP

Martin B. Stivers, PMP

George Sukumar

Craig M. Thiel, PMP

Srikanth U.S MS, PMP

Judy L. Van Meter

Dave Violette, MPM, PMP

William P. Wampler, PMP

CD Watson, PMP

Patrick Weaver, PMP, FAICD

Rebecca A. Winston, Esq

B.4.5 PMI Project Management Standards Program Member Advisory Group

The following individuals served as members of the PMI Standards Program Member Advisory Group during development of *The Standard for Program Management:*

Julia M. Bednar, PMP

Carol Holliday, PMP

Thomas Kurihara

Debbie O'Bray

Asbjorn Rolstadas, PhD

Cyndi Stackpole

Bobbye Underwood, PMP

Dave Violette, MPM, PMP

B.4.6   Production Staff

Special mention is due to the following employees of PMI:

Ruth Anne Guerrero, PMP, Former Standards Manager

Dottie Nichols, PMP, Former Standards Manager

Kristin L. Vitello, Standards Project Specialist

Nan Wolfslayer, Standards Project Specialist

Dan Goldfischer, Editor-in-Chief

Richard E. Schwartz, Former Product Editor

Barbara Walsh, Publications Planner

B.5 *The Standard for Program Management*—Second Edition

During the PMI Global Conference in Seattle, Washington, in 2006, a standards working session was held where *The Standard for Program Management* was reviewed for comments and suggestions to revise and improve upon the initial release. One of the most salient issues raised at this working session was the confusing nature of themes and the recognition that programs also have Knowledge Areas and tools and techniques inherently specific to managing programs, which cannot be adequately elaborated upon by mapping to the *PMBOK® Guide* Knowledge Areas.

Subsequently, a standards working session was held at the 2007 EMEA PMI Congress in Budapest in May to derive further structural and content recommendations in preparing for a standard revision and the production of *The Standard for Program Management* – Second Edition. In attendance from the Program Standard was Frank Parth (Program Standard PM), Doug Treasure (Program Standard Deputy PM) and Brenda Treasure (Volunteer Coordinator).

The workshop conducted was a joint session between the PMI portfolio and program standards, with an update on the PMI *PMBOK® Guide* – Fourth Edition also provided to the group of more than 50 attendees. The Portfolio and Program working groups then formed, based on attendee preference with approximately 30 members choosing to work on *The Standard for Program Management.* Some of the crucial areas discussed for potential inclusion, integration, or elimination included benefits realization and its importance at the program level, scope management and requirements management, reporting metrics, components, and earned value.

Following this, teams began formation for chapter revision and content development. A Core Team meeting was held in Denver, Colorado in June 2007 to further evaluate and firm up the structural changes to the standard. In September 2007, the Knowledge Areas for the Program Standard – Second Edition, were finalized and chapter content was initially developed, with an initial review draft of all Knowledge Areas submitted mid-month, and the initial chapters reviewed immediately thereafter.

The final draft was sent to PMI final editing in July 2008 and approved in September 2008 for publication by PMI.

APPENDIX C

CONTRIBUTORS AND REVIEWERS OF *THE STANDARD FOR PROGRAM MANAGEMENT* – SECOND EDITION

This appendix lists, alphabetically within groupings, those individuals who have contributed to the development and production of *The Standard for Program Management* – Second Edition. No simple list or even multiple lists can adequately portray all the contributions of those who have volunteered to develop *The Standard for Program Management* – Second Edition.

The Project Management Institute is grateful to all of these individuals for their support and acknowledges their contributions to the project management profession.

C.1 *The Standard for Program Management* – Second Edition Project Core Team

The following individuals served as members, were contributors of text or concepts, and served as leaders within the Project Core Team (PCT):

Frank R. Parth, MS, PMP, Project Manager

Doug Treasure, PMP, MMT, Deputy Project Manager

Paul Burgess, Operations Lead

Mohammed Taher Netarwala, BE Mechanical, PMP, Project Scheduler

Mark Paden, PMI, MAPM, Knowledge Area Team Lead

Penny Pickles, MA, PMP, Editor

Khalil Saeidzadeh, MPM, PMP, Sections 1 & 2 Team Lead

Glenn W. Strausser, MBA, PMP, Quality

Brenda E. Treasure, BBM, PMP, Resource Lead

Hubert J. van Goor, MSc, PMP, Architect

Kristin L. Vitello, Standards Project Specialist

C.2 *The Standard for Program Management* – Second Edition Project Sub-Teams

The following individuals served as contributors of text or concepts and as Knowledge Area chapter leaders of the Project Sub Teams (PST):

Ronald M. Askew, MPM, PMP   Srinivasan Chandrasekar, MBA, PMP

Elena Chirich   Eric Walter T. Chojnicki

Seamus M. Conlan, CEng MIMechE, PMP   Richard J. Flynn, PMP

W. Don Gottwald, PhD, PMP   Esther Messallem, PMP

Sivakami Shekar, PMP   Anca E. Slusanschi, MSc, PMP

Martin Wartenberg, MBA, PE

C.3 Significant Contributors

In addition to the members of the Project Core Team and the Sub-Team Leaders, the following individuals provided significant support on inputs and concepts:

Albert John Cacace MBA, PMP

Marius Grigore, MBA, PMP

Elizabeth Land, PMP

Beth Ouellette, MBA, PMP

C.4 Operation Team Members

In addition to those listed previously in Section C.3, the following team members assisted in project operations for *The Standard for Program Management* – Second Edition.

Operation Team Members:

Christine Boisvert

David Rogers, PMP

Sivakami Shekar

Vasant Shroff, MTech

Ashish Vazirani

C.5 *The Standard for Program Management* – Second Edition Project Content Reviewers

In addition to those listed previously, the following *The Standard for Program Management* – Second Edition Project Team Members performed reviews of drafts of *The Standard for Program Management* – Second Edition.

Content Reviewers:

James D. Betsinger Jr.	Sourav Chakraborty
Abby B. Hodge, MPM, PMP	Rodrigo Leite Martins, PMP
Darrel S. Rogan, PMP	Kuan-Hsun Wang, PMP

C.6 *The Standard for Program Management* – Second Edition Project Team Members

In addition to those listed previously, the following individuals participated on *The Standard for Program Management* – Second Edition Project Team.

Team Members:

Sorosh Ahmed, MBA, PMP	Srilekha Akula
Louai Al-Amir Salem, PMP	Pilar Sanchez Albaladejo, PMP
Nicholas Anderson	Marca Atencio, MBA, PMP
Sreenivas Atluri, PMP	Esteban Abdiel Francis Austin
Jaideep Agrawal, MBA, PMP	Hani A. Badr, MSc, PMP
Ravi Bansal, PMP, IBM Certified Senior PM	Celia Baula
Aaron B. Benningfield	Sanjiv Bhardwaj
Brad Bigelow, PMP, P2R	Michael C. Broadway, PMP
James N. Brooke, PhD, PMP	Terrance P. Bullock, PMP
Iris S. Burrell	Steve Butler
Qi Chen	Robert Crandlemire, PMP, PgMP
Wanda Curlee, DM, PgMP	Thomas Cutting, PMP
Dipanker Das	Ernani Marques da Silva, MBA, PMP
Raveesh Dewan	Alphonso Dinson
Nigel O. D'Souza, MSc, PMP	Jeffrey Dworkin
Jo Ann Estep, PMP	John A. Estrella, PhD, PMP
Joseph Fehrenbach, PMP	Daniel Fernandez

Martin Flank MBA, PMP

MV Giridhar

Murray Gough, MPD

Peter C. Grant

Joseph A. Griffin, PMP, MBA

Michael Haran, PMP

Elaine Rearick Holly

Mangesh Inamdar

Kimberly Anne Johnson

Julius E. Kanyamunyu, MBA, MSc

J. Paul Kelly III, PMP

Rameshchandra B. Ketharaju, CSQA

Sandeep Khanna

Srinivas Kolaganti

Ramki Krishnamurthy, MS, PMP

Charles Lebo, PMP

Nicholas Lloyd-Davies

Geoff S. Mattie, Six Sigma, MCSE

Masao Motegi

Biju Nair

Bobby K. Paramasivam, BS(Mech Eng), MBA, PMP

Shiri R. Persaud, PMP

Kerstin Pohl, PMP

Bellore R. Raghuram

Jay. R. Ramsuchit, PMP

Tom Reale, MBA, PMP

Gustavo de Abreu Ribas, MBA

Elmar J. Roberg, PMP

Fernán Rodríguez, PMP

Mohammad Shalan, PMP, ITIL

Amandeep Singh, PMP

Carolyn Francis, MBA, PMP

Robert Goode

Piyush Govil, BE, PMP

Philip A. Grech, PMP, GradDipPM

James A. Hallman

Henrique Moura, PMP

David A. Hillson, PhD, PMP

Michael O. Jablon, PMP

Shanker Jousula, PMP

Nikki Kelly

Tom Kerr, PMP

Diana Ketteridge BAppSc, PMP

Christopher A. Knapp, MEE, PMP

Mary Kosovich

Peter Kuchnicki

Juanita Jane Lightfoot, PMP

Durga Prasad Mangali, BE, PMP

Eric D. Mauricio, PMP

Anand Murali

Valerie O'Keeffe-Short, PMP, CHAM

Melissa Perez, PMP

Crispin ("Kik") Piney, BSc, PMP

Kate Pokorny, PMP

Rupesh Rahate

Dalbir Singh Rangi

Juliano Reis, MBA, PMP

Marco Rigo, PMP

Elaine J. Roberts

Agostino Schito, PMP

Jonathan Shinn MPM, MBA

Donald Six, PMP

Veldanda Swapna

Masanori Takahashi, MA, PMP

Sivasubramanian Thangarathnam, BE, PGDIM

Thierry Vanden Broeck, PMP

Dennis K. Van Gemert, MS, PMP

Jean-Jacques Verhaeghe, PMP

Albert Wong

Chao-Yong Zhang

M. Nabil Tahle, PE, PMP

Garry Tanuan

Rajesh Vaidyanathan, PMP

Surya Vangara, CISA, CISM

Satya Venkata Vanumu

J. Steven Waddell

Lucia Wong MBA, PMP

C.7 Final Exposure Draft Reviewers and Contributors

In addition to team members, the following individuals provided recommendations for improving the Exposure Draft of *The Standard for Program Management* – Second Edition:

Hanada Akira

Mohammed Abdulla Al-Kuwari, Eur Ing, PMP

Mohammed Safi Batley, MIM

Lynda Bourne, DPM, PMP

Chris Cartwright, MPM, PMP

Bruce C. Chadbourne PMP, PgMP

Allan Edward Dean, MBA, PMP

Bruce Ferguson MSc, MAICD

David P. Gent, CEng, PMP

Joelle A. Godfrey, PMP

Sheriff Hashem, PhD, PMP

Hideyuki Hikida, PMP

Zulfiqar Hussain, PE, PMP

Tony Johnson, PgMP, PMP

Thomas C. Keuten, PMP, OPM3-CC

Philippe Landucci, PMP

Yan Bello Méndez, PMP

Lawrence T. Michaels

Jeffrey S. Nielsen, PMP

Beth Ouellette, MBA, PMP

Hussain Ali Al-Ansari, Eur Ing, CEng

Ondiappan Arivazhagan "Ari," PMP, CSSBB

Stephen F. Bonk, PE, PMP

Gareth Byatt, MBA

Helena Cedersjö, MSc, PMP

Chiba, Tomio PMP

Billy D. Faubion, PhD, PMP

Quentin W. Fleming

Peter James Gilliland, PMP

Patti Harter, PMP

Mohamed S. Hefny, MSc, PMP

Travis J. Hughes, PMP

T.D. Jainendrakumar, PMP

Rameshchandra B. Ketharaju

Henry Kondo, PMP, CISA

K-G Lundquist, MSc, PMP

Louis J. Mercken, PMI Fellow, PMP

Christopher Miles , PMP, OPM3 Assessor

Kazuhiko Okubo, PE, PMP

Ramesh Pachamuthu, MSc, PMP

<table>
<tr><td>William J. Parkes, PMP</td><td>Major B. Howard Penix, USAF (retired), PMP</td></tr>
<tr><td>S. Ramani, PgMP, PMP</td><td>Gurdev S. Randhawa, PMP</td></tr>
<tr><td>Paul E. Shaltry, PMP</td><td>Kazuo Shimizu, PMP</td></tr>
<tr><td>Hilary Shreter, MBA, PMP</td><td>Michael Simmering</td></tr>
<tr><td>Sriraman Subramaniam, PMP</td><td>Shoji Tajima, PMP</td></tr>
<tr><td>Masanori Takahashi, PMP, MA</td><td>Massimo Torre, PhD, PMP</td></tr>
<tr><td>Srikanth U.S. MS, PGCPM</td><td>Aloysio Vianna da Vianna</td></tr>
<tr><td>Patrick Weaver, PMP, FAICD</td><td>Kevin R. Wegryn, PMP, CPM</td></tr>
<tr><td>Martin Weimarck, MSc, PMP</td><td>Clement C.L. Yeung, PMP</td></tr>
<tr><td>Azam M. Zaqzouq, MCT, PMP</td><td></td></tr>
</table>

C.8 PMI Standards Member Advisory Group (MAG)

The following individuals served as members of the PMI Standards Member Advisory Group (MAG) during development of *The Standard for Program Management* – Second Edition:

<table>
<tr><td>Julia M. Bednar, PMP</td><td>Chris Cartwright, MPM, PMP</td></tr>
<tr><td>Douglas Clark</td><td>Terry Cooke-Davies, PhD FCMI</td></tr>
<tr><td>Carol Holliday, MA, PMP</td><td>Deborah O'Bray, CIM (Hons)</td></tr>
<tr><td>Asbjørn Rolstadås, PhD, Ing</td><td>David W. Ross, PMP, PgMP</td></tr>
<tr><td>Paul E. Shaltry, PMP</td><td>David Violette, MPM, PMP</td></tr>
<tr><td>John Zlockie, MBA, PMP, PMI Standards Manager</td><td></td></tr>
</table>

C.9 Staff Contributors

Special mention is due to the following employees of PMI:

Christie Biehl, EdD, PMP, Former Project Manager

Steven L. Fahrenkrog, PMP, VP Regional Development

Amanda Freitick, Standards Program Administrator

Donn Greenberg, Publications Manager

Ruth Anne Guerrero, MBA, PMP, Former Standards Manager

Lisa M. Jacobsen, Project Manager, CAPM

Roberta Storer, Product Editor

Barbara Walsh, CAPM, Publications Planner

Nan Wolfslayer, AStd, Standards Compliance Specialist

Nancy Wilkinson, MBA, PMP, OPM3® Project Specialist

APPENDIX D

SUMMARY OF PROGRAM MANAGEMENT KNOWLEDGE AREAS

D.1 Chapter 4 – Program Integration Management

Program Integration Management includes the processes and activities needed to identify, define, combine, unify, and coordinate multiple components within the program as well as coordinate the various processes and program management activities within the Program Management Process Groups. In the program management context, integration includes characteristics of unification, consolidation, articulation and integrative actions that are crucial for completing the program, managing stakeholder expectations, and delivering program benefits. The Program Integration Management processes include:

- *Initiate Program*—The purpose of Initiate Program is to produce the information needed to begin effective program planning as a basis for efficient execution and obtain the authorization for this work approval of the program charter.

- *Develop Program Management Plan* —The process of consolidating and coordinating all subsidiary plans into a program management plan as well as updating the program roadmap. This plan will serve as the consolidated plan for executing, monitoring, and closing the program.

- *Develop Program Infrastructure*—The process of identifying, assessing, and developing the infrastructure required to support the program.

- *Direct and Manage Program Execution*—The process of managing the execution of the program management plan to achieve program objectives.

- *Manage Program Resources*—The process of tracking, assessing, and adapting to the use of resources throughout the program's life cycle.

- *Monitor and Control Program Performance*—The process of monitoring and controlling the program's execution to meet performance objectives as defined in the program management plan.

- *Manage Program Issues*—The process of addressing unplanned risks and events that may impact the program's planned directives. Issues are assessed and, if necessary, a change request is issued to address the issue or is referred to the Risk Management process, for example, for further analysis and planning.

- *Close Program*—The process of finalizing all activities across all of the Program Management Process Groups to formally close the program.

D.2 Chapter 5 – Program Scope Management

Program Scope Management identifies the deliverables, estimates the major risks, and establishes the relationship between product scope and program scope, while setting standards for clear achievable objectives. The Program Scope Management processes include:

- *Plan Program Scope*—The process of identifying and developing activities to produce deliverables and benefits that meet the program goals and objectives.

- *Define Program Goals and Objectives*—The process for establishing the overall goals and objectives of the program and ultimately what is to be delivered.

- *Develop Program Requirements*—The process for development and formal identification of the program requirements and specifications to deliver the program goals and objectives.

- *Develop Program Architecture*—The process of defining the structure of the program's components and identifying the interrelationships between all of the program components.

- *Develop Program WBS*—The process for subdividing the program into its constituent parts (components, deliverables, and activities) It provides a deliverable-orientated, hierarchical decomposition of the work to be executed and accomplished by each component of the program.

- *Manage Program Architecture*—The process for managing the relationships between all of the program components to ensure the program architecture remains up-to-date.

- *Manage Component Interfaces*—The process for maintaining the adherence of program delivery and its constituent parts and managing interrelationships between the program's components.

- *Monitor and Control Program Scope*—The process for ensuring the program's scope is controlled to meet the agreed-upon goals and realize the agreed program objectives and benefits identified in the program charter.

D.3 Chapter 6 – Program Time Management

Program Time Management involves processes for scheduling the defined program components and entities necessary to produce the final program deliverables. It includes determining the order in which the individual components are executed, the critical path for the program, and the milestones to be measured to keep the overall program on track and within the defined constraints. The Program Time Management processes include:

- *Develop Program Schedule*—The process of defining the program components needed to produce the program deliverables, determine the order in which the components must be executed, estimate the amount of time required to accomplish each component, and identify the major program level milestones during the performance period.

- *Monitor and Control Program Schedule*—The process of ensuring the program produces the required deliverables and solutions on time. Activities include tracking the start and finish dates as well as significant intermediate milestones against the planned time lines. Updating the schedule and reporting the impact of missed dates are part of this process.

D.4 Chapter 7 – Program Cost Management

This Knowledge Area is not included as part of *The Standard for Program Management*.

D.5 Chapter 8 – Program Quality Management

This Knowledge Area is not included as part of *The Standard for Program Management*.

D.6 Chapter 9 – Program Human Resource Management

This Knowledge Area is not included as part of *The Standard for Program Management*.

D.7 Chapter 10 – Program Communication Management

Program Communications Management includes the processes for ensuring timely and appropriate generation, collection, distribution, storage, retrieval, and ultimate disposition of program information. Program Communication Management is different from the project communications. Since it affects a wider array of stakeholders, different communications tools and marketing are required. The Program Communication Management processes include:

- *Plan Communications*—Determining the information and communications needs of the program stakeholders.

- *Distribute Information*—Making needed information available to program stakeholders in a timely manner.

- *Report Program Performance*—Collecting and distributing performance information. This includes status reporting, progress measurement, and forecasting.

D.8 Chapter 11 – Program Risk Management

Program Risk Management describes the processes involved with identifying, analyzing, and controlling risks for the program. The Program Risk Management processes include:

- *Plan Program Risk Management*—Deciding how to approach, plan, and execute the risk management activities for a program, including risks identified in the individual program components.

- *Identify Program Risks* —Determining which risks might affect the program and documenting their characteristics.

- *Analyze Program Risks* —Prioritizing risks for further analysis or action by assessing and tabulating their probability of occurrence and impact, analyzing the effect on overall program and its components, and managing interdependencies.

- *Plan Program Risk Responses*—Developing options and actions to enhance opportunities, and to reduce threats to program objectives.

- *Monitor and Control Program Risks*—Tracking identified risks, monitoring residual risks, identifying new risks, executing risk response plans, and evaluating their effectiveness throughout program life cycle.

D.9 Chapter 12 – Program Procurement Management

Program Procurement Management describes the processes, inputs, tools and techniques, and outputs associated with performing procurement for a program. The Program Procurement Management processes include:

- *Plan Program Procurements*—The process of (a) determining what to procure and when and (b) developing procurement strategies. This process precedes all other procurement efforts.

- *Conduct Program Procurements*—The process that details how to conduct the procurement activities of a program. It includes strategies, tools, methods, metrics gathering, reviews and update mechanisms, standard assessment parameters, and reporting requirements to be used by each component of the program in conducting the procurement activities of the program.

- *Administer Program Procurements*—The process involved in managing the contracts during the program to ensure that the deliverables meet requirements, deadlines, cost, and quality established in the contract.

- *Close Program Procurements*—Are those processes that formally close out each contract on the program after ensuring that all deliverables have been satisfactorily completed, that all payments have been made, and that there are no outstanding contractual issues.

D.10 Chapter 13 – Program Financial Management

Program Financial Management includes all of the processes involved in identifying the program's financial sources and resources, integrating the budgets of the individual program components developing the overall budget for the program, and controlling costs throughout the life cycle of both the component and program. The Program Financial Management processes include:

- *Establish Program Financial Framework*—Identifying the overall financial environment for the program and pinpointing the funds that are available according to identified milestones.

- *Develop Program Financial Plan*—Creating the processes for developing and managing the program budget and the payment schedules to the components.

- *Estimate Program Costs*—Developing the initial program cost estimates that will be presented to the decision makers for approval and further funding.

- *Budget Program Costs*—Developing the detailed budgets for the program and for the components based on the estimates provided by the components.

- *Monitor and Control Program Financials*—Influencing the factors that create cost variances, controlling those variances at the program level, and closing out the program and component finances.

D.11 Chapter 14 – Program Stakeholder Management

Program Stakeholder Management defines program stakeholders as individuals and organizations whose interests may be affected by the program outcomes, either positively or negatively. The Program Stakeholder Management processes include:

- *Plan Program Stakeholder Management*—Plan Stakeholder Management covers planning how stakeholders will be identified, analyzed, engaged, and managed throughout the life of the program.

- *Identify Program Stakeholders*—Identify Program Stakeholders addresses the systematic identification and analysis of program stakeholders and creates the stakeholder register.

- *Engage Program Stakeholders*—The process of engaging program stakeholders is where the program management team ensures that stakeholders are involved in the program.

- *Manage Program Stakeholder Expectations*—Manage Program Stakeholder Expectations is the process of managing communications to satisfy the requirements of, and resolve issues with, program stakeholders.

D.12 Chapter 15 – Program Governance Management

Program Governance Management ensures decision-making and delivery management activities are focused on achieving program goals in a consistent manner, addressing appropriate risks and fulfilling stakeholder requirements. The Program Governance Management processes include:

- *Plan and Establish Program Governance Structure*—Identifying governance goals and defining the governance structure, roles, and responsibilities.

- *Plan for Audits*—The process for ensuring the program is prepared for both external and internal audits of program finances, processes, and documents, and demonstrates compliance with approved organizational program management processes.

- *Plan Program Quality*—The process of identifying quality standards applicable to the program, the processes, and the standards to be applied, and ensuring compliance to these standards.

- *Approve Component Initiation*—The process of defining the decision-making structures and processes, which enable initiating and changing the program and/or components within the program.

- *Provide Governance Oversight*—The process for providing governance and auditability throughout the course of the program.

- *Manage Program Benefits*—The process for ensuring governance of expected program benefits is delivered consistently throughout the program life cycle.

- *Monitor and Control Program Changes*—The process for ensuring the appropriate level of governance is applied to decision making of proposed changes to the program plan.

- *Approve Component Transition*—The process for ensuring transition of knowledge, responsibilities, and benefit realization from the program to ongoing operations.

SECTION V

GLOSSARY AND INDEX

Glossary

Index

GLOSSARY

1. Inclusions and Exclusions

This glossary includes terms that are:

- Unique to program management (e.g., benefits management).

- Not unique to program management, but used differently or with a narrower meaning in program management than in general everyday usage (e.g., benefit, risk).

This glossary generally does not include:

- Application or industry area-specific terms.

- Terms used in program management which do not differ in any material way from everyday use (e.g., business outcome).

- Terms used in program management which do not differ from a similar term defined in the PMBOK® Guide – Fourth Edition, except that these terms are now used at a program level instead of a project level (e.g. a program charter and a project charter both serve the same purpose—to approve the start of the effort).

2. Common Acronyms

IPECC	The Initiating, Planning, Executing, Monitoring and Controlling, and Closing Process Groups
PMBOK	Project Management Body of Knowledge
PMO	Program Management Office
PMO	Project Management Office

3. Definitions

Many of the words here may have broader and, in some cases, different dictionary definitions to accommodate the context of program management.

Audit Plan. A document that describes the objectives and timing for audits and is updated with the results of each audit.

Benefit. An opportunity that provides an advantage to an organization, such as increased profits, improved operations, growth, or improved employee morale.

Benefits Management. Those activities and techniques used in defining, creating, maximizing, and sustaining the benefits provided by programs.

Benefits Realization Plan. A document detailing the expected benefits to be realized by a program and how these benefits will be achieved.

Best Practices Library. A repository for best practices in templates, processes, and methodologies that is made available to the program manager to help in selecting the most effective approach to manage the program.

Bidder Conferences. The meetings with prospective sellers prior to the preparation of a bid or proposal to ensure all prospective vendors have a clear and common understanding of the procurement. Also known as contractor conferences, vendor conferences, or pre-bid conferences.

Business Case. A documented economic feasibility study used to establish validity of the benefits of a selected component lacking sufficient definition and that is used as a basis for the authorization of further project management activities.

Business Outcome. A financial result (cost saving, opportunity, employee reduction, revenue growth, revenue retention) derived from implementing an organization's strategies.

Closing Processes [Program Management Process Group]. Those processes performed to formally terminate all activities of a program or phase, and transfer the completed product to others or close a cancelled program.

Component. A piece of the program. The majority of the components within a program are the individual projects that make up the program, but the program management office or other infrastructure required to manage the program is also a component.

Component Initiation Request. The formal request to begin work on a program component.

Component Transition Request. The formal request to transition a program component's product into the program.

Control. A means of comparing actual performance with planned performance, analyzing variances, assessing trends to effect process improvements, evaluating possible alternatives, and recommending appropriate corrective action as needed.

Corporate Governance. The process by which an organization directs and controls its operational and strategic activities, and by which the organization responds to the legitimate rights, expectations, and desires of its stakeholders.

Cost/Benefit Analysis (CBA). A financial analysis tool used to determine the benefits provided by a project against its costs.

Customer. The person or organization that will use the program's benefits, products or services, or results.

Executing Processes [Program Management Process Group]. Those processes performed to complete the work defined in the program management plan to accomplish the program's objectives defined in its scope statement.

Feasibility Study. An early engineering and financial analysis of a proposed project to determine its viability.

Governance Decision Register. A formal documentation of the meeting minutes, action item logs, and other decisions.

Initiating Processes [Program Management Process Group]. Those processes performed to authorize and define the scope of a new phase or program, or that can result in the continuation of halted program work.

Input [Process Input]. Any item, whether internal or external to the program, which is required by a process before that process proceeds. May be an output from a predecessor process.

Market Environmental Factors. Those influences that come from outside the organization and affect its activities. These can include influences such as the regulatory, social, and financial environments as well as market conditions.

Mechanism. A means used to perform a process. See also *tool* or *technique.*

Monitoring and Controlling Processes [Program Management Process Group]. Those processes performed to measure and monitor program execution so that corrective action can be taken when necessary to control the execution of the phase or program.

Multi-Project Management. Those aspects of program management associated with initiating and coordinating the activities of multiple projects and the management of project managers.

Operational Management. The ongoing organizational activities associated with supporting functional elements, as opposed to project elements. Operational management also includes support of products that the organization has created through project activity.

Output. A product, result, or service generated by a process. May be an input to a successor process.

Payment Control System. Those mechanisms and controls to ensure that evidence is presented and that required approvals are obtained before a payment request is authorized and executed.

Performing Organization. The enterprise whose personnel are most directly involved in doing the work of the program.

Phase Gate. A review process at the end of a program phase where an oversight group, such as a program board or steering committee, decides to continue, continue with modification, or stop a program.

Planning Processes [Program Management Process Group]. Those processes performed to define and mature the program scope, develop the management plan, and identify and schedule the activities that occur within the program.

Process. A set of interrelated actions and activities performed to achieve a specified set of products, results, or services.

Program. A group of related projects managed in a coordinated way to obtain benefits and control not available from managing them individually. Programs may include elements of related work outside of the scope of the discrete projects in the program.

Program Architecture. The structure of the program component products and their technical relationships with one another.

Program Financial Framework. The plan for identifying and coordinating the funding sources for the program, the conditions in which funds will be released, and how and to whom the money will be paid out.

Program Financial Plan. A document that is part of the program management plan, which includes funding schedules and milestones, the baseline budget, contract payments and schedules, financial metrics, financial reporting processes, how subcontractor payments will be managed, and all other financial-related efforts on the project.

Program Governance. The process of developing, communicating, implementing, monitoring, and assuring the policies, procedures, organizational structures, and practices associated with a given program.

Program Governance Plan. A plan that describes the governance, goals, structure, roles and responsibilities, and logistics for executing the governance process.

Program Management. The centralized coordinated management of a program to achieve the program's strategic objectives and benefits.

Program Management Plan. The full set of documents required to manage the program. The program management plan is distinct and separate from the project management plans required to manage the individual projects within the program.

Program Management Process. Program management processes accomplish program management by receiving inputs and generating outputs, with the use of tools and techniques. In order to ensure that the outputs are delivered as required, the processes need to operate subject to controls.

Program Management Process Group. The Process Groups for program management comprise Initiating, Planning, Executing, Monitoring and Controlling, and Closing processes.

Program Resource Plan. The plan for managing the program-level resources.

Program Stakeholders. Individuals and organizations that are actively involved in the program or whose interests may be positively or negatively affected by the program.

Program Transition Request. The request to turn the program's final product into an operational status or to transition it to the final user.

Project Management Process Group. A logical grouping of the project management processes described in the *PMBOK® Guide* – Fourth Edition. The Project Management Process Groups include Initiating Processes, Planning Processes, Executing Processes, Monitoring and Controlling Processes, and Closing Processes.

Qualified Sellers List. A list of vendors that have been pre-approved by the organization for the purchase of goods and services. Normal procurements should start by first assessing the qualified sellers list for purchases.

Roadmap. A chronological representation of a program's intended direction. It depicts key dependencies between major milestones, communicates the linkage between the business strategy and the program work, and provides a high-level view of key milestones and decision points.

Sponsor. The person or group that provides the financial resources, in cash or in-kind, for the program.

Stakeholder Register. A list of primary stakeholders on the program, their roles and responsibilities, and their needs and expectations of the program.

Strategic Directive. A document that formally expresses the organization's concept, vision, and mission for the program and its expected benefits. It may be written either at a high level or detailed.

Steering Committee. The group responsible for ensuring program goals are achieved and providing support to address program risks and issues. Sometimes this group is known as a program board or governance board.

Sustainment. Activities associated with ensuring that customers continue to receive utility from products.

Technique. A defined systematic procedure employed by a human resource to perform an activity to produce a product or result or deliver a service, and that may employ one or more tools.

Tolerance. The ranges set for the program or the program's components in cost, schedule, scope, risk, quality and other attributes that are associated with a specific level of responsibility. Tolerances permit the program manager to trade off these attributes among the different components, e.g. if one project is running slightly over budget, money from another project that is under budget may be moved to make up the shortfall. Also called margin or envelope.

Tool. Something tangible, such as a template or software program, used in performing an activity to produce a product or result.

Transition Plan. A plan that shows how a component's product will be implemented into the overall program. The program transition plan shows how the program's product will be implemented into production or turned over to the final user.

INDEX

A

AC. *See* Actual cost

Actual cost (AC), 133

Administer Program Procurements, 63, 185, 196, 198–203

Administration, 63, 198–203

Affinity diagrams, 168

Alignment, 6, 23, 265

American National Standards Institute (ANSI), xv

Analysis

architecture/cost tradeoff, 219

assumption, 167

benefits, 130, 265

business case, 167

cash flow, 130

change impact, 118

checklist, 167

communications requirements, 145

comparative advantage, 77

competitive analysis of service providers, 189

components, 85

cost, 222

cost/benefit, 77, 256

financial, 212

gap, 95

impact, 269

issues, 95, 97

make-or-buy, 190

operational cost, 216

organization, 233

procurement, 220

program dependency, 168

program impact, 234

quantitative risk, 175

requirements, 111

reserve, 219

risk, 54, 95, 163, 169–176

scenario analysis, 168

stakeholders, 230

total cost of ownership, 219

trend/probability, 95

Analyze Program Risks, 54, 160, 169–176

ANSI. *See* American National Standards Institute

Approve Component Initiation, 59, 243, 250, 257–259

Approve Component Transition, 68, 243, 269–271

Architecture, 57

baseline as input for risk analysis, 171

cost tradeoff analysis, 219

Executing Process Group, managing, 57

managing program, 117–118

planning process, 49

proposed changes to, 87

scope management, 112–114, 117–118

Assessments, 172–173

Assumption analysis, 167

Assumptions, 24, 38, 144

Audits, 52, 89, 182, 251–254

B

Benchmarking, 256

Benefits

management of, 264–267, 277

plan for, 109, 247

realization analysis, 130, 265

reporting on, 156

risk related to, 158

Benefits analysis, 130, 265

Best practices, 81

Bidder conferences, 195

Brainstorming, 111–112, 167, 233

Budgeting

allocation for procurements, 189

management system for, 202

Budget Program Costs, 51, 153, 221–223

risk management and, 164

Budget Program Costs, 51, 153, 221–223

Business case, 76, 105, 167

C

Capacity planning, 85

Cash flow analysis, 130

Categorization, 173
Cause-and-effect diagrams, 168
Change, 11
    control system, 200
    impact analysis, 118
Change requests, 132
Charters, 81, 105–106, 129, 131, 144, 247
Check points, 23
Checklist analysis, 167
Checklists, 256
Close Program Procurements, 68, 185, 203–206
Close Program, 37, 67, 73, 98–101
Closing Process Group, 8, 10, 40–41, 45, 60
    Approve Component Transition, 68, 243, 269–271
    Close Program Procurements, 68, 185, 203–206
    Close Program, 67, 98–101
Communication management, 303
    Distribute Information, 147–152
    Overview, 141–142
    Report Program Performance, 152–156
    Plan Communications, 142–147
Communications, 52
    communications requirements analysis, 145
    log for, 147
    messages, 149
    methods for, 146
    requirements analysis, 145
    skills in, 150
    strategy for, 147
Comparative advantage analysis, 77
Components, 7
    analysis of, 85
    Approve Component Initiation, 59, 257–259
    Approve Component Transition, 68, 269–271
    existing, in initiation process, 77
    Manage Component Interfaces, 57, 119–121
    overlap of, 18
    reviews of transition, 271
    risk management plan for, 166
    status of, 132
Computers, 220
Concept development, 42
Conduct Program Procurements, 59, 185, 192–197
Conflict management, 120, 241
Constraints, 24, 38, 144, 215
Contingencies, 179

Contractor, 214
Contracts, 232
    closure procedure for, 205
    management plan for, 90, 191, 201–202
    negotiation of, 195
    procedures for, 196
Coordination, 6
Cost
    analysis, 222
    management, xv, 303
    reporting system, 155
Cost/benefit analysis, 77, 256
Customer Acceptance Reviews, 109

D

Data gathering techniques, 174
Databases, 151, 162
Decision making, 122
Define Program Goals and Objectives, 23, 47, 107–109
Delphi technique, 167
Design reviews, 111
Develop Program Architecture, 49, 112–114
Develop Program Financial Plan, 50, 213–216
Develop Program Infrastructure, 48, 73, 84–86
Develop Program Management Plan, 48, 73, 79–83
Develop Program Requirements, 48, 110–112
Develop Program Schedule, 49, 127–131
Develop Program WBS, 49, 114–117
Diagramming techniques, 168
Direct and Manage Program Execution, 56, 72, 86–91, 153
Distribute Information, 58, 132, 141, 147–152
Distribution
    communications management, 149–151
    Executing Process Group, 58
Documentation, 87

E

Earned value (EV), 133
Earned value management (EVM), 94, 133, 225
EEF. *See* Enterprise Environmental Factors
Engage Program Stakeholders, 58, 228, 236–239
Enterprise Environmental Factors (EEF), 14–15
Enterprise external factors, 15
Environmental risk, 157

Establish Program Financial Framework, 43, 207, 210–213

Estimate to completion (ETC), 133

Estimate Program Costs, 50, 217–220

ETC. *See* Estimate to completion

EV. *See* Earned value

EVM. *See* Earned value management

Executing Process Groups, 8, 10, 40–41, 45, 55–60

    Approve Component Initiation, 59, 257–259

    Conduct Program Procurements, 59, 192–197

    Direct and Manage Program Execution, 56, 86–91

    Distribute Information, 58, 147–152

    Engage Program Stakeholders, 58, 236–239

    Manage Component Interfaces, 57, 119–121

    Manage Program Architecture, 57, 117–119

    Manage Program Resources, 57, 91–93

Execution of program, direction/management of, 86–91

Expert judgment, 77, 85, 106, 112, 116, 189, 220

F

Feasibility studies, 42, 77

Finance

    Budget Program Costs, 51, 153, 164, 189, 202, 221–223

    cash flow analysis, 130

    change requests for, 87

    cost reporting system, 155

    development of plan for, 50

    Initiating Process Group, establishing framework for, 43–44

    metrics for, 216

    Monitoring and Controlling Process Group and, 62

Financial analysis, 212

Financial management, 304–305

    Budget Program Costs, 51, 153, 164, 189, 202, 221–223

    Develop Program Financial Plan, 50, 213–216

    Establish Program Financial Framework, 43, 207, 210–213

    Estimate Program Costs, 50, 217–220

    Monitor and Control Program Financials, 62, 223–225

Focus groups, 108, 234

Forecasts, 154, 156

Funding, 15, 211

    constraints, 215

    methods, 212

G

Gap analysis, 95

Gate review requirements, 250

"Generally recognized," 4

Goals/objectives

    alignment between program/organization, 23

    in planning process, 47

    in scope management, 107–109

"Good practice," 4

Governance, 6, 305

    Approve Component Initiation, 59, 243, 250, 257–259

    Approve Component Transition, 68, 243, 269–271

    decision register, 263

    Manage Program Benefits, 66, 263–267

    Monitor and Control Program Changes, 64, 267–269

    overview, 243–244

    Plan for Audits, 52, 253–254

    Plan and Establish Program Governance Structure, 47, 245–251

    Plan Program Quality, 53, 254–257

    Planning Process Groups setting up, 47

    programs, 21, 25

    Provide Governance Oversight, 65, 259–262

    in risk management, 162

Governmental regulations, 15

A Guide to the Project Management Body of Knowledge (PMBOK® Guide), 3, 285

Guidelines, 85

H

Historical information, 38

Human resource management, 303

I

Identification

    root cause, 167

    of stakeholders, 47, 231–234

Identify Program Risks, 54, 160, 164–169

Identify Program Stakeholders, 47, 231–236

Impact analysis, 269

Influence diagrams, 168

Information

    Distribute Information, in communications management, 149–151

Executing Process Group distributing, 58

gathering techniques, 150, 167

presentation tools, 155

requests, 39

systems for, 82, 92, 145, 248

Information gathering techniques, 167

Infrastructure, Develop Program, 48, 73, 84–86

Initiate Program, 20, 43, 74–78

Initiating Process Group, 8–9, 40–45, 60

Establish Program Financial Framework, 43, 207, 210–213

Initiate Program, 20, 43, 74–78

Initiation

components, 59, 257–259

development of plan for, 23

Program Life Cycle, as part of, 24–25

strategy in, 76

tools/techniques for, 77

Inputs. *See* specific process

Interest rates, 15

Interfaces

change requests impact on, 87

Manage Component Interfaces, 57, 119–121

Interviewing, 108, 111, 167, 233

Issues, 24, 95–98

Issues analysis, 95, 97

J

Justification, 24

K

Knowledge

program manager, 12–14

technical, 113

transition of, 100

Knowledge Areas

Program Communication Management, 69, 141–156

Program Financial Management, 69, 207–226

Program Governance, 21, 25, 243–271

Program Integration Management, 69–101

Program Procurement Management, 69, 185–206

Program Risk Management, 53, 157–184

Program Scope Management, 103–124

Program Stakeholder Management, 47, 51, 227–241

Program Time Management, 125–134

L

Leadership, 13

Lessons learned, 39

database for, 151, 162

updates on, 151

M

Make-or-buy analysis, 190

Manage Component Interfaces, 57, 119–121

Manage Program Architecture, 57, 117–119

Manage Program Benefits, 66, 263–267

Manage Program Issues, 64, 95–98

Manage Program Resources, 57, 91–93

Manage Program Stakeholder Expectations, 12, 51, 62, 162, 239–241

Management, 11. *See also* Communication Management; Financial Management; Human Resource Management; Program Integration Management Knowledge Area; Program Management; Quality Management; Resources; Risk Management; Scope Management; Stakeholder Management; Time Management

benefits, 20, 264–267, 277

delivering/managing benefits, 30–31

Monitoring and Controlling Process Group, 40–41, 59–66

organizational differences, 31

sustainment of benefits in, 31–32

budget, 202

change requests as part of, 89, 110, 118

conflict, 120, 241

contracts, 90, 191

earned value, 94, 133, 225

Executing Process Group, 55–60

execution of program, 86–91

A Guide to the Project Management Body of Knowledge, 3, 285

The Organizational Project Management Maturity Model, 4

plan for contract, 191

plan for program communication, 146–147

plan for program schedule, 130–131

planning process, 116

portfolio, 4

interactions with program/project management, 10

program management and, 9

projects, 4

    interactions with portfolio/program management, 10

    program management and, 8

resources, 73, 91–93, 266

risk, 53

schedule management tools, 129

stakeholders, 12, 51, 162

The Standard for Portfolio Management, 4, 294

tools/techniques for, 92–93, 97, 241, 265–266

Market conditions, 15

Measurement, 266

Meetings, 85

    for planning of risk management, 163

    to review risk, 182

Messages, 149

Metrics, 133, 216

Military threat levels, 15

Monitor and Control Program Changes, 64, 267–269

Monitor and Control Program Financials, 62, 223–226

Monitor and Control Program Performance, 60, 93–95

Monitor and Control Program Risks, 63, 180–184

Monitor and Control Program Schedule, 61, 131–134

Monitor and Control Program Scope, 61, 121–124

Monitoring, 11

    changes, 267–269

    financials, 224–225

    Monitoring and Controlling Process Group, 8, 10, 40–41, 59-66

        Administer Program Procurements, 63, 198–203

        Manage Program Benefits, 66, 263–267

        Manage Program Issues, 64, 95–98

        Manage Program Stakeholder Expectations, 62, 239–241

        Monitor and Control Program Changes, 64, 267–269

        Monitor and Control Program Financials, 62, 223–226

        Monitor and Control Program Performance, 60, 93–95

        Monitor and Control Program Risks, 63, 180–184

        Monitor and Control Program Schedule, 61, 131–134

        Monitor and Control Program Scope, 61, 120–124

        Provide Governance Oversight, 65, 259–262

        Report Program Performance, 65, 152–156

    Monitor and Control Program Performance, 60, 93–95

    Monitor and Control Program Scope, 61, 120–124

O

Operational-level risk, 157

Operations, 216

OPM3®. See Organizational Project Management Maturity Model

Organization

    existing work of, 77, 81

    planning for, 248

    policies/guidelines for, 85

    process assets of, 38

    program aligned with goals of, 23

    structures/policies, 76

Organizational analysis, 233

Organizational process assets, 14

Organizational Project Management Maturity Model (OPM3®), xv, 4

Outcomes, 24

Outputs. *See* specific process

P

Performance

    forecasts, 156

    measurement of, 266

    monitor/control of program, 60, 73, 93–95

    reporting, 65, 89, 134, 153–156

Phase-gate reviews, 22

Phases, 6

Plan and Establish Program Governance Structure, 47, 245–251

Plan Communications, 52, 142–147

Plan for Audits, 52, 251–254

Planned value (PV), 133

Planning, 11

    architecture in, 49

    audits, 251–254

    benefits realization, 109

    capacity, 85

    communications management, 144–147

    contingencies, 179

    goals/objectives in process of, 47

    governance structure, 245–251

    Identification of stakeholders in process of, 47

    management of program schedule, 130–131

    management process of, 116

procurement management, 187–191
program management, 48, 73, 79–83
program management processes, 9, 51–53
program quality, 254–257
program transition, 100
resources, 86
risk management, 162–164
risk responses, 177–179
scope and, 46, 106
scope management, 104–106
for stakeholder management, 12, 51, 162, 228–231
techniques for, 83
Planning Process Groups, 8, 9, 40–41, 44–55, 60
    Analyze Program Risks, 54, 169–176
    Budget Program Costs, 51, 221–223
    Define Program Goals and Objectives, 23, 47, 107–109
    Develop Program Architecture, 49, 112–114
    Develop Program Financial Plan, 50, 213–216
    Develop Program Infrastructure, 48, 73, 84–86
    Develop Program Management Plan, 48, 73, 79–83
    Develop Program Requirements, 48, 110–112
    Develop Program Schedule, 49, 127–131
    Develop Program WBS, 49, 114–117
    Estimate Program Costs, 50, 217–220
    Identify Program Risks, 54, 160, 164–169
    Identify Program Stakeholders, 47, 231–236
    Plan and Establish Program Governance Structure, 47, 245–251
    Plan Communications, 52, 142–147
    Plan for Audits, 52, 251–254
    Plan for Program Quality, 53, 254–257
    Plan Program Procurements, 51, 187–191
    Plan Program Risk Management, 53–54, 161–164
    Plan Program Risk Responses, 55, 176–179
    Plan Program Scope, 104–106, 112–114, 302
    Plan Program Stakeholder Management, 12, 51, 162, 228–231
Plan Program Procurements, 51
Plan Program Quality, 254–257
Plan Program Risk Management, 53, 160–164
Plan Program Risk Responses, 55, 176–179
Plan Program Scope, 46, 104–106
Plan Program Stakeholder Management, 51, 228–231
PMBOK® Guide. *See A Guide to the Project Management Body of Knowledge*
PMO. *See* Program Management Office

PMP certification, 5
Policies, 85
Political climate, 15
Portfolio, 6–7, 9
Portfolio management. *See* Management
Portfolio managers, 4
Portfolio-related risk, 158
Probability/impact matrix, 173
Procedures, 196, 205
Process Groups, 8, 40–41. *See also* Specific Process Groups
Processes. *See* Program Management Processes
Procurement analysis, 220
Procurement management, 51, 83, 304
    Administer Program Procurements, 63, 198–203
    Close Program Procurements, 68, 185, 203–206
    Conduct Program Procurements, 59, 185, 192–197
    Plan Program Procurements, 51, 187–191
Product, 19, 104
Program
    benefits delivery, 28–29
    benefits management, 20
        delivering/managing benefits, 30–31
        organizational differences, 31
        sustainment of benefits in, 31–32
    budgeting for, 51, 153, 164, 189, 202, 221–223
    charter, 81, 105–106, 129, 144
    closure, 20, 98–101
    closure in, 29–30, 99
    external factors of impact on, 14
    governance, 21, 25
    impact analysis, 234
    Initiate Program, 20, 73–74
    Manage Program Resources, 57, 91–93
    performance reports, 39
    register for issues with, 90, 98
    scope of, 46, 104
    setup, 20, 25–28
    status reports, 39
    transition plan, 83
Program Communication Management, 141–146
    Distribute Information, 58, 147–152
    Plan Communications, 52, 142–147
    Report Program Performance, 65, 152–156
Program components. *See* Components
Program dependency analysis, 168

Program Financial Management, 207–226
    Budget Program Costs, 51, 221–223
    Develop Program Financial Plan, 50, 213–216
    Establish Program Financial Framework, 43, 210–213
    Estimate Program Costs, 50, 217–220
    Monitor and Control Program Financials, 62, 223–226
Program Governance, 243–271
    Approve Component Initiation, 59, 257–259
    Approve Component Transition, 68, 269–271
    Manage Program Benefits, 66, 263–267
    Monitor and Control Program Changes, 64, 267–269
    Plan and Establish Program Governance, 47, 245–251
    Plan for Audits, 52, 251–254
    Plan Program Quality, 53, 254–257
    Provide Governance Oversight, 65, 259–262
Program impact analysis, 234
Program Integration Management, 301
    Close Program, 37, 67, 73, 98–100, 185, 203–206
    Develop Program Infrastructure, 48, 73, 84–86
    Develop Program Management Plan, 48, 73, 79, 83
    Direct and Manage Program Execution, 56, 72, 86, 88–90, 153
    Initiate Program, 20, 43, 73–74
    Manage Program Issues, 95–98
    Manage Program Resources, 57
    Monitor and Control Program Performance, 93–95
Program Life Cycle, 20, 277
    characteristics of, 18–19
    closure in, 29–30
    delivery of program benefits in, 28–29
    governance across, 21
    initiation of program in, 24–25
    overview, 17–18
    phases of, 22–30
    pre-program preparations, 22–23
    product life cycle and, 19
    setup in, 25–28
Program management
    defined, 3–4, 6
    development of plan for, 48, 73, 79–83
    information systems, 82, 92, 145, 248
    interactions with portfolio/project management, 10–11
    plan for, 84, 154, 162, 194
    plan updates, 39

    portfolio management and, 9
    project management and, 8
Program Management Office (PMO), 11–12, 89, 93, 235
    in governance structure, 246
Program management processes, 9, 35, 51–53, 278
    Closing Process Group, 8, 10, 40–41, 45, 60, 66–68
        Approve Component Transition, 68, 269–270
        Close Program Procurements, 68, 203–206
        Close Program, 68, 98–101
    Executing Process Group, 60
        Approve Component Initiation, 59, 257–259
        Conduct Program Procurements, 59, 192–197
        Direct and Manage Program Execution, 56, 86–91
        Distribute Information, 58, 147–152
        Engage Program Stakeholders, 58, 236–239
        Manage Component Interfaces, 57, 119–121
        Manage Program Architecture, 57, 117–119
        Manage Program Resources, 57, 91–93
    Initiating Process Group, 8–9, 40–44
        Establish Program Financial Framework, 43, 207, 210–213
        Initiate Program, 20, 43, 74–78
    Monitoring and Controlling Process Group, 8, 10, 40–41, 59–66
        Administer Program Procurements, 63, 198–203
        Manage Program Benefits, 66, 263–267
        Manage Program Issues, 64, 95–98
        Manage Program Stakeholder Expectations, 62, 239–241
        Monitor and Control Program Changes, 64, 267–269
        Monitor and Control Program Financials, 62, 223–226
        Monitor and Control Program Performance, 60, 93–95
        Monitor and Control Program Risks, 63, 180–184
        Monitor and Control Program Schedule, 61, 131–134
        Monitor and Control Program Scope, 61, 121–124
        Provide Governance Oversight, 65, 259–262
        Report Program Performance, 65, 152–156
    Planning Process Groups, 8–9, 40–41, 44–55, 60
        Analyze Program Risks, 54, 169–176
        Budget Program Costs, 51, 221–223
        Define Program Goals and Objectives, 23, 47, 107–109
        Develop Program Architecture, 49, 112–114
        Develop Program Financial Plan, 50, 213–216

Develop Program Infrastructure, 48, 84–86
Develop Program Management Plan, 48, 79–83
Develop Program Requirements, 48, 110–112
Develop Program Schedule, 49, 127–131
Develop Program WBS, 49, 114–117
Estimate Program Costs, 50, 217–220
Identify Program Risks, 54, 160, 164–166
Identify Program Stakeholders, 47, 231–236
Plan and Establish Program Governance Structure, 47, 245–251
Plan Communications, 52, 142–147
Plan for Audits, 52, 251–254
Plan for Program Quality, 53, 254–257
Plan Program Procurements, 51, 187–191
Plan Program Risk Management, 53, 160–164
Plan Program Risk Responses, 55, 176–179
Plan Program Scope, 46, 104–106
Plan Program Stakeholder Management, 51, 228–231
Program Management Process Groups, 9, 35, 40, 51–53, 278
Program managers, 4, 12–14, 245
Program Procurement Management, 185–206
Administer Program Procurements, 63, 198–203
Close Program Procurements, 68, 203–206
Conduct Program Procurements, 59, 192–197
Plan Program Procurements, 51, 187–191
Program Risk Management, 157–184
Analyze Program Risks, 54, 160, 169–176
Identify Program Risks, 54, 160, 164–169
Monitor and Control Program Risks, 63, 180–184
Plan Program Risk Management, 53, 160–164
Plan Program Risk Responses, 55, 176–179
Program schedule. See Schedule
Program Scope Management, 103–124
Define Program Goals and Objectives, 47, 107–109
Develop Program Architecture, 49, 112–114
Develop Program Requirements, 48, 110–112
Develop Program WBS, 49, 114–117
Manage Component Interfaces, 57, 119–121
Manage Program Architecture, 57, 117–119
Monitor and Control Program Scope, 61, 121–124
Plan Program Scope, 46, 104–106
Program Stakeholder Management, 227–241
Engage Program Stakeholders, 58, 236–239
Identify Program Stakeholders, 47, 231–234

Manage Program Stakeholder Expectations, 62, 239–241
Plan Program Stakeholder Management, 51, 228–231
Program Time Management, 125–134. See also Time Management
Develop Program Schedule, 49, 127–131
Monitor and Control Program Schedule, 61, 131–134
Program Work Breakdown Structure (PWBS), 49, 149
in development of program schedule, 128
Program-level risk, 157
Programs, 3–7
Project management. See Management
Project Management Institute Code of Ethics and Professional Conduct, 5
Project managers, 4
in governance structure, 245
Project risk, 157
Projects, 247
configuration by Initiating Process Groups, 42
programs and, 3–7
Proposals, 195
Provide Governance Oversight, 65, 259–262
PV. See Planned value
PWBS. See Program Work Breakdown Structure

Q

Qualified sellers, 195
Quality management, 53, 172, 254–257, 303
Quantitative risk analysis, 175
Questionnaires, 111, 234

R

Register, 131
governance decision, 263
program issues, 90, 98
risk, 132, 168
stakeholder, 145, 234
Report Program Performance, 65, 152–156
Reporting
benefits realization, 156
cost, 155
final, 100
performance, 65, 89, 134, 153–156
time, 155
variance, 154

Request for proposals (RFPs), 195
Requirements, 109–110. *See also* Program Integration
    Management Knowledge Area; Program management
    processes
    analysis of, 111
    components, 112
    gate review, 250
    program, 112
    validation/verification, 112
Reserve analysis, 219
Resources, 6, 24, 57
    Manage Program Resources, 57, 91–93
    plan for, 86
Reviews, 85
    component transition, 271
    customer acceptance, 109
    design, 111
    gate, 250
    phase-gate, 22
    risk, 182
    status, 155, 225
RFPs. *See* Request for proposals
Risk, 6, 24
    analysis, 54, 95, 163, 169–176
    benefits-related, 158
    categorization, 173
    change requests impact on, 87
    data quality assessment, 172
    environmental risk, 157
    identification of, 54, 166–169
    meetings to review, 182
    monitoring/controlling, 63
    operational-level risk, 157
    plan for program management of, 53
    portfolio-related, 158
    probability assessment, 172
    program-level, 157
    project, 157
    quantitative analysis of, 175
    register for, 132
    responses to, 55
Risk management, 53, 266, 303–304
    Analyze Program Risks, 54, 160, 169–176
    Identify Program Risks, 54, 160, 164–169
    Monitor and Control Program Risks, 63, 180–184
    Plan Program Risk Management, 53, 160–164

Plan Program Risk Responses, 55, 176–179
    roles/responsibilities in, 163
Risk probability/impact assessment, 172
Risk urgency assessment, 173
Roadmap, 25, 81, 83, 90
Roles/responsibilities, 12, 163
Root cause identification, 167

S

Scenario analysis, 168
Schedule
    change requests to, 87
    development of, 49
    management plan for program, 130–131
    monitor/control of, 61
    PWBS in development of program, 128
    time management in development of program, 128–134
Schedule management tools, 129
Scope, 11, 24
    Monitoring and Controlling Process Group on, 61
    in planning process, 46, 106
Scope management, 302
    Define Program Goals and Objectives, 47, 107–109
    Develop Program Architecture, 49, 112–114
    Develop Program Requirements, 48, 110–112
    Develop Program WBS, 49, 114–117
    Manage Component Interfaces, 57, 119–121
    Manage Program Architecture, 57, 117–119
    Monitor and Control Program Scope, 61, 121–124
    Plan Program Scope, 46, 104–106
Sellers, 195
Service providers, 189
Skills
    communication, 150
    leadership, 13
    program manager, 12–14
Stakeholder analysis, 230
Stakeholder management, 4, 15, 24, 305
    engagement by Executing Process Group, 58
    Engage Program Stakeholders, 58, 236–239
    Identify Program Stakeholders, 47, 231–236
    impact and issue tracking tool, 238
    Manage Program Stakeholder Expectations, 62,
        239–241

Plan Program Stakeholder Management, 51, 228–231
requirements of, 247
The Standard for Portfolio Management, 4, 294
Status, 155, 225
Steering committee, 42
Strategy
alignment in, 265
benefits, 24
communications, 147
fit of program with, 24
program as part of, 5
stakeholder management, 236, 241
strategic directive in initiation of program, 76
understanding, in pre-program preparations, 23
Strengths, Weaknesses, Opportunities and Threats Analysis
(SWOT), 168
Success, 11
Supply, 6
Supporting details, 39
Surveys, 111, 234
SWOT. *See* Strengths, Weaknesses, Opportunities and
Threats Analysis
System(s)
change control, 200
configuration tools, 116
cost reporting, 155

evaluation of proposals, 195
information, 82, 92, 145, 248
management of budget, 202
time, 155

T

Task responsibility matrix, 116
Team, 86
Time management, 302
Develop Program Schedule, 49, 127–131
Monitor and Control Program Schedule, 61, 131–134
Timescale, 24
Tolerances, 82
Tools and techniques. *See specific process*
Transition, approval of, 68, 269–271

V

Variance report, 154
Vision, 24

W

Work, 6, 89